100 CROCHET PROJECTS

Jean Leinhauser and
Rita Weiss

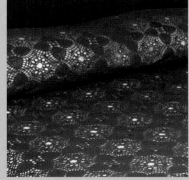

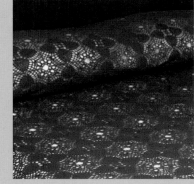

Sterling Publishing Co., Inc.
New York

Library of Congress Cataloging-in-Publication Data Available

10 9 8 7 6 5 4 3 2 1

Published by Sterling Publishing Co., Inc.
387 Park Avenue South, New York, NY 10016
© 2006 by The Creative Partners™ LLC
Distributed in Canada by Sterling Publishing
c/o Canadian Manda Group, 165 Dufferin Street,
Toronto, Ontario, Canada M6K 3H6
Distributed in the United Kingdom by GMC Distribution Services
Castle Place, 166 High Street, Lewes, East Sussex, England BN7 1XU
Distributed in Australia by Capricorn Link (Australia) Pty. Ltd.
P.O. Box 704, Windsor, NSW 2756, Australia

Sterling ISBN-13: 978-1-4027-2309-4
ISBN-10: 1-4027-2309-1

For information about custom editions, special sales, premium
and corporate purchases, please contact Sterling Special Sales
Department at 800-805-5489 or specialsales@sterlingpub.com.

Senior Technical Editor
Susan Lowman

Technical Editors
Janet Bates
Karen J. Hay,
Maxine Pike,
Carly Poggemeyer

Photo Stylist
Christy Stevenson

Photography
James Jaeger
Carol Wilson Mansfield
Marshall Williams

Book Design
Graphic Solutions, inc-chgo

Produced by
The Creative Partners,™ LLC.

The authors extend their thanks and appreciation
to these contributing designers:

Suzanne Atkinson, Orleans, Canada
Angela Best, Toronto, Canada
Vashti Braha, Longboat Keys, Florida
Carol Carlile, Windfall, Indiana
Belinda "Bendy" Carter, Marionville, Missouri
Valentine Devine, Los Alamos, New Mexico
Edie Eckman, Waynesboro, Virginia
Nazanin S. Fard, Novato, California
Noreen Crone-Findlay, Ardrossan, Canada
Laura Gebhardt, Pickering, Canada
Janie Herrin, Jacksonville, Florida
Tammy Hildebrand, Kernersville, North Carolina
C. Yvette Holmes, San Antonio, Texas
Susan Lowman, Prescott Valley, Arizona
Ruthie Marks, Ojai, California
Marty Miller, Greensboro, North Carolina
Dora Ohrenstein, New York, New York
Cheryl Oxsalida, North Bay Village, Florida
Kathleen Stuart, San Jose, California
Carol Sullivan, Lakeside, California
Myra Wood, Sherman Oaks, California
Joyce Renee Wyatt, Los Angeles, California
Zelda K, Mount Vernon, Ohio

The authors extend their thanks and appreciation to Kathleen Sams and
her associates at Coats & Clark, to Catherine Blythe and the design
department at Patons Yarns, to the design department at Lion Brand Yarn
and the design department at S. R. Kertzer Limited for sharing many of
their most creative designs with us.

Every effort has been made to ensure the accuracy of these instructions. We
cannot, however, be responsible for human error or variations in your work.

Wherever we have used a special yarn, we have given the brand name.
If you are unable to find these yarns locally, write to the following manu-
facturers who will be able to tell you where to purchase their products, or
consult their internet sites. We also wish to thank these companies for
supplying yarn for this book.

Bernat Yarns
320 Livingston Avenue South
Listowel, Ontario, Canada N4W 3H3
www.bernat.com

Berroco, Inc.
14 Elmdale Road
Uxbridge, Massachusetts 01569
www.berroco.com

Brown Sheep
10062 Country Road 16
Mitchell, Nebraska 69357
www.brownsheep.com

Caron International
Customer Service
P. O. Box 222
Washington, North Carolina 27889
www.caron.com

J&P Coats
Coats & Clark
Consumer Services, P.O. Box 12229
Greenville, South Carolina 29612-0229
www.coatsandclark.com

Lion Brand Yarn
34 West 15th Street
New York, New York 10011
www.lionbrand.com

Moda Dea Fashion Yarns
Coats & Clark
Consumer Services, P.O. Box 12229
Greenville, South Carolina 29612-0229
www.coatsandclark.com

Patons Yarns
2700 Dufferin Street
Toronto, Ontario, Canada M6B 4J3
www.patonsyarns.com

Plymouth Yarn Co., Inc
500 Lafayette Street
P.O. Box 28
Bristol, Pennsylvania 19007-0028
www.plymouthyarn.com

Red Heart Yarns
Coats & Clark
Consumer Services, P. O. Box 12229
Greenville, South Carolina 29612-0229
www.coatsandclark.com

TLC Yarns
Coats & Clark
Consumer Services, P. O. Box 12229
Greenville, South Carolina 29612-0229
www.coatsandclark.com

Twilleys of Stamford
S. R. Kertzer Limited
50 Trowers Rd
Woodbridge, Ontario L4L 7K6
Canada
www.kertzer.com

INTRODUCTION

Can you ever have too many crochet projects?

Never!

If you are a crocheter, chances are you have an insatiable need for just one more afghan pattern, one more pattern for baby booties, just one more summer top...

We know that most crocheters like to work on more than one project at a time, and therefore their families live with a strange assortment of lumpy bags strewn all over the house. Crocheters know these as PIGS—projects in grocery sacks.

And while they are working on those PIGS, the crocheter is undoubtedly fantasizing about WIM—works in mind, or projects that will get done someday, maybe.

As soon as the last Christmas gift is unwrapped, the dedicated crocheter is getting started on gifts for next year. A friend moved into new house? Of course that calls for an afghan in the new decorating colors. A baby on the way? My goodness, an entire layette needs to be crocheted.

Crocheters are generous with their time and talent. They enjoy making hats to keep disadvantaged children warm, or blankets for the homeless. And if they can find the time, they just might make a pretty scarf for themselves.

This new collection of designs has something for everyone— and then some! From fashion to a kitty toy, if you are a crocheter you will enjoy this book for years to come.

Jean Leinhauser   *Rita Weiss*

CONTENTS

Project Number   page

1 Citrus Chic   6

2 Pretty Petals Doily   10

3 Glitzy Capelet   12

4
} Prom Purses   14
5

6 Glitter Girl Bolero   16

7 Big Scary Spider Cat Toy   21

8 Wrap Up!   22

9
} Floral Potholder
   and Dish Cloth Set   24
10

11 Little Friend's Backpack   27

12
} Surely Chic   30
13

14 Kitchen Angel Dish Cloth   36

15 Square Deal Vest   38

16 Scarf in Style   41

17
} Rows of Bows   42
18

19 Entrelac Skull Cap   47

20 Slinky Tunic   50

21 Flower Garden Scarf   53

22 Dutch Treat   56

23 Lover's Knot Shrug   58

24 Rock-A-Bye Baby   61

25 Soft 'n Sweet   62

26 Felted Purse   64

27 Fast and Fun T-Top   66

28 Bedtime Roses   68

29 Grin and Bare It   72

30 Beauty in Geometry   76

31 Plum Granny Ripple   82

32 Harlequin Vest   86

33 Dad's Doily   90

34 Mesh Tunic   92

35 Bucket Bag   96

36 Magnificent in Mesh   98

37 A Little Something   101

38
39
} Let's Do Lunch   104
40
41

42 Four-Way Poncho   108

43 Awesome Blossom   110

44 Patchwork Tote   113

45 Sweet Summer Suit   116

46 Rose Garden   120

47 Quilt Block Pillow   123

48 Simply Shrug   126

49 Trendy Tank   128

50
51
} Romance of Yesteryear   132
52

53 **54** Two Trendy Tops 138

55 Stripes on Parade 146

56 **57** Cute Combo 148

58 Snowflake Earring 153

59 **60** Pretty Posies 154

61 Asymmetrical Poncho 159

62 Texas Roses 160

63 Tiny Bubbles Jacket 162

64 Beary Cute Jacket 165

65 Rainbow Cover-Up 168

66 Sweet Sachet 171

67 **68** Pick a Pretty Pair 172

69 Sheep Mittens 176

70 Ribbon Fringe Shawl 178

71 **72** **73** Summer Escape 180

74 A La Foo-Foo Potholder 188

75 Merry-Go-Round Blanket 190

76 Sunshine and Waves 192

77 Pinning Up Roses 197

78 By the Sea 198

79 Lazy Daisies for Baby 202

80 **81** **82** Lazy Daisies Layette 204

83 Bronze Beauty 209

84 **85** Flowers and Bears in the Dell 214

86 Loopy Poncho 216

87 Cozy Shrug 218

88 Flower Squares 220

89 Falling Leaves Wrap 225

90 Pineapple Roses 230

91 Robin's Hood 233

92 Shawl of Gold 234

93 All Buttoned Up 236

94 Loopy Tape Measure 240

95 Fun in the Sun Halter 242

96 **97** Fun Hat and Scarf 244

98 Town & Country Capelet 246

99 Baby on Board 248

100 Sophisticated Shell 250

General Directions 254

Index 256

#1 CITRUS CHIC

Designed by Tammy Hildebrand

Note: *Instructions are written for size Small; changes for sizes Medium and Large are in parentheses.*

SIZES	Small	Medium	Large
Body bust Measurements	32" - 34"	36" - 38"	40" - 42"
Finished bust Measurements	40"	44 $^1/_2$"	49"

MATERIALS

Sport weight yarn
  12 $^1/_2$ (13 $^1/_2$, 14 $^1/_2$) oz orange

Eyelash yarn
  8 (8 $^1/_2$, 9) oz orange
  7 $^1/_2$ (8, 8 $^1/_2$) oz copper

Note: *Photographed model made with Lion Brand® Microspun #186 Mango and Lion Brand® Fun Fur #133 Tangerine and #134 Copper*

Size K (6.5 mm) crochet hook
  (or size required for gauge)

One 1 $^1/_4$" long wooden shank
  button

Tapestry needle

GAUGE

9 dc = 4"

7 rows in pattern (dc, sc) = 4"

INSTRUCTIONS

Back

With one strand sport weight and one strand orange eyelash held together, ch 48 (54, 58).

Row 1 (right side): Dc in 4th ch from hook (3 skipped chs count as dc) and in each rem ch: 46 (52, 56) dc; ch 1, turn.

Row 2: Sc in first st and in each st across, changing eyelash yarn to copper in last sc: 46 (52, 56) sc; ch 3 (counts as dc on next row now and throughout), turn.

Row 3: Dc in next st and in each st across; ch 1, turn.

Row 4: Sc in first st and in each st across, changing eyelash yarn to orange in last sc; ch 3, turn.

Row 5: Rep Row 3.

Rows 6 through 21 (25, 25): Rep Rows 2 through 5 four, (five, five) times more.

Rows 22 (26, 26) and 23 (27, 27): Rep Rows 2 and 3.

Armhole Shaping

Row 1: Skip first st, sl st in next 5 sts, sc in next 34 (40, 44) sts, changing eyelash yarn to orange in last sc: 34 (40, 44) sc; ch 3, turn, leaving last 6 sts unworked.

Row 2: Dc in next 33 (39, 43) sts: 34 (40, 44) dc; ch 1, turn.

Row 3: Sc in first st and in each st across, changing eyelash yarn to copper in last sc; ch 3, turn.

Row 4: Dc in next st and in each st across; ch 1, turn.

Row 5: Sc in first st and in each st across, changing eyelash yarn to orange in last sc; ch 3, turn.

Row 6: Rep Row 4.

Rows 7 through 10: Rep Rows 3 through 6.

Rows 11 through 13: Rep Rows 3 through 5. At end of Row 13, finish off; weave in ends.

Right Front

With one strand sport weight and one strand orange eyelash, ch 26 (28, 31).

Row 1: Dc in 4th ch from hook (3 skipped chs count as dc) and in each rem ch: 24 (26, 29) dc; ch 1, turn.

Row 2: Sc in first st and in each st across, changing eyelash yarn to copper in last sc: 24 (26, 29) sc; ch 3 (counts as dc on next row now and throughout), turn.

Row 3: Dc in next st and in each st across; ch 1, turn.

Row 4: Sc in first st and in each st across, changing eyelash yarn to orange in last sc; ch 3, turn.

Row 5: Rep Row 3.

Rows 6 through 21 (25, 25): Rep Rows 2 through 5 four (five, five) times more.

Rows 22 (26, 26) and 23 (27, 27): Rep Rows 2 and 3.

Armhole Shaping

Row 1: Skip first st, sl st in next 5 sts, sc in next st and in each rem st across, changing eyelash yarn to orange in last sc: 18 (20, 23) sc; ch 3, turn.

Row 2: Dc in next 17 (19, 22) sts: 18 (20, 23) dc; ch 1, turn.

Row 3: Sc in first st and in each st across, changing eyelash yarn to copper in last sc; ch 1, turn.

Neckline Shaping

Row 1: Skip first st, sl st in next 6 sts, ch 3 (counts as dc), dc in next st and in each rem st across: 12 (14, 17) dc; ch 1, turn.

Row 2: Sc in first st and in each rem st to last 2 sts, changing eyelash yarn to orange in last sc: 10 (12, 15) sc; ch 3, turn, leaving last 2 sts unworked.

Row 3: Dc in next st and in each st across: 10 (12, 15) dc; ch 1, turn.

Row 4: Sc in first st and in each st across, changing eyelash yarn to copper in last sc; ch 1, turn.

Row 5: Rep Row 3.

Row 6: Sc in first st and in each st across, changing eyelash yarn to orange in last sc; ch 3, turn.

Rows 7 through 10: Rep Rows 3 through 6. At end of Row 10, finish off, leaving a long length for sewing.

Left Front

Rows 1 through 23 (27, 27): Rep Rows 1 through 23 (27, 27) of right front.

Armhole Shaping

Row 1: Sc in first st and in each st to last 6 sts, changing eyelash yarn to orange in last sc: 18 (20, 23) sc; ch 3, turn, leaving last 6 sts unworked.

Row 2: Dc in next st and in each st across: 18 (20, 23) dc; ch 1, turn.

Row 3: Sc in first st and in each st across, changing eyelash yarn to copper in last sc; ch 3, turn.

Neckline Shaping

Row 1: Dc in next st and in each st to last 6 sts: 12 (14, 17) dc; ch 1, turn, leaving last 6 sts unworked.

Row 2: Skip first st, sl st in next st, sc in next st and in each rem st across, changing eyelash yarn to orange in last sc: 10 (12, 15) sc; ch 3, turn.

Rows 3 through 10: Rep Rows 3 through 10 of neckline shaping on right front.

Sew shoulder seams with sport yarn. Sew side seams with sport yarn.

Sleeves (make 2)

Rnd 1: With wrong side facing, working in edges of rows and 12 unworked sts of arm-hole, join sport yarn and orange eyelash yarn with sc in first unworked st on Row 1 of armhole shaping at side seam, sc in next 5 unworked sts, sc in edge of Row 2 of arm-hole shaping, sc in edge of each sc row and each dc row around armhole, skip Row 1 of armhole shaping before next 6 unworked sts, sc in next 6 unworked sts; join with sl st in first sc; ch 3, turn.

Rnd 2: Dc in next st and in each st around, changing eyelash yarn to copper in last st; join with sl st in 3rd ch of turning ch-3; ch 1, turn.

Rnd 3: Sc in first st and in each st around; join with sl st in first sc; ch 3, turn.

Rnd 4: Dc in next st and in each st around, changing eyelash yarn to orange in last st; join with sl st in 3rd ch of turning ch-3; ch 1, turn.

Rnd 5: Rep Rnd 3.

Rnds 6 through 29 (33, 33): Rep Rnds 2 through 5 six (seven, seven) times more. At end of last rnd, finish off; weave in ends.

Cuff

Rnd 1: With right side facing, join sport yarn with sc in last st on last rnd of sleeve; *sc dec in next 2 sts; rep from * around; join with sl st in first sc. Do not turn.

Rnd 2: Ch 1, sc in same st as joining, sc in next st and in each st around; join with sl st in first sc. Finish off; weave in ends.

Edging

Row 1: With right side facing, join sport yarn with sc in edge of Row 1 on right front, work 1 sc in edge of each sc row and in unworked sts at neckline shaping and 2 sc in edge of each dc row to back, sc in each st across top of back neck to left front, work 1 sc in edge of each sc row and in unworked sts at neck-line shaping and 2 sc in edge of each dc row to bottom of left front. Finish off; weave in ends.

Row 2: With right side facing, join sport yarn with sc in first st on Row 1 of edging, sc in each st to neckline shaping; (sc, ch 5, sc) in next st, sc in each st to back; *sc dec in next 2 sts; rep from * across back; sc in each st to bottom of left front. Finish off; weave in ends.

With sport yarn and tapestry needle, sew button to top of left front at neckline shaping opposite ch-5 lp at neckline shaping on right front.

#2 PRETTY PETALS DOILY

Designed by Janie Herrin

SIZE
8" diameter

MATERIALS
Size 10 crochet cotton
  150 yds white

Size 7 (1.65 mm) steel crochet
  hook (or size required for
  gauge)

GAUGE
First 5 rounds = 2"

Beginning Cluster (beg Cl): Ch 2; (YO, insert hook in specified st and draw up a lp, YO and draw through first 2 lps on hook) twice; YO and draw through all 3 lps on hook: beg Cl made.

Cluster (Cl): (YO, insert hook in specified st and draw up a lp; YO and draw through first 2 lps on hook) 3 times; YO and draw through all 4 lps on hook: Cl made.

Picot: Ch 3, sl st in 3rd ch from hook: picot made

INSTRUCTIONS

Starting at center, ch 4, join with sl st to form ring.

Rnd 1: Ch 4 (equals first dc plus ch 1), (dc, ch 1) 11 times in ring, join with sl st in 3rd ch of beg ch-4: 12 ch-1 sps.

Rnd 2: Ch 1, sc in same st and in next ch-1 sp; *sc in next dc, sc in next ch-1 sp; rep from * around, join in beg sc: 24 sc.

Rnd 3: Work beg Cl in first sc, ch 4, skip next sc; *cl in next sc, ch 4, skip next sc; rep from * around, join in top of beg Cl: 12 ch-4 sps.

Rnd 4: Sl st in ch-4 sp, ch 1; (sc, 5 dc, sc) for petal in same sp and in each sp around, join in beg sc: 12 petals made.

Rnd 5: Sl st in next 3 dc, ch 1, sc in same st; (ch 2, work picot) twice, ch 2, skip next 6 sts; *sc in next dc, (ch 2, work picot) twice, ch 2, skip next 6 sts; rep from * around, join in beg sc: 24 picots.

Rnd 6: Sl st in next 2 chs, skip picot, sl st in next ch, sl st in same ch-2 sp (you will be between 2 picots), ch 12 (counts as tr and ch-8); *skip 2 picots, tr in sp between next picot pair, ch 8; rep from * around, join with sl st in 4th ch of beg ch-12: 12 ch-8 lps.

Rnd 7: Sl st in lp, ch 4, (dc, ch 1) 6 times in same lp; (dc, ch 1) 7 times in next lp and in each lp around; join in 3rd ch of beg ch 4: 84 dc, 84 ch-1 lps.

Rnd 8: Rep Rnd 2: 168 sc.

Rnd 9: Work beg Cl, ch 4, skip next 3 sc; *Cl in next sc, ch 4, skip next 3 sc; rep from * around, join in top of beg Cl: 42 Cl, 42 ch-4 sps.

Rnd 10: Sl st in sp, work beg Cl, ch 4; *Cl in next sp, ch 4; rep from * around, join in top of beg Cl: 42 ch-4 sps.

Rnd 11: Rep Rnd 4: 42 petals.

Rnd 12: Sl st in next 3 dc, ch 1, sc in same st; *ch 7, skip next 6 sts, sc in next dc; rep from * around, end with ch 3, tr in beg sc to form last lp: 42 ch-7 lps.

Rnd 13: Ch 5, (tr, ch 1) 3 times in same lp: shell made; sc in next lp, ch 1; *(tr, ch 1) 7 times in next lp, sc in next lp, ch 1; rep from * around, end with (tr, ch 1) 3 times in beg lp, sl st in 4th ch of beg ch-5: 21 shells.

Rnd 14: Work beg Cl in same place as joining, ch 4, skip next tr, Cl in next tr; *ch 4, sc in sc, (ch 4, skip next tr, Cl in next tr) 3 times; rep from * around, end with last ch 4, join in top of beg Cl: 63 Cl. Finish off; weave in ends.

Block; use spray starch if desired.

#3 GLITZY CAPELET

Designed by Jean Leinhauser

SIZE
One size fits most

MATERIALS
Worsted weight mohair blend yarn with metallic component 100 g (218 yds)

Bulky weight nylon metallic ribbon yarn 50 g (82 yds)

Note: *Photographed model was made with Sunbeam Paris Mohair Sparkle #1916 Cannes and Berroco® Quest™ #9809 Silver (Striping pattern occurs naturally in the mohair yarn.)*

Tapestry or yarn needle

Size H (5 mm) crochet hook

Size N (10 mm) crochet hook (or size required for gauge)

GAUGE
8 dc = 5" with mohair yarn and larger hook

INSTRUCTIONS

With mohair yarn and larger hook, ch 52; join with sl st to form a circle, being careful not to twist chain.

Rnd 1: Ch 1, sc in each ch around: 52 sc; join in beg sc.

Rnd 2: Ch 3, (dc, ch 1, 2 dc) in joining; *dc in next 12 sc, shell of (2 dc, ch 1, 2 dc) in next sc; rep from * around, ending dc in last 12 sc, join in 3rd ch of beg ch-3

Rnd 3: Ch 3, dc in next dc, in ch-1 sp work shell; *dc in each dc around, working shell in ch-1 sp of previous shells, join in 3rd ch of beg ch-3.

Rnds 4 through 9: Rep Rnd 3; at end of last rnd, finish off, weave in ends.

Note: Try on garment; if neckline is too large, work one rnd of sc, decreasing evenly as many sts as needed.

Rose (make 2)

With smaller hook and metallic ribbon yarn, ch 4, join with sl st to form a ring.

Rnd 1: Ch 3 (counts as a dc), 9 dc in ring: 10 dc; join with sl st in 3rd ch of beg ch-3.

Rnd 2: Ch 1, sc in joining, sc in each rem dc around: 10 sc; join in beg sc.

Rnd 3: *Ch 2, skip next sc, sc in next sc; rep from * around, sc in joining sl st of Rnd 2: 5 ch-2 lps.

Rnd 4: (Sl st, ch 2, 4 dc, ch 2, sl st) in each ch-2 sp around: 5 petals made; join in beg sc.

Rnd 5: Working behind petals, ch 1; *sc in back lp of next skipped sc on Rnd 3, ch 4; rep from * around, join in beg sc: 5 ch-4 lps.

Rnd 6: (Sl st, ch 2, 7 dc, ch 2, sl st) in each ch-5 lp around: 5 petals made; join in beg sl st.

Rnd 7: Ch 2; working behind petals of Rnd 6, *sl st in bottom back of center dc of next petal on Rnd 6, ch 5; rep from * around, join in beg sl st.

Rnd 8: *In next ch-5 sp work (sl st, ch 2, 9 dc, ch 2, sl st); rep from * around, join in beg sl st.

Finish off, leaving a long yarn end for sewing.

Finishing

Fold two opposite corners of capelet up to neckline and sew in place. Sew one rose at neckline at each side on top of folded corners.

SIZE

5 $\frac{1}{2}$" x 7 $\frac{1}{4}$"(white version)

5 $\frac{1}{4}$" x 7" (gold version)

MATERIALS

White version: Size 5 crochet cotton
100 yds

Gold version: Size 10 metallic crochet cotton
200 yds (used doubled)

Note: *Photographed models made with size 5 J&P Coats® Royale™ Silkessence Microfiber #2101 White or Size 10 J&P Coats® Royale™ crochet cotton, metallic gold*

Size 2 (2.25 mm) steel crochet hook (or size required for gauge)

GAUGE

5 ch-2 sps = 2" in mesh pattern

STITCH GUIDE

Block over block (BL over BL): Dc in next 3 dc.

Block over space (BL over sp): 2 dc in next ch-2 sp, dc in next dc.

Space over block (sp over BL): Ch 2, skip next 2 dc, dc in next dc.

Space over space (sp over sp): Ch 2, dc in next dc.

[Chart with shamrock/clover filet crochet pattern]

Row 7

 BL over BL   BL over sp

sp over BL   sp over sp

INSTRUCTIONS

Ch 51, using 2 strands held tog if using metallic thread, 1 strand if using white.

Row 1 (right side): Dc in 9th ch from hook; *ch 2, skip 2 chs, dc in next ch; rep from * across: 15 ch-2 sps, counting beg ch as dc and ch-2 sp; turn.

Rows 2 through 5: Ch 5 (equals first dc plus ch-2), dc in next dc; *ch 2, dc in next dc; rep from * across; turn.

Row 6: Ch 5, (dc in next dc, ch 2) 7 times; (dc in next dc, 2 dc in next sp) twice; dc in next dc, ch 2, dc in next dc; (BL over sp) twice, (sp over sp) twice: 11 sps, 4 blocks; turn.

Beginning with Row 7 of chart, start following chart; turn at end of each row and work ch-5 at beg of each row.

At end of last row, do not finish off, ch 1, turn.

Edging

Rnd 1: Sc in first dc; *2 sc in next sp, sc in next dc; rep from * across.

Fold piece in half so that first row and last row meet, and wrong sides are tog. Working now across side and into sps on both front and back at same time, sc in first sp, (5 dc in next sp, sc in next sp) 7 times; working across bottom, 2 sc in same sp as last sc, (5 dc in next sp, sc in next sp) 7 times; working across opposite side and into both lps as before, 2 sc in same sp as last sc, (5 dc in next sp, sc in next sp) 7 times; join with a sl st in beg sc on front and in last dc on back at same time.

Flap (worked across back only)

Row 1: Sl st into first sp, ch 1, 2 sc in same sp; (sc in next dc, 2 sc in next sp) 14 times, sc in last dc, ch 3, turn.

Row 2: Skip first sc, sc in each rem sc to last sc, skip last sc; ch 3, turn.

Rep Row 2 until 4 sc remain; at end of last row, ch 3, turn.

Last Row: Skip first sc, sc in next 2 sc, skip last sc. Finish off; weave in ends.

Straps

With right side facing, join thread with sl st in last sc of front, and into last dc of mesh row on back; tightly ch 100, join with sl st to opposite side, ch 100, join in beg sl st. Finish off.

#6 GLITTER GIRL BOLERO

Designed by Dora Ohrenstein

MATERIALS

Worsted weight metallic blend yarn
7 (8 1/2, 10 1/2) oz silver/copper
(main color)

Worsted weight boucle type yarn with
metallic and eyelash components
1 3/4 oz silver/gold/copper for all
sizes (trim color)

Note: *Photographed model made with
Berroco® Jewel FX™ #6903 Moonstones
(main color) and Trendsetter Yarns
Sorbet #1028 Silver/Gold/Copper (trim
color)*

Stitch markers or contrast yarn

Sewing needle and thread

Safety pin

Size H (5 mm) crochet hook (or size
required for gauge)

GAUGE

7 V-sts = 5" with worsted weight yarn

Note: *Instructions are written for size Small; changes
for sizes Medium and Large are in parentheses*

SIZES	Small	Medium	Large
Body bust Measurements	28" - 32"	34" - 36"	40" - 42"
Finished Bust Measurements	33"	38 1/2 "	44"

INSTRUCTIONS

Note: The garment begins at the hemline and is worked in one piece to armholes, where it is then divided with fronts and back worked separately.

Body

With worsted weight yarn, ch 92 (110, 128).

Row 1 (right side): Dc in 5th ch from hook; * skip 2 chs, V-st in next ch; rep from * to last 3 last chs; skip 2 chs, dc in last ch; ch 3, turn: 28 (34, 40) V-st.

Row 2: V-st in each V-st across; dc in turning ch; ch 3, turn.

Row 3: (V-st in next V-st) 14 (17, 20) times; V-st between last V-st worked and next V-st; (V-st in next V-st) 14 (17, 20) times; dc in turning ch; ch 3, turn: 29 (35, 41) V-st.

Row 4: (V-st in next V-st) 2 (3, 4) times; 2 V-st in next V-st; (V-st in next V-st) 3 (4, 5) times; 2 V-st in next V-st; (V-st in next V-st) 15 (17, 19) times; 2 V-st in next V-st; (V-st in next V-st) 3 (4, 5) times; 2 V-st in next V-st; (V-st in next V-st) 2 (3, 4) times; dc in turning ch; ch 3, turn: 33 (39, 45) V-st.

Row 5: (V-st in next V-st) 16 (19, 22) times; 2 V-st in next V-st; (V-st in next V-st) 16 (19, 22) times; dc in turning ch; ch 3, turn: 34 (40, 46) V-st.

Row 6: (V-st in next V-st) 3 (4, 5) times; V-st between last V-st worked and next V-st; (V-st in next V-st) 5 (6, 7) times; V-st between last V-st worked and next V-st; (V-st in next V-st) 18 (20, 22) times; V-st between last V-st worked and next V-st; (V-st in next V-st) 5 (6, 7) times; V-st between last V-st worked and next V-st; (V-st in next V-st) 3 (4, 5) times; dc in turning ch; ch 3, turn: 38 (44, 50) V-st.

Row 7: (V-st in next V-st) 19 (22, 25) times; V-st between last V-st worked and next V-st; (V-st in next V-st) 19 (22, 25) times; dc in turning ch; ch 3, turn: 39 (45, 51) V-st.

Row 8: (V-st in next V-st) 3 (4, 5) times; 2 V-st in next V-st; (V-st in next V-st) 5 (6, 7) times; 2 V-st in next V-st; (V-st in next V-st) 19 (21, 23) times; 2 V-st in next V-st; (V-st in next V-st) 5 (6, 7) times; 2 V-st in next V-st; (V-st in next V-st) 3 (4, 5) times; dc in turning ch; ch 3, turn: 43 (49, 55) V-st.

Row 9: (V-st in next V-st) 21 (24, 27) times; 2 V-st in next V-st; (V-st in next V-st) 21 (24, 27) times; dc in turning ch; ch 3, turn: 44 (50, 56) V-st.

For Sizes Medium and Large Only

Row 10: (V-st in next V-st) 25 (28) times; V-st between last V-st worked and next V-st; (V-st in next V-st) 25 (28) times; dc in turning ch; ch 3, turn: 51 (57) V-st.

Row 11: (V-st in next V-st) 25 (28) times; 2 V-st in next V-st; (V-st in next V-st) 25 (28) times; dc in turning ch; ch 3, turn: 52 (58) V-st.

For Size Large Only

Row 12: (V-st in next V-st) 29 times; V-st between last V-st worked and next V-st; (V-st in next V-st) 29 times; dc in turning ch; ch 3, turn: 59 V-st.

Row 13: (V-st in next V-st) 29 times; 2 V-st in next V-st; (V-st in next V-st) 29 times; dc in turning ch; ch 3, turn: 60 V-st.

For All Sizes

Row 10 (12, 14): Skip first V-st; (V-st in next V-st) 3 (4, 5) times; V-st between last V-st worked and next V-st; (V-st in next V-st) 7 (8, 9) times; V-st between last V-st worked and next V-st; (V-st in next V-st) 22 (26, 30) times; V-st between last V-st worked and next V-st; (V-st in next V-st) 7 (8, 9) times; V-st between last V-st worked and next V-st; (V-st in next V-st) 3 (4, 5) times; skip last V-st; dc in turning ch; ch 3, turn: 46 (54, 62) V-st.

Row 11 (13, 15): V-st in next V-st 11 (13, 15) times; V-st in next V-st, mark same st for start of Right Front section; V-st in next V-st 22 (26, 30) times; V-st in next V-st, mark same st for start of Back section; V-st in next V-st 11 (13, 15) times; dc in turning ch; ch 3, turn.

Begin separation at armhole.

Left Front

Row 12 (14, 16) (wrong side): Skip first V-st; (V-st in next V-st) 10 (12, 14) times; dc in next V-st (same st marked for start of Back Section, do not move marker); ch 3, turn: 10 (12, 14) V-st.

Row 13 (15, 17): V-st in each V-st across; dc in turning ch; ch 3, turn.

Row 14 (16, 18): Skip first V-st; (V-st in next V-st) 9 (11, 13) times; dc in turning ch; ch 3, turn: 9 (11, 13) V-st.

Rows 15 (17, 19) through 23 (27, 31): V-st in each V-st across; dc in turning ch; ch 3, turn. At end of last row, finish off; weave in ends.

Back

Row 12 (14, 16) (wrong side): Join worsted weight yarn with sl st in V-st marked for start of Back section, ch 3, remove marker; (V-st in next V-st) 22 (26, 30) times; dc in next V-st (same st marked for start of Right Front Section, do not move marker); ch 3, turn: 22 (26, 30) V-st.

Row 13 (15, 17): (V-st in next V-st) 11 (13, 15) times; V-st between last V-st worked and next V-st; (V-st in next V-st) 11 (13, 15) times; dc in turning ch; ch 3, turn: 23 (27, 31) V-st.

Row 14 (16, 18): V-st in each V-st across; dc in turning ch; ch 3, turn.

Row 15 (17, 19): (V-st in next V-st) 11 (13, 15) times; 2 V-st in next V-st; (V-st in next V-st) 11 (13, 15) times; dc in turning ch; ch 3, turn: 24 (28, 32) V-st.

Row 16 (18, 20): V-st in each V-st across; dc in turning ch; ch 3, turn.

Row 17 (19, 21): (V-st in next V-st) 12 (14, 16) times; V-st between last V-st worked and next V-st; (V-st in next V-st) 12 (14, 16) times; dc in turning ch; ch 3, turn: 25 (29, 33) V-st.

Row 18 (20, 22): V-st in each V-st across; dc in turning ch; ch 3, turn.

Row 19 (21, 23): (V-st in next V-st) 12 (14, 16) times; 2 V-st in next V-st; (V-st in next V-st) 12 (14, 16) times; dc in turning ch; ch 3, turn: 26 (30, 34) V-st.

Row 20 (22, 24): V-st in each V-st across; dc in turning ch; ch 3, turn.

For Size Small Only
Row 21: V-st in each V-st across; dc in turning ch; ch 3, turn; proceed to shoulder shaping, Left Shoulder.

For Sizes Medium and Large Only
Row 23 (25): (V-st in next V-st) 15 (17) times; V-st between last V-st worked and next V-st; (V-st in next V-st) 15 (17) times; dc in turning ch; ch 3, turn: 31 (35) V-st.

Row 24 (26): V-st in each V-st across; dc in turning ch; ch 3, turn.

Row 25 (27): (V-st in next V-st) 15 (17) times; 2 V-st in next V-st; (V-st in next V-st) 15 (17) times; dc in turning ch; ch 3, turn: 32 (36) V-st.

For Size Medium Only
Proceed to shoulder shaping, Left Shoulder.

For Size Large Only
Row 28: V-st in each V-st across; dc in turning ch; ch 3, turn.

Row 29: (V-st in next V-st) 18 times; V-st between last V-st worked and next V-st; (V-st in next V-st) 18 times; dc in turning ch; ch 3, turn: 37 V-st.

Begin shoulder shaping.

Left Shoulder

Row 22 (26, 30): (V-st in next V-st) 9 (11, 13) times; dc between last V-st worked and next V-st; ch 3, turn: 9 (11, 13) V-st.

Row 23 (27, 31): V-st in each V-st across; dc in turning ch; finish off, weave in ends.

Right Shoulder

Row 22 (26, 30) (wrong side): With wrong side facing, join worsted weight yarn with sl st between V-st 17 (21, 24) and V-st 18 (22, 25) of previous row, ch 3; (V-st in next V-st) 9 (11, 13) times; dc in turning ch; ch 3, turn: 9 (11, 13) V-st.

Row 23 (27, 31): V-st in each V-st across; dc in turning ch; finish off, weave in ends.

Right Front

Row 12 (14, 16) (wrong side): Join worsted weight yarn with sl st in V-st marked for start of Right Front section, ch 3, remove marker; (V-st in next V-st) 10 (12, 14) times; skip last V-st; dc in turning ch, ch 3, turn: 10 (12, 14) V-st.

Row 13 (15, 17): V-st in each V-st across; dc in turning ch; ch 3, turn.

Row 14 (16, 18): (V-st in next V-st) 9 (11, 14) times; skip last V-st; dc in turning ch, ch 3, turn: 9 (11, 13) V-st.

Rows 15 (17, 19) through 23 (27, 31): V-st in each V-st across; dc in turning ch; ch 3, turn. At end of last row, finish off; weave in ends.

With right sides tog, sew fronts to back across shoulders.

Sleeves

Note: Sleeves are attached directly to garment and worked in rounds from armhole to wrist, with first rnd worked over sts at end of armhole rows.

Left Sleeve

With wrong side facing and bottom of garment to the right, locate bottom row of Left armhole.

Rnd 1 (wrong side): Join worsted weight yarn with sl st in end st of bottom row of Left armhole; (ch 1, sc) in same row; (ch 5, skip next row, sc in end st of next row) 11 (13, 15) times; (ch 2, dc) in beg sc (counts as ch-5 sp); ch 1, do not turn: 12 (14, 16) ch-5 sps.

Rnd 2: Sc into first ch-5 sp; (ch 5, sc in next ch-5 sp) 11 (13. 15) times; (ch 2, dc) in beg sc (counts as ch-5 sp); ch 1, do not turn.

Rep Rnd 2 twenty times more or to desired length, minus 1". Finish off; weave in ends.

Sleeve Edging

With wrong side facing, join trim yarn with sl st in last st worked.

Rnd 1 (wrong side): Sc in first ch-5 sp; (ch 5, sc in next ch-5 sp) 11 times; (ch 2, dc) in beg sc, ch 1, do not turn.

Rnd 2: Rep Rnd 1. Finish off; weave in ends.

Work Right sleeve and edging same as Left.

Trim

Holding bolero with wrong side of garment facing and hem at top, join trim yarn with sl st in any st in center back of body.

Rnd 1: Sc evenly around outside edge of garment, adjusting sts as needed to keep work flat and working 3 sc in corners; join in beg sc. Finish off; weave in ends.

Front Fastener

With trim yarn, ch 4; join with sl st to form a ring.

Rnd 1: Ch 3 (count as a dc), 11 dc in ring; sl st in top of ch-3: 12 dc.

Finish off, weave in ends.

With sewing needle and thread, attach fastener to left front of bolero. When wearing bolero, use safety pin to attach fastener to right front of bolero.

#7 BIG SCARY SPIDER CAT TOY

Designed by Jean Leinhauser

MATERIALS

Worsted weight yarn
   1 oz black

Note: *Photographed model made with Caron® Wintuk® #3009 Black*

Size I (5.5 mm) crochet hook
   (or size required for gauge)

GAUGE

6 dc = 2"

INSTRUCTIONS

Ch 4.

Rnd 1 (right side): 15 dc in 4th ch from hook: 16 dc, counting beg ch-4 as a dc; join with a sl st in 4th ch of beg ch-4.

Rnd 2: *Ch 16, hdc in 2nd ch from hook and in each rem ch; skip next dc on Rnd 1, sc in next dc; rep from * 7 times more: 8 legs made; join in sc at base of beg ch-16. Finish off; weave in ends.

Cord

Leaving an 8" yarn end, ch 75.

Row 1: Sc in 2nd ch from hook and in each rem ch: 74 sc. Finish off, leaving a 6" yarn end. Weave end back through chs. Tie a knot at end of cord.

From right side, draw beg 8" yarn end through center of Rnd 1 to wrong side, and sew in place securely.

WRAP UP!

Designed by Zena Low for Bernat® Yarns

SIZE
About 18" wide x 63" long
   plus fringe

MATERIALS:
Bulky weight yarn
   14 oz lt. blue

Note: Photographed model made with Bernat® Solo #57128 Water

Size L (8 mm) crochet hook
   (or size required for gauge)

GAUGE:
In pattern, 9 sts = 4" in patt

5 rows = 4"

INSTRUCTIONS

Ch 44 loosely.

Row 1 (right side): Dc in 6th ch from hook (counts as a dc and ch-1 sp); *ch 1, skip next ch, dc in next ch; rep from * across: 21 dc; ch 3 (counts as dc on next row), turn. Place marker in last ch-1 sp (2nd ch of foundation ch).

Row 2: Dc in first ch-1 sp; *ch 1, skip next dc, dc in next ch-1 sp; rep from * to last dc; dc in last dc: 22 dc; ch 4 (counts as a dc and ch-1 sp on next row), turn.

Row 3: Skip next dc, dc in first ch-1 sp; *ch 1, skip next dc, dc in next ch-1 sp; rep from * to last 2 dc; ch 1, skip next dc, dc in last dc: 21 dc; ch 3, turn.

Rows 4 through 7: Rep Rows 2 and 3 two times more.

Row 8: *Skip next ch-1 sp, 3 dc in next dc, skip next ch-1 sp, dc in next dc; rep from * across, working last dc in 3rd ch of turning ch-4: 41 dc; ch 3, turn.

Row 9: *Skip next dc, 3 dc in next dc (middle dc of 3 dc on last row), skip next dc, dc in next dc; rep from * across, working last dc in 3rd ch of turning ch-3: 41 dc; ch 4, turn.

Row 10: Skip next dc, dc in next dc (middle dc of 3 dc on last row); *ch 1, skip next dc, dc in next dc; rep from * to end of row: 21 dc; ch 3, turn.

Rows 11 through 73: Rep Rows 2 through 10 seven times more.

Rows 74 through 79: Rep Rows 2 through 7 once. At end of Row 79, ch 1, turn instead of ch 3, turn. Do not finish off.

Fringe

Sl st in first ch-1 sp, ch 24, sl st in first ch to form lp, sl st in next dc; *sl st in next ch-1 sp, ch 24, sl st in first ch to form lp, sl st in next dc; rep from * to last ch-1 sp working last sl st in 3rd ch of turning ch-4: 20 fringes. Finish off.

With right side facing, join yarn with sl st in marked ch-1 sp at other end of wrap, ch 24, sl st in first ch to form lp, sl st in free lp of ch at base of next dc; *sl st in next ch-1 sp, ch 24, sl st in first ch to form lp, sl st in free lp of ch at base of next dc; rep from * to last ch-1 sp, working last sl st in 41st ch of foundation ch: 20 fringes. Finish off; weave in all ends.

#FLORAL POTHOLDER AND DISH CLOTH SET

Designed by Jean Leinhauser

SIZE

Potholder: 9" diameter

Dish cloth: 10 1/2" diameter

MATERIALS

Sport or DK weight cotton yarn
  3 oz white
  1/2 oz green
  1 oz pink

Note: *Photographed model made with Patons® Grace®, #231 Snow, #203 Lime and #207 Fuschia*

Size D (3.25 mm) crochet hook (or size required for gauge) for potholder

Size E (3.5 mm) crochet hook (or size required for gauge) for dish cloth

GAUGE

4 dc = 3/4" with size D hook

4 dc = 1" with size E hook

POTHOLDER

INSTRUCTIONS

Front

With green and smaller hook, ch 4.

Rnd 1: 11 dc in 4th ch from hook: 12 dc, counting beg 3 skipped chs as a dc; join with a sl st in 4th ch of beg ch-4; finish off green.

Rnd 2: Join white in any dc; ch 3 (counts as a dc here and throughout), dc in same st; 2 dc in each dc around: 24 dc; join in 3rd ch of beg ch-3.

Rnd 3: Ch 3, 2 dc in next dc; *dc in next dc, 2 dc in next dc; rep from * around: 36 dc; join as before; finish off white.

Rnd 4: Join green in any dc, ch 6 (counts as a dc and ch-3 sp), dc in next dc; *ch 3, dc in next dc; rep from * around: 36 dc and 36 ch-3 sps; finish off green.

Rnd 5: Join pink with a sc in any ch-3 sp; in same sp work 5 dc, sc: first petal made; *in each of next 5 ch-3 sps work petal of (sc, 5 dc, sc); remove lp from hook, insert hook from front to back between 3rd and 4th petals just made, and working behind petals, place dropped lp back on hook and draw through, ch 1: flower made. *Work petal in next 6 ch-3 sps, drop lp from hook, insert hook between 3rd and 4th petals just made and draw dropped lp through, ch 1: another flower made; rep from * around, join with a sl st in beg sc: 6 flowers made; finish off pink.

Rnd 6: Join white in ch-1 at end of any flower; ch 7 (counts as a tr and ch-3 sp), tr in same ch; *in center dc of each of next 3 flat petals work (dc, ch 3, dc); (tr, ch 3, tr) in next ch-1 at end of next flower; rep from * around, ending last rep (dc, ch 3, dc) in center dc of each of last 3 flat petals, join in 4th ch of beg ch-7.

Rnd 7: Sl st into next ch-3 sp; ch 3 (counts as a dc), 3 dc in same sp; 4 dc in each ch-3 sp around, join in 3rd ch of beg ch-3.

Rnd 8: Ch 3 (counts as a dc), dc in each of next 3 dc, ch 1; *dc in each of next 4 dc, ch 1; rep from * around, join as before. Finish off; weave in all ends.

Back

With white and smaller hook, ch 4.

Rnd 1: 11 dc in 4th ch from hook: 12 dc; join as before.

Rnd 2: Ch 3, dc in joining; 2 dc in each dc: 24 dc; join.

Rnd 3: Ch 3, 2 dc in next dc; *dc in next dc, 2 dc in next dc: 36 dc; join.

Rnd 4: Ch 3, dc in next dc, 2 dc in next dc; *dc in next 2 dc, 2 dc in next dc: 48 dc; join.

Rnd 5: Ch 6 (counts as a dc and ch-3 sp), skip next dc, dc in next dc; *ch 3, skip next dc, dc in next dc; rep from * around, ending ch 3, skip next dc, join in 3rd ch of beg ch-6.

Rnd 6: Sl st into next ch-3 sp; in sp work ch 4, 3 tr, ch 1; (4 tr, ch 1) in each rem ch-3 sp around; join.

Rnd 7: Ch 3 (counts as a dc), dc in next 3 tr, ch 1; *dc in next 4 tr, ch 1; rep from * around: join.

Rnd 8: Rep Rnd 7 working dc in dc; do not finish off, proceed to Assembly.

Assembly

Hold Front and Back with wrong sides tog.

Edging

Rnd 1: Working through both Front and Back and carefully matching sts, join white with sl st in any dc of Rnd 8; ch 1, sc in joining and in each dc and each ch-1 sp around; join, finish off white.

Rnd 2: Join green with sl st in any sc, ch 1; sc joining and in each sc around; join, ch 12 for hanging lp, sl st in joining. Finish off green; weave in all ends.

DISH CLOTH

INSTRUCTIONS

With larger hook and green, ch 4.

Rnd 1: 11 dc in 4th ch from hook: 12 dc, counting beg skipped chs as a dc; join with sl st 4th ch of beg ch-4.

Rnd 2: Ch 3 (counts as a dc), dc in joining; 2 dc in each dc around, join in 3rd ch of beg ch-3: 24 dc; finish off green.

Rnd 3: Join white with sl st in any dc; ch 3, 2 dc in next dc; *dc in next dc, 2 dc in next dc; rep from * around, join: 36 dc.

Rnd 4: Ch 3, dc in next dc, 2 dc in next dc; *dc in next 2 dc, 2 dc in next dc; rep from * around, join: 48 dc; finish off white.

Rnd 5: Join pink with sl st in any dc; ch 1, sc in joining; sc in each dc around, join; finish off pink.

Rnd 6: Join white in any dc; ch 3, dc in next 2 dc, 2 dc in next dc; *dc in next 3 dc, 2 dc in next dc; rep from * around, join with sc in 3rd ch of beg ch.

Rnd 7: *Ch 4, skip next 2 dc, sc in next dc; rep from * around, join in last sc of Rnd 6.

Rnd 8: Sl st into next ch-4 sp; ch 3, 3 dc in same sp, ch 1; * 4 dc in next ch-4 sp, ch 1; rep from * around; join.

Rnd 9: Rep Rnd 8, working 2 chs between each 4-dc group.

Rnd 10: Rep Rnd 8, working 3 chs between each 4-dc group.

Rnd 11: Rep Rnd 8, working 4 chs between each 4-dc group.

Rnd 12: Ch 1, sc in joining; sc in each dc around, working 4 sc in each ch-4 sp; join, finish off white.

Rnd 13: Join pink in any sc; ch 1, sc in joining; sc in each sc around, join. Finish off;

Weave in all ends.

#11 LITTLE FRIEND'S BACKPACK

Designed by Kathleen Stuart

SIZE
8" wide x 11" high x 4" deep

MATERIALS
Worsted weight yarn
  7 oz off-white
  3 1/2 oz blue/off-white

Note: Photographed model made with Bernat® Denimstyle #3006 Canvas and #3117 Stonewash

Size J (6 mm) crochet hook
  (or size required for gauge)

One 1 1/2" toggle button

Stitch markers

GAUGE
18 rows = 4"

16 sts = 4"

PATTERN STITCHES
Reverse sc (rev sc): Insert hook in st to right of last st and draw up a lp, YO and draw through 2 lps on hook: rev sc made.

Sc decrease (sc dec): (Insert hook in next st and draw up a lp) twice, YO and draw through all 3 lps on hook: sc dec made.

To change color: Work st until 2 lps rem on hook, drop old color, pick up new color and draw through both lps on hook, cut dropped color.

INSTRUCTIONS

Note: When working in rnds, do not join unless otherwise noted; mark first stitch in each rnd with a stitch marker.

Bottom
With blue/off-white, ch 14.

Row 1 (wrong side): Sc in 4th ch from hook (counts as ch-1 sp and sc); *ch 1, skip next ch, sc in next ch; rep from * across: 6 sc and 6 ch-1 sps; ch 2 (counts as ch-1 sp on next row now and throughout), turn.

Row 2 (right side): *Skip next sc, sc in skipped foundation ch below next ch-1 sp, ch 1; rep from * across, end with sc in 2nd ch of 3 skipped chs at beg of Row 1: 6 sc and 6 ch-1 sps; ch 2, turn.

Row 3: *Skip next sc, sc in sc one row below next ch-1 sp, ch 1; rep from * across, end with sc in first ch of turning ch-2: 6 sc and 6 ch-1 sps; ch 2, turn.

Rows 4 through 32: Rep Row 3 twenty nine times more. At end of last row, do not ch 2 or turn.

Front, Back and Sides

Rnd 1: Work 3 sc in edge of last sc on Row 32; 30 sc evenly across left-hand edge, 3 sc in corner ch sp; sc in free lp of foundation ch at base of first sc on Row 1, sc in free lp of next 9 foundation chs, 3 sc in free lp of last foundation ch; 30 sc evenly across right-hand edge, 3 sc in edge of last sc on Row 31; *sc in next sc, sc in sc one row below next ch-1 sp; rep from * across Row 32: 92 sc.

Rnd 2: Working in back loops only: sc in next 3 sc; *sc in next 3 sc, sc dec next 2 sc*; rep from * to * 5 times more; sc in next 16 sc; rep from * to * 6 times more; 2 sc in next sc, sc in last 12 sc: 81 sc.

Rnd 3: Sc in first sc; *ch 1, skip next sc, sc in next sc; rep from * around: 41 sc and 40 ch-1 sps.

Rnd 4: Ch 1, skip next sc; *sc in sc one row below next ch-1 sp, ch 1, skip next sc; rep from * around: 40 sc and 41 ch-1 sps.

Rnd 5: Sc in sc one row below next ch-1 sp; *ch 1, skip next sc, sc in sc one row below next ch-1 sp; rep from * around, changing to off-white in last sc: 41 sc and 40 ch-1 sps.

Rnds 6 through 51: With off-white, rep Rnds 4 and 5 twenty three times more.

Rnd 52: Sc in first sc; *sc in sc one row below next ch-1 sp, sc in next sc; rep from * around, changing to blue/off-white in last sc: 81 sc.

Rnd 53: Working in back lps only: sc in first sc and in each sc around: 81 sc; join with sl st in first sc.

Rnd 54: Ch 3, skip first sc, dc in next sc, ch 1, skip next sc; *dc in next 2 sc, ch 1, skip next sc; rep from * around: 54 dc and 27 ch-1 sps; join with sl st in 3rd ch of beg ch-3.

Rnd 55: Sc in same ch as joining, sc in next dc, sc in next ch-1 sp; *sc in next 2 dc, sc in next ch-1 sp; rep from * around: 81 sc. Finish off; weave in ends.

Flap

Row 1 (right side): Working in front lps only: join off-white with sc in 6th sc on Rnd 53, sc in next 29 sc on Rnd 53, leaving rem sc unworked: 30 sc; ch 2 (counts as ch-1 sp on next row now and throughout), turn.

Row 2: Skip first sc, sc in next sc; *ch 1, skip next sc, sc in next sc; rep from * across: 15 sc and 15 ch-1 sps; ch 2, turn.

Row 3: *Skip next sc, sc in sc one row below next ch-1 sp, ch 1; rep from * across, end with sc in first ch of turning ch-2: 15 sc and 15 ch-1 sps; ch 2, turn.

Rows 4 through 22: Rep Row 3 nineteen times more.

Row 23: *Skip next sc, sc in sc one row below next ch-1 sp, ch 1; rep from * across to last 3 sts (ch, sc, ch), sc in sc one row below next ch-1 sp, skip next sc, sc in first ch of turning ch-2: 15 sc and 14 ch-1 sps; ch 1 (does not count as st on next row now and through-out), turn.

Row 24: Sc in first sc, ch 1; *skip next sc, sc in sc one row below next ch-1 sp, ch 1; rep from * across to last 3 sts (ch, sc, ch), sc in sc one row below next ch-1 sp, skip next sc, sc in first ch of turning ch-2: 15 sc and 13 ch-1 sps; ch 1, turn.

Row 25: Sc in first sc, ch 1; *skip next sc, sc in sc one row below next ch-1 sp, ch 1; rep from * across to last 2 sts (ch, sc), sc dec in last 2 sts, working first part of sc dec in sc one row below next ch-1 sp and second part in last sc: 14 sc and 13 ch-1 sps; ch 2, turn.

Row 26: *Skip next sc, sc in sc one row below next ch-1 sp, ch 1; rep from * across to last 2 sts (ch, sc), sc dec in last 2 sts, working first part of sc dec in sc one row below next ch-1 sp and second part in last sc: 13 sc and 13 ch-1 sps; ch 2, turn.

Rows 27 through 30: Rep Rows 23 through 26. At end of Row 30: 11 sc and 11 ch-1 sps. Finish off; weave in ends.

Flap Edging

With right side facing, join blue/off-white with sc in edge of last sc on Row 1 of flap, work rev sc in rows ending with ch sps along edge of flap, rev sc in last sc dec on Row 30 and in next 5 ch-1 sps on Row 30, ch 6, sl st in last rev sc to form button lp, rev sc in rem ch-1 sps on Row 30, work rev sc in rows ending with ch sps along other edge of flap. Finish off; weave in ends.

Tie Cord

With blue/off-white, make a chain 26" long, sc in 2nd ch from hook and in each sc across. Finish off; weave in ends. Weave cord through ch sps on Rnd 54 of backpack.

Strap

With blue/off-white, ch 2.

Rnd 1: 6 sc in 2nd ch from hook: 6 sc, join and form a ring.

Rnd 2: *Sc in next sc, 2 sc in next sc; rep from * around; join: 9 sc.

Rnd 3: Sc in each sc around; do not join. From now on, work in sc around, forming a tube until strap measures 40". Finish off; weave in ends. Fold strap in half and tack together 2" below fold. Sew this folded loop to center back edge of flap. Sew ends of strap to back bottom edge of backpack about 5" apart.

Finishing

Fold flap down and mark where button needs to be placed. Sew button to front of backpack.

SKIRT

SIZES	Small	Medium	Large
Body Waist Measurements	24" - 26"	28" - 30"	32" - 34"
Finished Waist Measurements	25"	29"	33"
Body Hip Measurements	28" - 30"	32" - 34"	36" - 38"
Finished Hip Measurements	29"	33"	37"

MATERIALS

Worsted weight yarn
   6 (7, 8) oz white

Size J (6 mm) crochet hook
   (or size required for gauge)

Three $1/2$" diameter white buttons

GAUGE

11 sts = 4" in pattern (sc, dc)

9 rows = 4" in pattern (sc, dc)

STITCH GUIDE

V-stitch (V-st): (Dc, ch 1, dc) in specified st: V-st made.

Beginning V-stitch (beg V-st): Ch 4, dc in same st as joining: beg V-st made.

Shell: (3 dc, ch 1, 3 dc) in specified st: shell made.

INSTRUCTIONS

Front

Starting at top, ch 35 (41, 47).

Row 1 (right side): Sc in 2nd ch from hook and in each ch across: 34 (40, 46) sc; ch 1, turn.

Row 2: Sc in first sc, dc in next sc; *sc in next sc, dc in next sc; rep from * across: 17 (20, 23) sc and 17 (20, 23) dc; ch 1, turn.

Row 3: Sc in first dc, dc in next sc; *sc in next dc, dc in next sc; rep from * across; ch 1, turn.

Row 4: Rep Row 3, ending with ch 3 (counts as first dc on next row now and throughout), turn.

Row 5: Sc in first dc; *dc in next sc, sc in next dc; rep from * across to last st; work (dc, sc) in last st: 18 (21, 24) sc and 18 (21, 24) dc; ch 3, turn.

Row 6: Skip first sc, sc in next dc; *dc in next sc, sc in next dc; rep from * across, ending with sc in 3rd ch of turning ch-3; ch 3, turn.

Rows 7 and 8: Rep Row 6 two times more. At end of Row 8, ch 1 instead of ch 3. Place markers at beg and end of Row 8.

Row 9: (Sc, dc) in first sc; *sc in next dc, dc in next sc; rep from * across; work (sc, dc) in 3rd ch of turning ch-3: 19 (22, 25) sc and 19 (22, 25) dc; ch 1, turn.

Row 10: Sc in first dc, dc in next sc; *sc in next dc, dc in next sc; rep from * across; ch 1, turn.

Rows 11 and 12: Rep Row 10 two times more. At end of Row 12, ch 3, turn.

Row 13: Rep Row 5: 20 (23, 26) sc and 20 (23, 26) dc.

Rep Row 6 until piece measures about 12", or to desired length. At end of last row, do not ch 3. Finish off; weave in ends.

Back
Work same as front.

Assembly
Sew side seams, leaving opening on one side from top to marker.

Bottom Edging
Rnd 1: With right side facing, join with sc in any st on last row, work 75 (87, 99) more sc evenly around: 76 (88, 100) sc; join with sl st in first sc.

Rnd 2: Ch 1, sc in same st as joining, skip next sc, shell in next sc; *skip next sc, sc in next sc, skip next sc, shell in next sc; rep from * around: 19 (22, 25) sc and 19 (22, 25) shells; skip last sc; join with sl st in first sc.

Rnd 3: Work beg V-st, shell in ch-1 sp of next shell; *V-st in next sc, shell in ch-1 sp of next shell; rep from * across: 19 (22, 25) V-sts and 19 (22, 25) shells; join with sl st in 4th ch of beg V-st.

Rnd 4: Work beg V-st, shell in ch-1 sp of next shell; *V-st in ch-1 sp of next V-st, shell in ch-1 sp of next shell; rep from * across; join with sl st in 4th ch of beg V-st.

Rep Rnd 4 once more, or to desired length. At end of last rnd, finish off; weave in ends.

Finishing
Row 1: With right side facing, join with sc in edge of Row 8 on side seam with opening at top, work 9 more sc evenly spaced in edge of rows to top: 10 sc; ch 1, turn.

Row 2: Sc in first sc and in each sc across; ch 1, turn.

Row 3: Sc in first sc and in each sc across to last sc, work 3 sc in last sc, working across top, sc in edge of Rows 2 and 1, sc around each sc on Row 1 at top of skirt, working down opening on other side, sc in edge of same row; *ch 3, sc in edge of next 4 rows; rep from * once; ch 3, sc in edge of Row 8. Finish off; weave in ends.

Sew buttons on finishing Row 1 across from buttonholes.

SHRUG

SIZE
26" (26", 27") wide x 54" (56", 58") long

MATERIALS
Worsted weight yarn
 9 (9 ½, 10) oz white
Size J (6 mm) crochet hook
 (or size required for gauge)
Stitch markers

GAUGE
11 sts = 4" in pattern (sc, dc)
9 rows = 4" in pattern (sc, dc)

STITCH GUIDE

V-stitch (V-st): (Dc, ch 1, dc) in specified st: V-st made.

Beginning V-stitch (beg V-st): Ch 4, dc in same st as joining: beg V-st made.

Shell: (3 dc, ch 1, 3 dc) in specified st: shell made.

Note: *Shrug is worked from side to side, starting at one cuff and ending at the other.*

INSTRUCTIONS

First Sleeve
Starting at cuff, ch 23 (23, 25).

Row 1 (wrong side): Sc in 2nd ch from hook and in each ch across: 22 (22, 24) sc; ch 1, turn.

Row 2 (right side): Sc in first sc, dc in next sc; *sc in next sc, dc in next sc; rep from * across: 11 (11, 12) sc and 11 (11, 12) dc; ch 1, turn.

Row 3: Sc in first dc, dc in next sc; *sc in next dc, dc in next sc; rep from * across; ch 3 (counts as first dc on next row now and throughout), turn.

Row 4: Sc in first dc; *dc in next sc, sc in next dc; rep from * across to last st; work (dc, sc) in last st: 12 (12, 13) sc and 12 (12, 13) dc; ch 3, turn.

Row 5: Skip first sc, sc in next dc; *dc in next sc, sc in next dc; rep from * across, ending with sc in 3rd ch of turning ch-3; ch 3, turn.

Rows 6 and 7: Rep Row 5 two times more. At end of Row 7, ch 1 instead of ch 3.

Row 8: (Sc, dc) in first sc; *sc in next dc, dc in next sc; rep from * across to last st; (sc, dc) in 3rd ch of turning ch-3: 13 (13, 14) sc and 13 (13, 14) dc; ch 1, turn.

Rows 9 and 10: Sc in first dc, dc in next sc; *sc in next dc, dc in next sc; rep from * across; ch 1, turn.

Rep Rows 3 through 10 until piece measures about 14" to 15", ending with a Row 10. At end of last row: 19 (19, 20) sc and 19 (19, 20) dc. Place markers at beg and end of last row.

Body

Row 1: Sc in first dc, dc in next sc; *sc in next dc, dc in next sc; rep from * across; ch 1, turn.

Rep Row 1 until body measures about 19" (21", 23"). Place markers at beg and end of last row.

Second Sleeve

Rows 1 through 3: Rep Row 1 of body 3 times more.

Row 4: Skip first dc, dc in next sc; *sc in next dc, dc in next sc; rep from * across, ending with sc dec in last 2 sts: 18 (18, 19) sc and 18 (18, 19) dc; ch 3 (counts as dc on next row now and throughout), turn.

Row 5: Skip first sc dec, sc in next dc; *dc in next sc, sc in next dc; rep from * across; ch 3, turn.

Rows 6 and 7: Skip first sc, sc in next dc; *dc in next sc, sc in next dc; rep from * across, ending with sc in 3rd ch of turning ch-3; ch 3, turn. At end of Row 7, ch 1 instead of ch 3.

Row 8: Skip first sc, sc in next dc; *dc in next sc, sc in next dc; rep from * across, ending with dc dec in last 2 sts: 17 (17, 18) sc and 17 (17, 18) dc; ch 1, turn.

Row 9: Sc in first dc dec, dc in next sc; *sc in next dc, dc in next sc; rep from * across; ch 1, turn.

Rows 10 and 11: Sc in first dc, dc in next sc; *sc in next dc, dc in next sc; rep from * across; ch 1, turn.

Rep Rows 4 through 11 until sleeve measures about 14" to 15", ending by working a Row 9. At end of last row: 11 (11, 12) sc and 11 (11, 12) dc.

Cuff Row: Sc in first dc, sc in next sc; *sc in next dc, sc in next sc; rep from * across: 22 (22, 24) sc. Finish off; weave in ends.

Assembly

Sew sleeve seams from cuffs to markers, leaving body open between markers.

Cuff Trim

For Sizes Small and Medium Only
Rnd 1: With right side facing, join with sc in any sc on cuff row, sc in next 8 sc, sc dec in next 2 sc, sc in next 9 sc, sc dec in last 2 sc: 20 sc; join with sl st in first sc.

For Size Large Only
Rnd 1: With right side facing, join with sc in any sc on cuff row, sc in next sc and in each sc around: 24 sc; join with sl st in first sc.

For All Sizes

Rnd 2: Ch 1, sc in same st as joining, skip next sc, shell in next sc; *skip next sc, sc in next sc, skip next sc, shell in next sc; rep from * around: 5 (5, 6) sc and 5 (5, 6) shells; skip last sc; join with sl st in first sc.

Rnd 3: Work beg V-st, shell in ch-1 sp of next shell; *V-st in next sc, shell in ch-1 sp of next shell; rep from * across: 5 (5, 6) V-sts and 5 (5, 6) shells; join with sl st in 4th ch of beg V-st.

Rnd 4: Work beg V-st, shell in ch-1 sp of next shell; *V-st in ch-1 sp of next V-st, shell in ch-1 sp of next shell; rep from * across; join with sl st in 4th ch of beg V-st.

Rep Rnd 4 to desired length. At end of last rnd, finish off; weave in ends.

Collar and Trim

Rnd 1: With right side facing, join with sc in edge of any row on body, work 79 (87, 95) more sc evenly spaced in edges of rows on body: 80 (88, 96) sc.

Rnd 2: Rep Rnd 2 of cuff trim: 20 (22, 24) sc and 20 (22, 24) shells.

Rnd 3: Rep Rnd 3 of cuff trim: 20 (22, 24) V-sts and 20 (22, 24) shells.

Rnd 4: Rep Rnd 4 of cuff trim.

Rep Rnd 4 three times more, or to desired length. At end of last rnd, finish off; weave in ends.

KITCHEN ANGEL DISH CLOTH

Designed by Janie Herrin

SIZE
4 1/2" tall without halo

MATERIALS
Sport or DK weight yarn
  1 3/4 oz white,
  30 yds contrast color

***Note:** Photographed model made with Patons®
Grace® #60006 Snow and #60416 Pink*

1/2 yd 3/8" wide ribbon

Size D (3.25 mm) crochet hook (or size
  required for gauge)

GAUGE
11 dc = 2"

INSTRUCTIONS

Head

With white, ch 4 (counts as first dc).

Rnd 1: 10 dc in 4th ch from hook, join with sl st to 4th ch of beg ch-4: 11 dc.

Rnd 2 (wings and halo): Ch 3 (mark ch for st placement later), 2 dc in same st, 3 dc in next dc, ch 1; working around post of last dc made, work (sc, hdc, dc, tr); ch 2, sl st in top of last tr made, ch 3, sl st around same dc post as previous sts, sl st in next dc on head and in next 2 dc; ch 12 for halo, skip 3 sts, sl st in next 3 sts and around post of next dc (see st placement) ch 5, sl st in 3rd ch from hook; working around post, work (tr, dc, hdc, sc) sl st in FLO of next dc. (Note: This dc may be hidden somewhat under previous sts, push wing back so as not to skip).

Skirt

Rnd 1: Ch 5 (counts as first dc plus ch 2), working in FLO, dc in same st, ch 2; in FLO of each of next 3 sts, (dc, ch 2) twice in each st, turn; working behind sts just made and into free lps, work (dc, ch 2) twice in each of next 4 dc, join to 3rd ch of beg ch-5: 16 dc and 16 ch-2 sps.

Rnd 2: Sl st in ch-2 sp, ch 5, dc in same sp, ch 2; * (dc, ch 2) twice in next sp; rep from * around, join in 3rd ch of beg ch-5: 32 dc and 32 ch-2 sps.

Rnd 3: Rep Rnd 2: 64 dc and 64 ch-2 sps.

Rnd 4: Ch 3; *2 dc in next sp, dc in dc; rep from * around, ending with sl st in top of beg ch-3.

Rnd 5: Ch 4; *dc in next dc, ch 1; rep from * around, join in 3rd ch of beg ch-4.

Rnd 6: Ch 5; *dc in next dc, ch 2; rep from * around, join in 3rd ch of beg ch-5.

Rnd 7: Sl st in sp, ch 3, 2 dc in same sp, ch 1; *3 dc in next sp, ch 1; rep from * around, join tin top of beg ch-3; finish off.

Rnd 8: Join contrast color with sc in any ch-1 sp, ch 4; *sc in next sp, ch 4; rep from * around, join in beg sc. Finish off; weave in ends.

Tie ribbon into a bow and attach bow at waist.

#15 SQUARE DEAL VEST

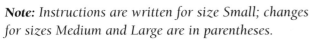

Note: *Instructions are written for size Small; changes for sizes Medium and Large are in parentheses.*

SIZES	Small	Medium	Large
Body Chest Measurements	30" - 32"	34" - 36"	38" - 40"
Finished Chest Measurements	32"	36"	40"

MATERIALS

Size 5 crochet cotton
   200 (220, 250) yds

Note: *Photograhed model made with Twilleys Lyscordet #86 Beige*

For size Small
   Size D (3.25 mm) crochet hook
   Size E (3.5 mm) crochet hook

For size Medium
   Size E (3.5 mm) crochet hook
   Size F (3.75 mm) crochet hook

For size Large
   Size F (3.75 mm) crochet hook
   Size G (4 mm) crochet hook

GAUGE

Measured diagonally,
   one square = 4" (4 1/2", 5")

INSTRUCTIONS

First Square

Rnd 1: With larger hook, ch 4, join with sl st to form a ring.

Rnd 2: Ch 1, 7 sc in ring, join with sc in beg sc.

Rnd 3: (Ch 3, sc in same place as last sc, sc in each of next 2 sc) 3 times; ch 3, sc in same place as last sc, sc in next sc, sc in beg ch-3 lp: 4 corner ch-3 lps.

Rnd 4: (Ch 3, sc in same corner lp, sc in each of next 3 sc, sc in corner lp) 4 times.

Rnd 5: (Ch 3, sc in same corner lp, sc in each of next 5 sc, sc in corner lp]) 4 times.

Rnd 6: (Ch 3, sc in same corner lp, ch 3, skip 3 sc, sc in next sc; ch 3, skip 3 sc, sc in next corner lp) 4 times.

Rnd 7: *Ch 3, sc in same corner lp; (sc in next sc, 3 sc in ch-3 lp) twice; sc in next sc, sc in next corner lp; rep from * 3 times more.

Rnd 8: *Ch 3, sc in same corner lp; (ch 3, skip 3 sc, sc in next sc] twice; ch 3, skip 3 sc, sc in next corner lp; rep from * 3 times more.

Rnd 9: *Ch 3, sc in same corner lp; (ch 1, skip 1 sc, 3 sc in next ch-3 sp) 3 times; ch 1,skip 1sc, sc in next corner lp; rep from * 3 times more, join with sl st in center ch of corner ch-3 lp. Finish off; weave in ends.

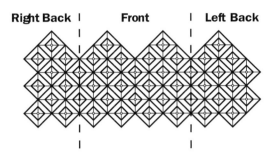

Right Back | Front | Left Back

Second Square

Work Rnds 1 through 8 same as First Square.

Rnd 9 (joining rnd): *Ch 3, sc in same corner lp; (ch 1, skip 1 sc, 3 sc in next ch –3 lp) 3 times; ch 1, skip 1 sc, sc in next corner lp; rep from * once more.

Place First Square, right side up, next to Second Square and join as follows: ch 1, sl st in corresponding corner lp of previous square, ch 1, sc in same place as last sc; (sl st in corresponding ch lp of previous square, skip 1 sc, 3 sc in next ch lp) 3 times; sl st in corresponding ch lp of previous square, skip 1 sc, sc in next corner lp, ch 1, sl st in corresponding corner lp of next square, ch 1, sc in same corner lp as last sc, complete rnd as for First Square. Finish off; weave in ends.

Make a total of 44 squares, joining them on one or more sides in this manner as required, following placement shown in Fig. Join the two side edges tog to complete the Front and Back.

Bottom Border

Rnd 1: With right side of work facing, with smaller hook, join yarn in ch-3 sp at one lower point, ch 1; * work I 5 sc evenly down side edge of square to inner corner, sc3tog at corner, 15 sc evenly up side edge of next square to point, 3 sc in 3 ch sp at point; rep from * around, ending 3 sc in same ch-3 sp as beg of rnd, join with sl st in beg sc.

Rnd 2: Ch 1, sc in first sc; * (ch 3, sl st in last sc: picot made; sc in each of next 3 sc) 4 times; picot, sc in next sc, 3 sctog at corner, sc in each of next 2 sc; (picot, sc in each of next 3 sc])4 times; picot, sc in next sc, 2 sc in next sc (which is the 2nd of 3 sc at point); picot, sc in same sc, sc in each of next 2 sc; rep from * around, ending sl st in beg sc. Finish off.

First Armhole Border and Strap

With right side of work facing, with hook, join yarn in ch-3 sp at point of Left Front.

Rnd 1: Ch 48(52, 54); ch, join with sl st to point of Left Back, being careful not to twist ch; work 30 sc evenly down armhole edge to underarm, sc3tog at corner, 30 sc evenly up armhole edge to point of Left Front, sc in each of 48 (52, 54) ch, sl st in next sc.

Rnd 2: Ch 1; (sc in each of next 3 sc, picot) 9 times; sc in each of next 2 sc, sc3tog at underarm; (sc in each of next 3 sc, picot) 9 times, sc in each sc to point of Left Front. Finish off.

Second Armhole Border and Strap

Work to match first border and strap, beginning at point of Right Back.

Neck Border

With right side of work facing, with smaller hook, join yarn in neck edge at point of Left Front.

Rnd 1: Ch 1; work 30 sc evenly down neck edge to center front, sc3tog at corner; work 30 sc evenly up neck edge to point of Right Front, sc in base of each chain of strap to point of Right Back; work 30 sc evenly down neck edge to center back, sc3tog at center back; work 30 sc evenly up neck edge to point of Left Back, sc in base of each chain of strap, ending sl st in beg sc of rnd.

Rnd 2 (first half): Ch 1; (sc in each of next 3 sc, picot)9 times; sc in each of next 2 sc, sc3tog at center front; (sc in each of next 3 sc, picot) 9 times; sc in each sc to point of Right Front. Finish off.

Rnd 2 (2nd half): Join yarn in neck edge at point of Right Back and work same as first half along back neck edge.

Weave in all yarn ends.

#16 SCARF IN STYLE

Designed by Susan Lowman

SIZE
7 1/2" wide x 55" long before fringe

MATERIALS
Worsted weight cotton yarn
 4 1/2 oz red
 4 oz pink
 4 oz white

Note: Photographed model made with Lily® Sugar 'n Cream® #15 Wine, #46 Rose Pink and #1 White

Size H (5 mm) crochet hook
 (or size required for gauge)

GAUGE
8 dc = 2 1/4"

6 rows = 2 1/4"

STITCH GUIDE

Front post tr (FPtr): YO twice, insert hook from front to back to front around post of specified st, YO and draw up a lp, (YO and draw through 2 lps on hook) 3 times: FPtr made.

Back post tr (BPtr): YO twice, insert hook from back to front to back around post of specified st, YO and draw up a lp, (YO and draw through 2 lps on hook) 3 times: BPtr made.

To change color: Work st until 2 lps rem on hook, drop first color, pick up new color and draw through both lps on hook, cut dropped color.

INSTRUCTIONS

With red, ch 28.

Row 1: Sc in 2nd ch from hook and in each ch across: 27 sc; ch 3 (counts as first dc of next row throughout pattern), turn.

Row 2: Dc across: 27 dc; ch 1, turn.

Row 3: Sc in each dc across, sc in 3rd ch tch, change to pink, ch 1, turn.

Row 4: Sc in first sc, (*FPtr around post of dc 1 row below next st, skip next sc, sc in next sc*; BPtr around post of dc 1 row below next st, skip next sc, sc in next sc) 6 times; rep from * to * once; ch 3, turn.

Row 5: Rep Row 2.

Row 6: Rep Row 3, change to white in last st.

Rows 7 through 9: Rep Rows 4 through 6, change to red in last st on Row 9.

Rows 10 through 12: Rep Rows 4 through 6, changing to pink in last st on Row 12.

Work Rows 4 through 12, fifteen times more. Finish off; weave in ends.

Fringe

Following fringe instructions on page 255, cut strands of each color 10" long. Knot 6 strands (2 strands of each color) in every other stitch on each short end of scarf. Trim fringe.

41

ROWS OF BOWS

Designed by Edie Eckman

MATERIALS

Sport weight yarn

11 1/4 (12 1/2, 15, 17 1/2) oz white

2 1/2 oz yellow

2 1/2 oz orange

2 1/2 oz green

Note: *Photographed model made with Lion Brand® MicroSpun #101 Lily White, #158 Buttercup, #186 Mango and #194 Lime*

Size J (6 mm) crochet hook (or size required for gauge)

Stitch markers

Five buttons, 5/8" diameter

GAUGE

15 dc = 4"; in patt (2 rows sc, 1 row dc)

12 rows = 4"

Note: *Instructions are written for size 2; changes for sizes 4,6 and 8 are in parentheses.*

CARDIGAN SIZES	2	4	6	8
Body Chest Measurements	21"	23"	25"	26 1/2"
Finished Chest Measurements	23 1/2"	25 1/2"	27 1/2"	29"

BAG SIZE

4 1/2" wide x 5" high plus strap

CARDIGAN

INSTRUCTIONS

Back

Starting at bottom, with white, ch 47 (51, 54, 58).

Row 1 (right side): Sc in 2nd ch from hook and in each ch across: 46 (50, 53, 57) sc; ch 1, turn.

Row 2: Sc in first st and in each st across; ch 3 (counts as dc on next row now and throughout), turn.

Row 3: Skip first st, dc in next st and in each st across: 46 (50, 53, 57) dc; ch 1, turn.

Row 4: Sc in first st and in each st across; ch 1, turn.

Rep Rows 3 through 4 until piece measures about 7" (8", 9", 10"), ending by working a Row 2. At end of last row: ch 1, turn.

Armhole Shaping

Row 1: Skip first st, sl st in next 3 (3, 3, 4) sts, ch 3 (counts as dc), dc in next st and in each st across to last 3 (3, 3, 4) sts, leaving last 3 (3, 3, 4) sts unworked: 40 (44, 47, 49) sc; ch 1, turn.

Row 2: Sc in first st and in each st across; ch 1, turn.

Row 3: Sc in first st and in each st across; ch 3 (counts as dc on next row now and throughout), turn.

Row 4: Skip first st, dc in next st and in each st across: 40 (44, 47, 49) dc; ch 1, turn.

Rep Rows 2 through 4 until piece measures about 12" (14", 15 1/2", 17 1/2"), ending by working a Row 3.

Neck Shaping

Row 1: Skip first st, dc in next 10 (12, 12, 13) sts: 11 (13, 13, 14) dc. Finish off; weave in ends. Skip next 18 (18, 21, 21) sts, join white with sl st in next st, ch 3 (counts as dc), dc in next st and in each st across: 11 (13, 13 14) dc. Finish off; weave in ends.

Front A
(Left front for sizes 2 and 6,
Right front for sizes 4 and 8)
Starting at bottom, with white, ch 24 (26, 28, 29).

Row 1 (right side): Sc in 2nd ch from hook and in each ch across: 23 (25, 27, 28) sc; ch 1, turn.

Row 2: Sc in first st and in each st across; ch 3 (counts as dc on next row), turn.

Row 3: Skip first st, dc in next st and in each st across: 23 (25, 27, 28) dc; ch 1, turn.

Row 4: Sc in first st and in each st across; ch 1, turn.

Rep Rows 2 through 4 until piece measures about 7" (8", 9", 10"), ending by working a Row 2. At end of last row: ch 1, turn.

Armhole Shaping

Row 1: Skip first st, sl st in next 3 (3, 4, 4) sts, ch 3 (counts as dc), dc in next sc and in each sc across: 20 (22, 23, 24) dc; ch 1, turn.

Row 2: Sc in first st and in each st across: 20 (22, 23, 24) sc; ch 1, turn.

Row 3: Sc in first st and in each st across: ch 3 (counts as dc on next row now and through-out), turn.

Row 4: Skip first st, dc in next st and in each st across; ch 1, turn.

Rep Row 2 through 4 until piece measures about 10" (12", 13 1/2", 15 1/4"), ending at front edge by working a Row 3.

Neck Shaping

Row 1: Skip first sc, dc in next st and in each st across to last 6 (6, 7, 7) sts, leaving last 6 (6, 7, 7) sts unworked: 14 (16, 16, 17) dc; ch 1, turn.

Row 2: Skip first st, sl st in next st, ch 1, sc in same st as sl st, sc in each st across: 13 (15, 15, 16) sc; ch 1, turn.

Row 3: Sc in first st and in each st across to last st, leaving last st unworked: 12 (14, 14, 15) sc; ch 1, turn.

Row 4: Skip first st, sl st in next st, ch 3 (counts as dc), dc in next st and in each st across: 11 (13, 13, 14) dc; ch 1, turn.

Row 5: Sc in first st and in each st across; ch 1, turn.

Row 6: Sc in first st and in each st across; ch 3, turn.

Row 7: Skip first st, dc in next st and in each st across: ch 1, turn.

Rep Rows 5 through 7 as needed until piece measures 12 1/2" (14 1/2", 16", 18"). At end of last row, do not ch 1. Finish off; weave in ends.

Front B
(Right front for sizes 2 and 6, Left front for sizes 4 and 8)
Starting at bottom, with white, ch 24 (26, 28, 29).

Rows 1 through 5: Rep Rows 1 through 5 of Front A.

Rep Rows 2 through 4 until piece measures about 7" (8", 9", 10"), ending by working a Row 2. At end of last row: ch 3, turn.

Armhole Shaping

Row 1: Skip first st, dc in next st and in each st across to last 3 (3, 4, 4) sts, leaving last 3 (3, 4, 4) sts unworked: 20 (22, 23, 24) dc; ch 1, turn.

Rows 2 through 6: Rep Rows 2 through 4 of armhole shaping on Front A.

Rep Rows 2 through 4 until piece measures about 10" (12", 13 1/2", 15 1/4"), ending at front edge by working a Row 3. At end of last row: ch 1, turn.

Neck Shaping

Row 1: Skip first st, sl st in next 6 (6, 7, 7) sts, ch 3 (counts as dc), dc in next st and in each st across: 14 (16, 16, 17) dc; ch 1, turn.

Row 2: Sc in first st and in each st across to last st, leaving last st unworked: 13 (15, 15, 16) sc; ch 1, turn.

Row 3: Skip first st, sl st in next st, ch 1, sc in same st as sl st, sc in each st across: 12 (14, 14, 15) sc; ch 3, turn.

Row 4: Skip first st, dc in next st and in each st across to last st, leaving last st unworked: 11 (13, 13, 14) dc; ch 1, turn.

Rows 5 through 7: Rep Rows 5 through 7 of neck shaping on Front A.

Rep Row 5 through 7 as needed until piece measures 12 1/2" (14 1/2", 16", 18"). At end of last row, do not ch 1. Finish off; weave in ends.

Sleeves (make 2)

Starting at bottom, with white, ch 24 (28, 30, 31).

Row 1 (right side): Sc in 2nd ch from hook and in each ch across: 23 (27, 29, 30) sc; ch 1, turn.

Row 2: Sc in first st and in each st across; ch 3 (counts as dc on next row now and throughout), turn.

Row 3: Dc in first st and in each st across to last st, 2 dc in last st: 25 (29, 31, 32) dc; ch 1, turn.

Row 4: Sc in first st and in each st across; ch 1, turn.

Rows 5 and 6: Rep Rows 2 and 3. At end of Row 6: 27 (31, 33, 34) dc.

Rows 7 through 30 (33, 36, 39): Rep Rows 4 through 6 eight (nine, ten, eleven) times more. At end of last row: 43 (49, 53, 56) dc.

Row 31 (34, 37, 40): Rep Row 4.

Row 32 (35, 38, 41): Rep Row 2.

Row 33 (36, 39, 42): Skip first st, dc in next st and in each st across; ch 1, turn.

Rep Rows 31 (34, 37, 40) through 33 (36, 39, 42) until sleeve measures about 12 1/2" (13 1/2", 14 1/4", 15"). At end of last row, do not ch 1. Finish off; weave in ends.

Bows

Make about 16-24 each from yellow and orange, depending upon sweater size and placement of bows.

With appropriate color, ch 40, sc in 2nd ch from hook and in each ch across: 39 sc. Finish off; weave in ends.

Finishing

Sew shoulder seams. Sew sleeves to front and back with center of sleeves at shoulder seams. Sew side and sleeve seams.

Sleeve Border

With right side facing, join green with sl st in free lp of first ch on bottom edge of sleeve, ch 1, sc in free lp of each ch around bottom edge of sleeve; join with sl st in first sc. Finish off; weave in ends. Rep on second sleeve.

Sweater Border

Place 5 markers for buttonholes along right front center edge of sweater, with top and bottom markers 1/2" from neck and bottom edge and other 3 markers evenly spaced between top and bottom markers.

Row 1: With right side facing, join white with sl st in free lp of first ch at bottom of right side, ch 1, sc in same sp and in free lp of each ch across bottom edge, 3 sc in corner, sc evenly up Right Front edge, 3 sc in corner st at beg of right neck shaping, sc evenly around neck, 3 sc in corner st at beg of left neck shaping, sc evenly down Left Front edge to bottom corner, 3 sc in corner, sc in free lp of each ch along bottom of Left Front and Back; join with sl st in first sc. Finish off; weave in ends.

Row 2: With right side facing, join green with sl st in first sc, ch 1, sc in same sp as joining, sc in each st around entire edge, working 3 sc in each corner st and making buttonholes with (ch 1, skip next sc, sc in next sc) at markers; join with sl st in first sc. Finish off; weave in ends.

Tie bows evenly spaced along dc rows on fronts following photograph, or as desired. Tie a single row of bows along bottom dc row on back.

Sew buttons to Left Front center edge on Row 1 of border, aligning with buttonholes on Right Front edge.

BAG

INSTRUCTIONS

With white, ch 17.

Row 1 (right side): Sc in 2nd ch from hook and in each ch across: 16 sc; ch 1, turn.

Row 2: Sc in first st and in each st across; ch 3 (counts as dc on next row), turn.

Row 3: Skip first st, dc in next st and in each st across: 16 dc; ch 1, turn.

Row 4: Sc in next st and in each st across; ch 1, turn.

Rows 5 and 6: Rep Rows 2 and 3.

Rep Rows 4 through 6 until piece measures 10". At end of last row, do not ch 1. Finish off; weave in ends.

Fold bag in half with wrong sides together and pin. Join green with sl st through both layers in bottom right-hand corner, ch 1, sc in same sp, sc along right-hand edge through both layers to top corner. Make about 18" ch, or desired length, sc along left-hand edge through both layers to bottom corner. Finish off; weave in ends.

Tie bows onto bag following photograph, or as desired.

#19 ENTRELAC SKULL CAP

Designed by Joyce Renee Wyatt

STITCH GUIDE

Sc decrease (sc dec): (Insert hook in specified st, YO and pull up a lp) twice, YO and pull through all 3 lps on hook: sc dec made.

3 Sc decrease (3 sc dec): (Insert hook in specified st, YO and pull up a lp) 3 times, YO and pull through all 4 lps on hook: 3 sc dec made.

INSTRUCTIONS

Headband
(starting at bottom of hat)
With J hook, ch 54 loosely; join with sl st in 1st ch to form a ring; ch 1, turn.

Rnd 1 (right side): Sc in back lp of first ch and in back lp of each ch around: 54 sc; sl st in first sc. Do not turn.

Rnds 2 and 3: Ch 1, sc in same sc as joining, sc in each sc around; sl st in first sc. Do not turn.

Rnd 4: With L hook, ch 1, sc in same sc as joining, sc in each sc around: 54 sc; sl st in first sc. Do not turn.

Triangle #1

Row 1: With right side facing and L hook, ch 1, sc loosely in first sc; turn.

Row 2: 2 sc in sc: 2 sc; ch 1, turn.

Row 3: 2 sc in first sc, sc in next sc: 3 sc; skip next sc on Rnd 4 of Headband, sl st in next sc on Rnd 4 of Headband; turn.

Row 4: 2 sc in first sc, sc in next 2 sc: 4 sc; ch 1, turn.

Row 5: 2 sc in first sc, sc in next 3 sc: 5 sc; skip next sc on Rnd 4 of Headband, sl st in next sc on Rnd 4 of Headband; turn.

Row 6: 2 sc in first sc, sc in next 4 sc: 6 sc; ch 1, turn.

Row 7: 2 sc in first sc, sc in next 5 sc: 7 sc; skip next sc on Rnd 4 of Headband, sl st in next sc on Rnd 4 of Headband; turn.

Row 8: Sc in each sc across; ch 1, turn.

Row 9: Sc in each sc across: 7 sc; skip next sc on Rnd 4 of Headband, sl st in next sc on Rnd 4 of Headband. Do not turn.

Triangles #2 through #6

Row 1: Sc loosely in next sc on Rnd 4 of Headband; turn.

Rows 2 through 9: Rep Rows 2 through 9 of Triangle #1. At end of Row 9 on Triangle #6, sl st in first sc on Triangle #1. Finish off and weave in ends.

Square #1

Row 1: With wrong side facing and working across edge of triangle, join with sl st in edge of last sc on Row 8 of Triangle #1, ch 1, sc in edge of same sc as joining, sc in edge of next 6 rows: 7 sc; sl st in last sc on Row 9 of Triangle #6; turn.

Row 2: Sc in each sc across; ch 1, turn.

Row 3: Sc in each sc across, sl st in next 2 sc on Row 9 of same triangle as last sl st; turn.

Rows 4 through 7: Rep Rows 2 and 3 two times more.

Row 8: Rep Row 2.

Row 9: Sc in each sc across. Do not turn.

Squares #2 through #6

Row 1: Sc in edge of last sc on Row 8 of same triangle as last sl st, sc in edge of next 6 rows: 7 sc; sl st in last sc on Row 9 of next triangle; turn.

Rows 2 through 9: Rep Rows 2 through 9 of Square #1. At end of Row 9 on Square #6, sl st in edge of first sc on Row 1 of Square #1. Finish off and weave in ends.

Decrease Square #1

Row 1: With right side facing and working across edge of square, join with sl st in edge of last sc on Row 8 of Square #6, ch 1, sc in edge of same sc as joining, sc in edge of next 6 rows; 7 sc; sl st in last sc on Row 9 of next square; turn.

Row 2: Sc in each sc across; ch 1, turn.

Row 3: Sc in next 2 sc, sc dec in next 2 sc, sc in next 3 sc: 6 sc; 3 sc dec in next 3 sc on Row 9 of same square as last sl st; turn.

Row 4: Skip 3 sc dec, sc in each sc across; ch 1, turn.

Row 5: Sc in next 2 sc, sc dec in next 2 sc, sc in next 2 sc: 5 sc; 3 sc dec in next 3 sc on Row 9 of same square as last 3 sc dec; turn.

Row 6: Rep Row 4.

Row 7: Sc in each sc across: 5 sc. Do not turn.

Decrease Squares
#2 through #6

Row 1: Sc in edge of last sc on Row 8 of same square as last 3 sc dec, sc in edge of next 6 rows: 7 sc; sl st in last sc on Row 9 of next square; turn.

Rows 2 through 7: Rep Rows 2 through 7 of Decrease Square #1. At end of Row 7 of Decrease Square #6, sl st in edge of first sc of Decrease Square #1. Finish off and weave in ends.

Decrease Triangle #1

Row 1: With wrong side facing and working across edge of decrease square, join with sl st in edge of last sc on Row 6 of Decrease Square #1, ch 1, sc in edge of same sc as joining, sc in edge of next 4 rows: 5 sc; sc dec in last 2 sc on Row 7 of next Decrease Square; turn.

Row 2: Skip sc dec, sc in each sc across; ch 1, turn.

Row 3: Sc in next 2 sc, sc dec in next 2 sc, sc in next sc: 4 sc; 3 sc dec in next 3 sc on Row 7 of same Decrease Square as last sc dec; turn.

Row 4: Skip 3 sc dec, sc in each sc across; ch 1, turn.

Row 5: Sc in next sc, sc dec in next 2 sc, sc in next sc: 3 sc. Do not turn.

Decrease Triangles
#2 through #6

Row 1: Sc in edge of last sc on Row 6 of same Decrease Square as last 3 sc dec, sc in edge of next 4 rows: 5 sc; sc dec in last 2 sc on Row 7 of next Decrease Square; turn.

Rows 2 through 5: Rep Rows 2 through 5 of Decrease Triangle #1. At end of Row 5 on Decrease Triangle #6, sl st in edge of first sc on Decrease Triangle #1. Finish off and weave in ends.

Closing Rnds

Rnd 1: With right side facing, join with sl st in last sc on Row 4 of Decrease Triangle #1, ch 1, sc in same sc as joining, sc in next 2 sc on same Decrease Triangle, (*sc in edge of last sc on Row 4 of same Decrease Triangle, sc in edge of next 2 rows of same Decrease Triangle*, sc in next 3 sc on next Decrease Triangle) 5 times, rep from * to * once: 36 sc; sl st in first sc. Do not turn.

Rnd 2: Ch 1, sc dec in same sc as joining and in next sc, (sc dec in next 2 sc) 17 times: 18 sc; sl st in first sc. Do not turn.

Rnd 3: Ch 1, sc dec in same sc as joining and in next sc, (sc dec in next 2 sc) 8 times: 9 sc; sl st in first sc. Finish off, leaving a long end.

Finishing

Draw end through rem sc on Rnd 3 and fasten securely. Weave in ends.

#20 SLINKY TUNIC

Designed by Belinda "Bendy" Carter for Berroco

Note: *Instructions are written for size Small; changes for sizes Medium and Large are in parentheses.*

SIZES	Small	Medium	Large
Body bust Measurements	32" - 34"	36" - 38	40" - 42"
Finished bust Measurements	40"	44"	48"

MATERIALS

Worsted weight yarn
  14 (15 $^3/_4$, 17 $^1/_2$) oz variegated
  7 (8 $^3/_4$, 8 $^3/_4$) oz blue

Note: *Photographed model made with Berroco® Quest™ #9932 St Barts and Berroco® Crystal™ FX #4704 Caribe*

Size J (6 mm) crochet hook
  (or size required for gauge)

Small safety pin

GAUGE

10 sts = 4"

PATTERN STITCHES

Lover's Knot (LKN): Insert hook in specified st and draw up a an elongated lp to height of beg ch on current row, holding base of elongated lp with thumb and middle finger of hand holding yarn, YO and draw through elongated lp, insert hook in single strand to left of elongated lp and draw up a lp, YO and draw through all 3 lps on hook: LKN made.

Sc decrease (sc dec): (Insert hook in specified st and draw up a lp) two times, YO and draw through all 3 lps on hook: sc dec made.

INSTRUCTIONS

Back

With variegated, ch 51 (57, 61).

Row 1 (right side): Sc in back ridge of 2nd ch from hook and in back ridge of each ch across: 50 (56, 60) sc; ch 1, turn

Row 2: Sc in first sc; *sc in front lp of next sc, sc in back lp of next sc; rep from * across to last st; sc in last sc; ch 1, turn.

Rows 3 and 4: Rep Row 2 two times more. At end of Row 4, do not ch 1. Drop lp from hook.

Note: If needed, place dropped lp on safety pin to keep it from pulling out.

Row 5: With right side facing, join blue with sl st in first st, ch 4, work LKN in next st and in each st across to last st, tr in last st. Drop lp from hook. Do not turn.

Row 6: With right side facing, draw dropped variegated lp through 4th ch of beg ch-4 on last row, ch 1, sc in same ch; *sc in front lp of next st, sc in back lp of next st; rep from * across to last st; sc in last st; ch 1, turn.

Row 7: Rep Row 2. At end of row, do not ch 1 and turn. Drop lp from hook.

Row 8: With wrong side facing, draw dropped blue lp through first sc on last row, ch 4, work LKN in next st and in each st across to last st, tr in last st. Drop lp from hook. Turn.

Row 9: With right side facing, draw dropped variegated lp through top of end tr on last row, ch 1, sc in top of same tr; *sc in front lp of next st, sc in back lp of next st; rep from * across to last st; sc in last st; ch 1, turn.

Rows 10 through 12: Rep Row 2 three times more. At end of Row 12, do not ch 1. Drop lp from hook.

Row 13: With right side facing, draw dropped blue lp through last sc on last row, ch 4, work LKN in next st and in each st across to last st, tr in last st. Drop lp from hook. Do not turn.

Rep Rows 6 through 13 until piece measures 27" (27 1/2", 28"), ending by fastening off blue loop and working a variegated row. At end of last row, finish off; weave in ends.

Front

Work same as back.

Assembly

Sew shoulder seams, leaving center 10" open for neck. Place markers on sides of back and front 8" (8 1/2", 9") down from shoulder seams.

Sleeves (make 2)

Row 1: With right side facing, join variegated with sl st in marked st, ch 1, sc in same st as joining, work 39 (41, 43) more sc evenly spaced across to next marked st: 40 (42, 44) sc; ch 1, turn.

Rows 2 through 6: Rep Rows 2 through 6 of Back.

Row 7: Sc dec in first 2 sts; *sc in back lp of next sc, sc in front lp of next sc; rep from * across to last 2 sts; sc dec in last 2 sts: 38 (40, 42) sc. Drop lp from hook. Do not turn.

Rows 8 and 9: Rep Rows 8 and 9 of Back.

Row 10: Sc dec in first 2 sts; *sc in back lp of next sc, sc in front lp of next sc; rep from * across to last 2 sts; sc dec in last 2 sts: 36 (38, 40) sc; ch 1, turn.

Row 11: Sc in first st; *sc in back lp of next sc, sc in front lp of next sc; rep from * across to last st; sc in last st; ch 1, turn.

Row 12: Sc dec in first 2 sts; *sc in front lp of next sc, sc in back lp of next sc; rep from * across to last 2 sts; sc dec in last 2 sts: 34 (36, 38) sc. Drop lp from hook. Turn.

Row 13: Rep Row 13 of Back.

Rows 14 through 21: Rep Rows 6 through 13 of Sleeve.

At end of Row 20: 28 (30, 32) sc.

Rows 22 through 29: Rep Rows 6 through 13 of Sleeve.

At end of Row 28: 22 (24, 26) sc.

Rows 30 and 31: Rep Rows 6 and 7 of Sleeve: 20 (22, 24) sc.

For Size Small Only
Rep Rows 8 through 13 of Back, then Rows 6 through 13 of Back as necessary until sleeve measures about 17 1/2", or to desired length, ending by working a variegated row. At end of last row, finish off; weave in ends.

For Sizes Medium and Large Only
Rows 32 and 33: Rep Rows 8 and 9 of Back.

Row 34: Rep Row 10 of Sleeve: 20 (22) sc.

Rep Rows 11 through 13 of Back, then Rows 6 through 13 of Back as necessary until sleeve measures about 17 1/2", or to desired length, ending by working a variegated row. At end of last row, finish off; weave in ends.

Sew side and sleeve seams.

#21 FLOWER GARDEN SCARF

Designed by Jean Leinhauser

SIZE
60" long

MATERIALS
Worsted weight yarn
   3 oz green
   1 oz yellow
   2 oz deep rose
   2 oz med rose
   2 oz lt rose
   2 oz white
   2 oz lavender

Sewing pins

Size H (5 mm) crochet hook
   or size required for gauge

GAUGE
7 dc = 2"

INSTRUCTIONS

Note: The green base of the scarf is composed of three motifs; the first two are worked only once, then the third is repeated for the length of the scarf. Flowers are made separately and sewn to the base.

First Motif

With green, ch 6, join with sl st to form a ring.

Row 1: Ch 3 (counts as a dc), 13 dc in ring: 14 dc; ch 1, turn.

Row 2: Sc in first dc (mark this sc), sc in next dc; (ch 4, sc in each of next 2 dc) 6 times, working last sc in 3rd ch of turning ch; ch 6, turn; do not finish off.

Second Motif

Row 1: Sl st in first free ch-4 lp of First Motif, ch 3, turn.

Row 2: 13 dc in ch-6 lp, sl st in the first (marked) sc of first motif, ch 1, turn.

Row 3: Sc in first 2 dc, (ch 4, sc in each of next 2 dc) 6 times, working last sc in 3rd ch of turning ch; sl st in next free ch-4 lp of adjoining motif; ch 6, turn; do not finish off.

Designed by Janie Herrin

SIZE

45" x 60" before fringe

MATERIALS

Worsted weight yarn
  26 oz medium blue
  26 oz white

Note: Photographed model made with Red Heart® Super Saver® #885 Delft Blue and #316 Soft White

Size H (5 mm) crochet hook
  (or size required for gauge)

GAUGE

Square = 7 $^1/2$" x 7 $^1/2$"

INSTRUCTIONS

Square (make 48)

With blue, ch 5, join with sl st to form a ring.

Rnd 1: Ch 3, 2 dc in ring; (ch 2, 3 dc in ring) 3 times, ch 2, sl st in top of beg ch-3 to form last ch-2 sp: 12 dc and 4 ch-2 sps.

Rnd 2: Ch 5, dc in last sp made; * in next ch-2 sp work (V-st, ch 2, V-st); rep from * 2 times more, V-st in next sp, ch 2, sl st in 3rd ch of beg ch-5.

Rnd 3: Ch 3, 2 dc in last sp made; *ch 1, skip V-st, 3 dc in next sp between V-sts, ch 1, skip next V-st; (3 dc, ch 2, 3 dc) in next corner ch-2 sp; rep from * around, ending with 3 dc, ch 2, join with sl st in beg ch-3; finish off blue.

Rnd 4: Join white with sl st in any corner sp, ch 3, (dc, ch 2, 2 dc) in same sp; *dc in each of next 3 dc, (tr in ch-2 sp of V-st two rows below, dc in each of next 3 dc) twice (2 dc, ch 2, 2 dc) in next corner sp, rep from * around ending with sl st in top of beg ch-3.

Rnd 5: Sl st to corner sp, (ch 5, dc, ch 2, V-st) in same corner sp; *(skip 3 sts, V-st in next dc) 3 times, in next corner sp work (V-st, ch 2, V-st); rep from * around ending with sl st in 3rd ch of beg ch-5: 20 V-sts.

Rnd 6: Ch 4 (counts as first dc plus ch-1); *skip next V-st, in next corner sp work (2 dc, ch 2, 2 dc), ch 1; (skip next V-st, 3 dc in next sp between V-sts, ch 1) 4 times, rep from * around ending with 2 dc in last sp, join with sl st to beg dc; finish off white.

Rnd 7: Join blue with sl st in any corner sp, ch 3, (dc, ch 2, 2 dc) in same sp; *dc in each of next 2 dc, (tr in ch-2 sp of V-st two rows below, dc in each of next 3 dc) across to last 2 dc before corner, dc in last 2 dc, (2 dc, ch 2, 2 dc) in next corner sp; rep from * around ending with sl st in top of beg ch-3. Finish off; weave in ends.

Joining

With blue, holding two squares with right sides facing, sew tog with overcast stitch, working in outer loops only and carefully matching stitches. Make 6 strips of 8 squares each; then join strips in same manner.

Fringe

Following fringe instructions on page 255, cut strands of white 20" long. Using 3 strands in each knot, tie 14 knots evenly spaced across each square on each short end of afghan. Trim fringe.

#23 LOVER'S KNOT SHRUG

Designed by C. Yvette Holmes

SIZE
22" wide x 38" long

MATERIALS
Sport weight yarn
   10 oz lt. blue

Metallic fur yarn,
   3 1/2 oz lt. blue

Note: Photographed model made with Aunt Lydia® Shimmer #9559 Light Blue and Moda Dea™ Zing™ #1181 Blue Ice

Size I (5.5 mm) crochet hook
   (or size required for gauge)

Size J (6 mm) crochet hook

Stitch markers

GAUGE
13 hdc = 4" with smaller hook
   and sport yarn

4 LKN lps = 5" with smaller
   hook and sport yarn

INSTRUCTIONS

First sleeve

With I hook and sport yarn, ch 35.

Row 1 (wrong side): Sc in 2nd ch from hook and in each ch across: 34 sc; ch 2 (counts as hdc on next row now and throughout), turn.

Row 2 (right side): Hdc in next st and in each st across: 34 hdc; ch 2, turn.

Rows 3 through 7: Rep Row 2 five times more.

Row 8: Hdc in first st, hdc in next st and in each st across to last 2 sts, 2 hdc in next st, hdc in last st: 36 hdc; ch 2, turn.

Rows 9 through 16: Rep Row 8 eight times more: 2 hdc more in each row than in previous row. At end of Row 16: 52 hdc; ch 1, turn.

Body

Row 1: Work beg LKN, skip first hdc, sc in next hdc; *work 2 LKN, skip 2 hdc, sc in next hdc; rep from * to last 2 sts; work 2 LKN, skip next hdc, sc in last hdc: 18 LKN lps; turn.

Row 2: Work beg LKN; *sc in first sc of next LKN lp, work 2 LKN; rep from * across, ending by working sc in 2nd sc of beg LKN lp: 18 LKN lps; turn.

Rep Row 2 until piece measures about 31" long from beg, ending by working a right side row. At end of last row, ch 1, turn.

Second Sleeve

Row 1: Hdc in each elongated lp of each LKN lp and in each sc at base of each LKN lp across, working last hdc in 2nd lp of beg LKN: 52 hdc; ch 2, turn. Note: Do not work hdc in last sc of previous row or in first lp of beg LKN.

Row 2: Hdc dec in next 2 sts, hdc in next st and in each st across to last 3 sts, hdc dec in next 2 sts, hdc in last st: 50 hdc; ch 2, turn.

Rows 3 through 10: Rep Row 2 eight times more: 2 hdc less in each row than in previous row. At end of Row 10: 34 hdc.

Row 11: Hdc in next st and in each st across: 34 hdc; ch 2, turn.

Rows 12 through 15: Rep Row 11 four times more. At end of Row 15; ch 1, turn.

Row 16: Sc in first hdc and in each hdc across: 34 sc. Finish off; weave in ends.

Edging

With right side facing and I hook, join sport yarn with sc in edge of last sc on Row 1 of first sleeve, sc in edge of each row on first sleeve, sc in each elongated lp of each LKN lp and in each sc at base of each LKN lp across to second sleeve, sc in edge of each row on second sleeve.

Rep edging on other edge of shrug, starting with sc in edge of last sc on Row 16 of second sleeve and ending with sc in edge of first sc on Row 1 of first sleeve.

#25 SOFT 'N SWEET

Designed by Zelda K

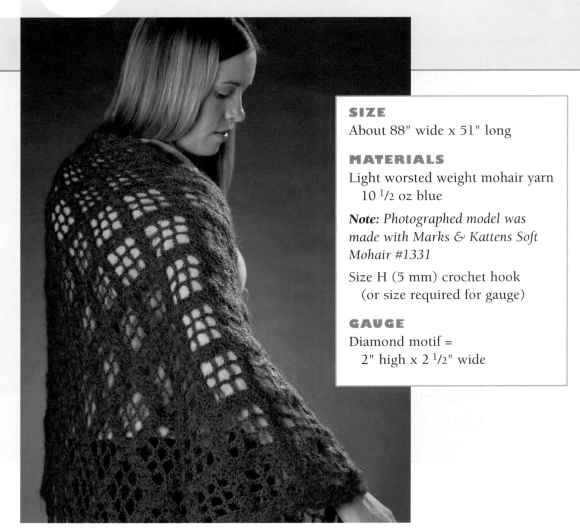

SIZE
About 88" wide x 51" long

MATERIALS
Light worsted weight mohair yarn
  10 ¹/₂ oz blue

Note: *Photographed model was made with Marks & Kattens Soft Mohair #1331*

Size H (5 mm) crochet hook
  (or size required for gauge)

GAUGE
Diamond motif =
  2" high x 2 ¹/₂" wide

INSTRUCTIONS

Beg at bottom edge, ch 4.

Row 1 (right side): Work beg shell in 4th ch from hook: 1 shell; ch 3, turn.

Row 2: Work beg shell in first dc, skip next dc, sc in next dc (center dc of shell), skip next dc, shell in 4th ch of foundation ch: 2 shells; ch 3, turn.

Row 3: Work beg shell in first dc, sc in center dc of first shell, ch 5, sc in center dc of next shell, shell in 3rd ch of turning ch-3: 2 shells and 1 ch lp; ch 3, turn.

Row 4: Work beg shell in first dc, sc in center dc of first shell; *ch 5, sc in center st of next ch lp or shell; rep from * across to last shell; shell in 3rd ch of turning ch-3: 2 shells and 2 ch lps; ch 3, turn.

Row 5: Rep Row 4: 2 shells and 3 ch lps; ch 3, turn.

Row 6: Work beg shell in first dc, sc in center dc of first shell, shell in next sc, sc in center ch of next ch lp, (ch 5, sc in center ch of next ch lp) 2 times, shell in next sc, sc in center dc of next shell, shell in 3rd ch of turning ch-3: 4 shells and 2 ch lps; ch 3, turn.

Row 7: Work beg shell in first dc, sc in center dc of first shell; *ch 5, sc in center st of next ch lp or shell**, shell in next sc, sc in center st of next ch lp or shell; rep from * across, ending last rep at **; shell in 3rd ch of turning ch-3: 4 shells and 3 ch lps; ch 3, turn.

Row 8: Work beg shell in first dc, sc in center dc of first shell; *(ch 5, sc in center st of next ch lp or shell) 2 times**, (shell in next sc, sc in center st of next ch lp or shell) 2 times; rep from * across, ending last rep at **; shell in 3rd ch of turning ch-3: 4 shells and 4 ch lps; ch 3, turn.

Row 9: Work beg shell in first dc, sc in center dc of first shell; *(ch 5, sc in center st of next ch lp or shell) 3 times**, shell in next sc, sc in center dc of next shell; rep from * across, ending last rep at **; shell in 3rd ch of turning ch-3: 3 shells and 6 ch lps; ch 3, turn.

Row 10: Work beg shell in first dc, sc in center dc of first shell; *shell in next sc, sc in center ch of next ch lp, (ch 5, sc in center ch of next ch lp) 2 times, shell in next sc, sc in center dc of next shell; rep from * across; shell in 3rd ch of turning ch-3: 6 shells and 4 ch lps; ch 3, turn.

Row 11: Rep Row 7: 6 shells and 5 ch lps; ch 3, turn.

Row 12: Work beg shell in first dc, sc in center dc of first shell; *(ch 5, sc in center st of next ch lp or shell) 2 times**, (shell in next sc, sc in center st of next ch lp or shell) 2 times; rep from * across, ending last rep at **; shell in 3rd ch of turning ch-3: 6 shells and 6 ch lps; ch 3, turn.

Row 13: Work beg shell in first dc, sc in center dc of first shell; *(ch 5, sc in center st of next ch lp or shell) 3 times**, shell in next sc, sc in center dc of next shell; rep from * across, ending last rep at **; shell in 3rd ch of turning ch-3: 4 shells and 9 ch lps; ch 3, turn.

Row 14: Work beg shell in first dc, sc in center dc of first shell; *shell in next sc, sc in center ch of next ch lp, (ch 5, sc in center ch of next ch lp) 2 times, shell in next sc, sc in center dc of next shell; rep from * across; shell in 3rd ch of turning ch-3: 8 shells and 6 ch lps; ch 3, turn.

Rep Rows 7 through 14 until piece measures about 50" from bottom point to center of last row, ending final rep with a Row 13. At end of each row: 4 more shells and 4 more ch lps than 8 rows before. Do not finish off.

Edging

Work beg shell in first dc, sc in center dc of first shell; *shell in next sc, sc in center st of next shell or ch lp; rep from * across to last shell; 10 dc in 3rd ch of turning ch-3; working down side of shawl, sc in base of same shell; **shell in base of next shell, sc in base of next shell***; rep from ** to bottom point; 10 dc in point, sc in base of next shell; rep from ** to *** up other side of shawl to top; 5 dc in same dc as beg shell; join with sl st in 3rd ch of beg ch-3. Finish off; weave in ends.

#26 FELTED PURSE

Designed by Marty Miller

SIZE

13" wide x 12 $^1/_2$" high before
  felting, 10" wide x 10 $^1/_2$"
  high after felting

MATERIALS

Worsted weight wool yarn
  4 oz purple
  Eyelash yarn
  180 yds multi-color

Note: *Photographed model made
with Brown Sheep Lamb's Pride
#65 Sapphire and Sandnes
Funny #9367 Clown*

Size N (10 mm) crochet hook
  (or size required for gauge)

Stitch marker

GAUGE

6 sc = 3 $^1/_8$"

11 sc rnds = 4 $^3/_4$"

INSTRUCTIONS

Note: Do not join rnds unless otherwise noted. Mark beg of each rnd with stitch marker and move marker up in each rnd.

Starting at bottom with one strand of each yarn held together, ch 25 loosely.

Rnd 1 (right side): 2 sc in 2nd ch from hook, sc in next 22 chs, 3 sc in last ch, working in free lps on other side of foundation ch, skip first ch where 3 sc are worked, sc in next 22 chs, sc in next ch: 50 sc

Rnd 2: Sc in next sc and in each sc around.

Rep Row 2 until bag measures 9 ½". At end of last rnd, join with sl st in first sc with worsted yarn, dropping eyelash yarn.

Note: Sl st should be at end of one side.

Edging and Handles

Rnd 1: With one strand of worsted yarn, ch 1, sc in same sc as joining, sc in next sc and in each sc around: 50 sc; join with sl st in first sc.

Rnds 2 through 4: Rep Rnd 1.

Rnd 5: Ch 1, sc in same sc as joining, sc in next 4 sc, ch 15, skip next 15 sc, sc in next 10 sc, ch 15, skip next 15 sc, sc in last 5 sc: 20 sc and 30 chs; join with sl st in first sc. Note: Ch-15 sps should be in center of sides for handles.

Rnd 6: Ch 1, sc in same sc as joining, sc in next 4 sc, sc in next 15 chs, sc in next 10 sc, sc in next 15 chs, sc in last 5 sc: 50 sc; join with sl st in first sc.

Rnd 7: Ch 1, sc in same sc as joining, sc in next sc and in each sc around; join with sl st in first sc.

Rnd 8: Rep Rnd 7. Finish off; weave in ends.

Felting purse

Place bag in zippered pillow case to protect washing machine from wool lint. Set water level at low and use hottest water possible. Add a little clear liquid laundry detergent. Put in something for bag to agitate against like an old towel or two, an old pair of jeans, a pair of rubber beach shoes, a few rubber balls, or something similar. Add a little boiling water to washing machine. Let washing machine agitate for a while, but check the felting process every few minutes. Do not let bag go through spin cycle. You may have to repeat this washing process 2 or 3 times. Keep checking felting progress, and add more boiling water if necessary. When bag is felted to your satisfaction, rinse in sink with cold water and set on rack to dry. Put crumpled newsprint or plain paper in bag to help wick water away from inside and to shape bag. Remember, felting is not a "scientific" process. Every washing machine will handle it differently.

FAST AND FUN T-TOP

Note: *Instructions are written for size X-Small; changes for sizes Small, Medium and Large are in parentheses.*

SIZES	X-Small	Small	Medium	Large	X-Large
Body Bust Measurements	30"	32"	34"	36"	38"
Finished Bust Measurements	32"	34"	36"	38"	40"

MATERIALS
Worsted weight yarn
  8 (8, 9, 10, 10) oz red

Note: *Photographed model made with Bernat® Berella "4"® #8929 Geranium*

Sewing pins

Size H (5 mm) crochet hook
  (or size required for gauge)

GAUGE
14 dc = 4"

INSTRUCTIONS

Top Section (make 2)

Starting at bottom edge, ch 93 (95, 105, 111, 115).

Row 1: Dc in 4th ch from hook and in each rem ch: 91 (93, 103. 109, 113) dc; ch 3 (counts as first stitch of following row here and throughout pattern), turn.

Row 2: Dc in each dc, ch 3, turn.

Repeat Row 2 until piece measures 7" (7 1/2", 8", 8 1/2", 8 1/2"); ch 3, turn. Mark this last row as the wrong side.

Shape First Shoulder

Row 1 (right side): Dc in next 29 (29, 34, 36, 38) dc, ch 3, turn, leaving rem sts unworked .

Rows 2 and 3: Dc in each dc, ch 3, turn.

Row 4: Dc in 7 (8, 9, 10, 11) dc; hdc in next 5 (6, 6, 7, 8) dc, sc in each dc. Finish off; weave in ends.

Shape Second Shoulder

Row 1 (wrong side): Hold piece with wrong side facing; join yarn with sl st in first st at right; ch 3, dc in next 29 (29, 34, 36, 38) dc, ch 3, turn, leaving rem sts unworked for neckline.

Rows 2 and 3: Dc in each dc, ch 3, turn.

Row 4: Dc in 7 (8, 9, 10, 11) dc; hdc in next 5 (6, 6, 7, 8) dc; sc in each rem dc. Finish off; weave in ends.

Set these two pieces aside.

Bottom Section (make 2)

Ch 39 (40, 42, 44, 46).

Row 1: Dc in 4th ch from hook and in each rem ch: 37 (38, 40, 42, 44) dc; ch 3, turn.

Row 2: Dc in each dc, ch 3, turn.

Rep Row 2 until piece measures 16 1/2" (17 1/2", 18 1/2", 19 1/2", 20 1/2") from starting ch. Mark last row for right side. Finish off; weave in ends.

Finishing

Hold one top section with neck edge at top. Fold piece in half vertically to find center, and mark center at bottom edge with a straight pin. Hold one bottom section with rows running up and down (not from side to side) and fold vertically to find center; mark center on one edge with a straight pin.

Matching center markers, place the two pieces with right sides together and pin together, being careful not to stretch either piece. Remaining sections at each end of top will form the sleeves. Sew the two pieces together with overcast st, being sure not to pull sts too tightly. Join other two garment pieces in same manner.

Hold front and back with right sides together. Sew shoulder, underarm and side seams.

Neck Edging

Hold garment with right side facing and neckline at top; join yarn with sl st in one shoulder seam; ch 1, work sc around neck opening, working one sc in the side of each row at seams, and in each dc; at end, join with sl st in beg sc. Finish off, weave in ends.

Sleeve Edging (make 2)

Hold garment with right side facing and one sleeve opening at top; join yarn in underarm seam; ch 1, work sc around opening, adjusting sts as need to keep work flat; at end, join with sl st in beg sc.

Bottom Edging

Hold garment with right side facing and bottom opening at top. Join yarn with sl st in side seam; ch 1, work sc evenly in side of each dc around opening, adjusting sts as needed to keep work flat; at end, join with sl st in beg sc. Finish off; weave in all ends.

Because this beautiful bedspread is made in squares, the size can be adjusted to fit any bed. The squares are joined as you crochet, so there is no tedious sewing together later.

Size	Bed Size
66" x 99"	Twin
77" x 99"	Full
88" x 99"	Queen
99" x 99"	King

MATERIALS

Size 10 crochet cotton

10,800 yds for Twin size (make 216 squarres)

12,600 yds for Full size (make 252 squares)

14,400 yds for Queen size (make 288 squares)

16,200 yds for King size (make 324 squares)

Note: Photographed model made with J&P Coats Opera, #554 Tapestry Rose

Size 6 (1.80 mm) steel crochet hook (or size required for gauge)

GAUGE

Rnds 1 through 3 of Square = 1 $\frac{3}{4}$"

Completed 13-rnd Square = 5 $\frac{1}{2}$" x 5 $\frac{1}{2}$"

INSTRUCTIONS

First Square

Note: All rnds are worked from the right side; do not turn.

Ch 12, join with sl st to form a ring.

Rnd 1: Ch 3, 31 dc in ring: 32 dc made, counting beg ch-3 as a dc; sl st in top of beg ch-3.

Rnd 2: Ch 1, sc in joining; (ch 12, skip 7 dc, sc in next dc) 3 times; ch 12, skip 7 dc; sl st in beg sc.

Rnd 3: Sl st in next ch-12 sp, ch 4 (counts as a tr), 9 tr in same ch-12 sp, ch 5; (10 tr in next ch-12 sp, ch 5) 3 times; sl st in 4th ch of beg ch-4. Note: each 10-tr group forms the base of a pineapple.

STITCH GUIDE

Cluster (CL): (YO 2 times; insert hook in specified st or sp and draw up a lp; YO and draw through first 2 lps on hook twice) 3 times; YO and draw through all 4 lps on hook: CL made.

Rnd 4: Ch 5, (tr in next tr, ch 1) 8 times, tr in next tr; * [ch 3, sc in next ch-5 sp, ch 3; (tr in next tr, ch 1) 9 times, tr in next tr] 3 times; ch 3, sc in next ch-5 sp, ch 3, sl st in 4th top ch of beg ch-5.

Rnd 5: Sl st in next ch-1 sp, in next tr work (sl st, ch 1, sc); ch 3, sc in next tr; * † (ch 3, sc in next tr) 7 times, ch 5; skip next ch-3 sp, next sc, next ch-3 sp, next tr, and next ch-1 sp †; (sc, ch 3, sc) in next tr; rep from * 2 times more, then rep from † to † one time; sl st in beg sc.

Rnd 6: In next ch-3 sp work (sl st, ch 1, sc) * †; (ch 3, sc in next ch-3 sp) 7 times; ch 3, 3 dc in next ch-5 sp; ch 3 †, sc in next ch-3 sp; rep from * two times more; rep from † to † once, sl st in beg sc.

Rnd 7: In next ch-3 sp work (sl st, ch 1, sc); * † (ch 3, sc in next ch-3 sp) 6 times; ch 3, 3 dc in next ch-3 sp, ch 7, 3 dc in next ch-3 sp, ch 3 †; sc in next ch-3 sp; rep from * twice more, then rep from † to † once; sl st in beg sc.

Rnd 8: In next ch-3 sp work (sl st, ch 1, sc); * † (ch 3, sc in next ch-3 sp) 5 times; ch 3, 3 dc in next ch-3 sp, ch 7, sc in next ch-7 sp, ch 7, 3 dc in next ch-3 sp, ch 3 †; sc in next ch-3 sp; rep from * two times more, then rep from † to † one more time; sl st in beg sc.

Rnd 9: In next ch-3 sp work (sl st, ch 1, sc); * † (ch 3, sc in next ch-3 sp) 4 times; ch 3, 3 dc in next ch-3 sp; (ch 7, sc in next ch-7 sp) two times; ch 7, 3 dc in next ch-3 sp, ch 3 †; sc in next ch-3 sp; rep from * two times more, then rep from †to † one time; sl st in beg sc.

Rnd 10: In next ch-3 sp work (sl st, ch 1, sc); * † (ch 3, sc in next ch-3 sp) 3 times; ch 3, 3 dc in next ch-3 sp, ch 5, sc in next ch-7 sp, ch 5, in next ch-7 sp work (CL, ch 5) 3 times; sc in next ch-7 sp, ch 5, 3 dc in next ch-3 sp; ch 3 †; sc in next ch-3 sp; rep from * two times more, then rep from † to † one time; sl st in beg sc.

Rnd 11: In next ch-3 sp work (sl st, ch 1, sc); * †(ch 3, sc in next ch-3 sp) twice; ch 3, 3 dc in next ch-3 sp, (ch 7, sc in next ch-5 sp) twice; ch 5, sc in next ch-5 sp, ch 12, sc in next ch-5 sp, ch 5, sc in next ch-5 sp, ch 7, sc in next ch-5 sp, ch 7; 3 dc in next ch-3 sp, ch 3 †; sc in next ch-3 sp; rep from * two more times, then rep from † to † one more time; sl st in beg sc.

Rnd 12: In next ch-3 sp work (sl st, ch 1, sc); * † ch 3, sc in next ch-3 sp, ch 3, 3 dc in next ch-3 sp; ch 7, (sc in next ch-7 sp, ch 7) twice; 3 sc in next ch-5 sp (near the ch-12 sp); in next ch-12 sp work (3 sc, ch 3, 3 sc, ch 5, 3 sc, ch 3, 3 sc); 3 sc in next ch-5 sp (near the ch-12 sp), ch 7; (sc in next ch-7 sp, ch 7) twice; 3 dc in next ch-3 sp †; ch 3, sc in next ch-3 sp; rep from * two times more, then rep from † to † one more time; ch 1, hdc in beg sc.

Rnd 13: Ch 1, sc in sp formed by joining hdc, ch 7, skip next ch-3 sp, sc in next ch-3 sp, ch 7; * † (sc in next ch-7 sp, ch 7) 3 times; sc in next ch-3 sp, ch 7, sc in next ch-5 sp, ch 7, sc in next ch-3 sp, ch 7; (sc in next ch-7 sp, ch 7) 3 times †; sc in next ch-3 sp, ch 7, skip next ch-3 sp, sc in next ch-3 sp, ch 7; rep from * two times more, then rep from † to † once; sl st in beg sc. Finish off; weave in ends.

Second Square

Rep Rnds 1 through 12 of First Square. On next rnd, Second Square will be joined to First Square.

Rnd 13: Ch 1, sc in sp formed by joining hdc, ch 7, skip next ch-3 sp, sc in next ch-3 sp, ch 7, (sc in next ch-7 sp, ch 7) 3 times; sc in next ch-3 sp, ch 7, se in next ch-5 sp, ch 3; hold wrong sides of completed square and this square tog, and carefully matching sts, join as follows: on completed square, sl st in corresponding ch-7 sp, ch 3; on working square, sc in next ch-3 sp; † ch 3, on completed square, sl st in next ch-7 sp, ch 3; on working square, sc in next ch-7 sp †; rep from † to † twice more; ch 3; on completed square, sl st in next ch-7 sp, ch 3; on working square, sc in next ch-3 sp, ch 3; on completed square, sl st in next ch-7 sp, ch 3; on working square, skip next ch-3 sp, sc in next ch-3 sp; rep from † to † 3 times more, ch 3; on completed square, sl st in next ch-7 sp, ch 3; on working square, sc in next ch-3 sp, ch 3; on completed square, sl st in next ch-7 sp, ch 3; on working square, sc in next ch-5 sp; †† ch 7, sc in next ch-3 sp, ch 7, (sc in next ch-7 sp, ch 7) 3 times; sc in next ch-3 sp, ch 7, skip next ch-3 sp, se in next ch-3 sp, ch 7; (sc in next ch-7 sp, ch 7) 3 times; sc in next ch-3 sp, ch 7, sc in next ch-5 sp ††; rep from †† to †† once more; ch 7, sc in next ch-3 sp, ch 7, (sc in next ch-7 sp, ch 7) 3 times; sl st in beg sc. Finish off; weave in ends.

Third Square (two-sided joining)

Work same as First Square through Rnd 12. On following rnd, Third Square will be joined on 2 sides.

Rnd 13: Ch 1, sc in sp formed by joining hdc, ch 7, skip next ch-3 sp, sc in next ch-3 sp, ch 7; (sc in next ch-7 sp, ch 7) 3 times; sc in next ch-3 sp, ch 7, se in next ch-5 sp; * ch 3; hold completed square and working square with wrong sides tog, and carefully matching sts, join as follows: on completed square, sl st in corresponding ch-7 sp, ch 3; on working square, sc in next ch-3 sp, † ch 3; on completed square, sl st in next ch-7 sp, ch 3; on working square, sc in next ch-7 sp †; rep from † to † twice more; ch 3, on completed square, sl st in next ch-7 sp, ch 3; on working square, sc in next ch-3 sp, ch 3; on completed square, sl st in next ch-7 sp, ch 3; on working square, skip next ch-3 sp, sc in next ch-3 sp; rep from † to † 3 times; ch 3; on completed square, sl st in next ch-7 sp, ch 3; on working square, sc in next ch-3 sp, ch 3; on completed square, sl st in next ch-7 lp, ch 3; on working square, sc in next ch-5 lp; rep from * once more; ch 7, sc in next ch-3 sp, ch 7, (sc in next ch-7 lp, ch 7) 3 times; sc in next ch-3 sp, ch 7, skip next ch-3 sp, sc in next ch-3 sp, ch 7, (sc in next ch-7 lp, ch 7) 3 times; se in next ch-3 sp, ch 7, sc in next ch-5 lp, ch 7, sc in next ch-3 sp, ch 7, (sc in next ch-7 lp, ch 7) 3 times; sl st in beg sc. Finish off; weave in ends.

Additional Squares

Work and join additional squares in same manner as Second and Third Squares, joining sides in same way and working corner joins where needed.

When all squares for desired size of bedspread are joined, work border.

Border

With right side facing and one short end at top, join thread with sc in ch-7 lp in upper right-hand corner.

Rnd 1: Ch 4, sc in next sp, ch 4; in next sp work (CL, ch 5) 3 times; * (sc in next sp, ch 5) two times; in next sp work (CL, ch 5) 3 times; rep from * around, ending last rep as needed; sl st in beg sc. Finish off.

Rnd 2: Join with sc in any ch-5 lp; ch 5, * sc in next ch-5 lp, ch 5; rep from * around; sl st in beg sc. Finish off; weave in ends. Block if needed.

#29 GRIN AND BARE IT

Designed by Tammy Hildebrand

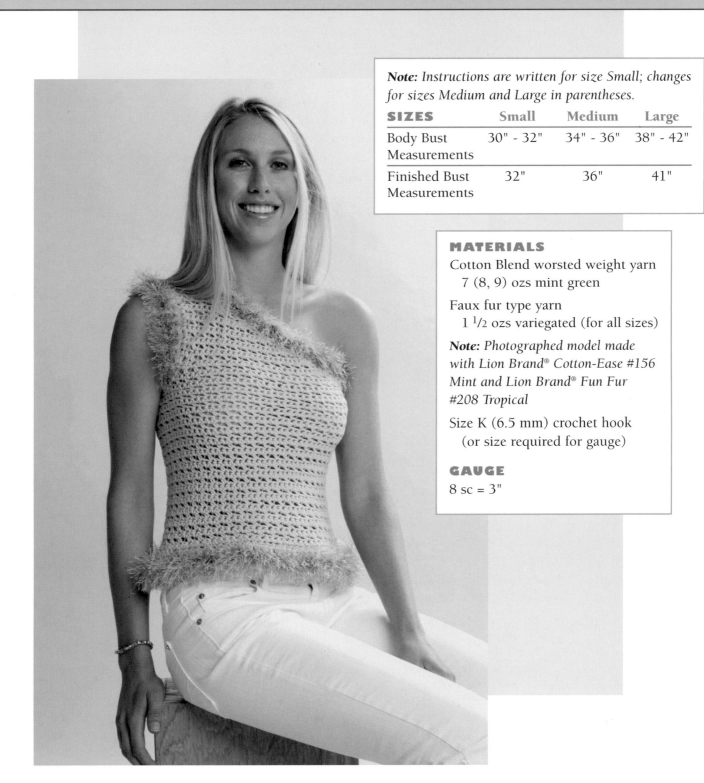

Note: *Instructions are written for size Small; changes for sizes Medium and Large in parentheses.*

SIZES	Small	Medium	Large
Body Bust Measurements	30" - 32"	34" - 36"	38" - 42"
Finished Bust Measurements	32"	36"	41"

MATERIALS

Cotton Blend worsted weight yarn
  7 (8, 9) ozs mint green

Faux fur type yarn
  1 ¹/₂ ozs variegated (for all sizes)

Note: *Photographed model made with Lion Brand® Cotton-Ease #156 Mint and Lion Brand® Fun Fur #208 Tropical*

Size K (6.5 mm) crochet hook
  (or size required for gauge)

GAUGE

8 sc = 3"

INSTRUCTIONS

Note: Garment is worked in one piece to the armholes in joined and turned rnds.

Beginning at bottom edge, with worsted weight yarn ch 86 (98, 110); join with sl st to form a circle, being careful not to twist ch.

Rnd 1: Ch 1, sc in joining and each ch around: 86 (98, 110) sc; join with sl st in beg sc, ch 1, turn.

Rnd 2: Sc in first sc, ch 1, skip next st; * sc in next sc, ch 1, skip next sc; rep from * around, join in beg sc, ch 1; turn: 43 (49, 55) sc, 43 (49, 55) ch-1 sps.

Rnd 3: Sc in each st and ch-1 sp, join. Ch-1, turn: 86 (98, 110) sc.

Rep Rnds 2 and 3, 13 (14, 15) times; then rep Rnd 2 once more.

Divide for Front and Back

Front

Row 1: Sc in first st, sc in next 36, (42, 48) sc and ch-1 sps, ch 1; turn, leaving rem sts unworked: 37 (43, 49) sts.

Row 2: Skip first st, sc in next st; *ch 1, skip next st, sc in next st; rep from * to last st, leave last st unworked, ch 1; turn: 18 (21, 24) sc, 17 (20, 23) ch-1 sps.

Row 3: Skip first st; *sc in next ch-1 sp, sc in next st; rep from * across, ch 1; turn: 34 (40, 46) sc.

Row 4: Sc in first st; *ch 1, skip next st, sc in next st; rep from * until 3 sts rem, ch 1; turn: 16 (19, 22) sc, 15 (18, 21) ch-1 sps.

Row 5: Rep row 3: 30 (36, 42) sc.

Row 6: Rep Row 4: 14 (18, 20) sc; 13 (16, 19) ch-1 sps.

Rows 7 through 16: Rep Rows 3 and 4 in sequence; at end of row 16: 4 (7, 10) sc and 3 (6, 9) ch-1 sps.

For Size Small Only

Row 17: Sc in each st and sp across, ch 1, turn: 7 sc.

Row 18: Sc in first st; *ch 1, skip next st, sc in next st; rep from * across; join with sl st in first sc, ch 1, turn: 4 sc, 3 ch-1 sps.

Rows 19 to 22: Rep Rows 17 and 18 twice. Finish off.

For Sizes Medium and Large Only

Row 17: Rep Row 3: (12, 18) sc.

Row 18: Rep Row 4: (5, 8) sc, (4, 7) ch-1 sps.

Row 19: Rep Row 3: (8, 14) sc.

For Size Medium Only

Row 20: Rep Row 3: 7 sc.

Row 21: Sc in first st; *ch 1, skip next st, sc in next st; rep from * across; ch 1; turn: 4 sc, 3 ch-1 sps.

Row 22: Sc in each st and ch-1 sp across, ch 1, turn: 7 sc.

Rows 23 to 24: Rep Rows 21 and 22 once.

Row 25: Rep Row 21. Finish off.

For Size Large Only
Row 20: Rep Row 4: 6 sc, 5 ch-1 sps.

Row 21: Rep Row 3: 10 sc.

Row 22: Rep Row 4: 4 sc, 3 ch-1 sps.

Row 23: Sc in each st and ch-1 sp across, ch 1, turn: 7 sc.

Row 24: Sc in first st; *ch 1, skip next st, sc in next st; rep from * across; ch 1, turn: 4 sc, 3 ch-1 sps

Rows 25 to 28: Rep Rows 23 and 24 twice. Finish off.

Back

Row 1: Skip next 6 unworked sts and ch-1 sps after Row 1 of Front, join yarn with sc in next st or sp, sc in next 36 sts and ch-1 sps, ch 1; turn: 37 (43, 49) sc.

Row 2: Skip first st, sc in next st; *ch 1, skip next st, sc in next st; rep from * to last sc, leaving last st unworked, ch 1; turn: 18 (21, 24) sc, 17 (20, 23) ch-1 sps.

Row 3: Sc in first st, sc in each ch-1 sp and sc across to last ch-1 sp, ch 1, turn, leaving last sp and last st unworked: 33 (39, 45) sc.

Row 4: Skip first st, sc in next st; *ch 1, skip next st, sc in next st; rep from * to last sc, leaving last st unworked, ch 1, turn: 16 (19, 22) sc, 15 (18, 21) ch-1 sps.

Rows 5 through 16: Rep Rows 3 and 4 six times: 4 (7, 10) sc, 3 (6, 9) ch-1 sps.

For Size Small Only
Row 17: Sc in each sc and ch-1 sp across, ch 1, turn: 7 sc.

Row 18: Sc in first st; *ch 1, skip next st, sc in next st; rep from * across, ch 1, turn: 4 sc, 3 ch-1 sps.

Rows 19 through 22: Rep Rows 17 and 18 twice

Row 23: Rep Row 17 once more.

Finish off, leaving a long yarn length for sewing.

For Size Medium and Large Only
Rows 17 and 18: Rep Rows 3 and 4 once: (9, 15) sc.

For Size Medium Only
Row 19: Rep Row 3: 7 sc.

Row 20: Sc in first st; *ch 1, skip next st, sc in next st; rep from * across, ch 1, turn: 4 sc, 3 ch-1 sps.

Row 21: Sc in each sc and ch-1 sp across, ch 1; turn: 7 sc.

Row 22: Sc in first st; *ch 1, skip next st, sc in next st; rep from * across, ch 1, turn: 4 sc, 3 ch-1 sps.

Rows 23 and 24: Rep Rows 21 and 22 once.

Row 25: Rep Row 21.

Finish off, leaving a long yarn length for sewing.

For Size Large Only
Rows 19 to 22: Rep Rows 3 and 4 twice: 4 sc, 3 ch-1 sps.

Row 23: Sc in each sc and ch-1 sp across, ch 1; turn: 7 sc.

Row 24: Sc in first st; *ch 1, skip next st, sc in next st; rep from * across. Ch 1, turn.

Rows 25 and 26: Rep Rows 23 and 24.

Row 27: Rep Row 23.

Finish off, leaving a long length for sewing.

Finishing

For all sizes, hold garment with wrong sides tog and carefully matching sts, sew shoulder seam.

Neckline Edging

Rnd 1: With right side facing and working in row ends, join worsted-weight yarn with sc in shoulder seam; sc evenly around neckline, working in ends of rows, sts and ch-1 sps and adjusting sts as needed to keep work flat; join with sl st in beg-sc; ch 3, do not turn.

Rnd 2: Dc in next sc and in each st around, join with sl st in top of beg ch-3.

Rnd 3: Ch 1, sc in joining and in each st around, join with sl st in beg sc. Finish off; weave in ends.

Neckline Fur Trim

Join faux fur yarn with sc around post (vertical bar) of any dc of Rnd 2, (sc, ch 3, sc) in next sc of Rnd 3; *sc around post of next dc, (sc, ch 3, sc) in next sc; rep from * around, join with sl st in beg-sc. Finish off, weave in ends

Armhole Edging

Rnd 1: Join worsted weight yarn with sc in first unworked sp at underarm, sc in next 5 sps, sc in each row end, join with sl st in beg sc, ch 1; do not turn.

Rnd 2: Ch 1, sc in joining amd in next 5 sts, dc in each st around to end; join with sl st in beg ch 1; ch 1, turn.

Rnd 3: Ch 1; sc in joining and each st around, join with sl st in beg sc. Finish off; weave in ends.

Armhole Fur Trim

Join faux fur yarn with sc in first sc of Rnd 3, sc in next 5 sts, sc around post of first dc of Rnd 2, (sc, ch 3, sc) in next sc of Rnd 3; *sc around post of next dc, (sc, ch 3, sc) in next sc; rep from * around, join with sl st in beg sc. Finish off; weave in ends.

Waist Edging

Hold garment with right side facing and bottom at top.

Rnd 1: Working in free lps of starting ch, join worsted weight yarn with sc in any lp, sc in same lp and each lp around, join with sl st in beg-sc; ch 3, do not turn.

Rnd 2: Dc in each st around; join with sl st in top of beg ch-3, ch 1.

Rnd 3: Sc in each st across, join with sl st in beg sc. Finish off; weave in ends.

Waist Fur Trim

Join faux fur with sc around post of any dc of Rnd 2, (sc, ch 3, sc) in next sc of Rnd 3; *sc around post of next dc, (sc, ch 3, sc) in next sc; rep from * around; join with sl st in beg-sc. Finish off; weave in all ends.

#30 BEAUTY IN GEOMETRY

Designed by Dora Ohrenstein

Note: *Instructions are written for Medium; changes for Large are in parentheses.*

SIZES	Medium	Large
Body Bust Measurements	34" - 38"	40" - 44"
Finished Bust Measurements	40"	47"

MATERIALS

DK or sport weight yarn

 1 3/4 (2 3/4) oz golden yellow (A)
 3 1/2 (5 1/2) oz olive (B)
 3 1/2 (5 1/2) oz beige (C
 3 1/2 (5 1/2) oz pale yellow (D
 3 1/2 (5 1/2) oz mocha (E
 3 1/2 (5 1/2) peach (F)
 1 3/4 (2 3/4) oz off white (G)

Note: *Photographed model made with Karabella Vintage Cotton #320 Calendula (A) #365 Raw Linen (C) #340 Straw (D) #311 Beige (F) and Karabella Zodiac #402 Silver-grey green (B) #419 Camel (E) and #424 Off White (G)*

Stitch markers or contrast yarn

Sewing pins

Size E (3.5 mm) crochet hook
  (or size required for gauge)

GAUGE

18 dc = 4"

2 dc tog: (YO, insert hook in next st and draw up a lp; YO and draw through first 2 lps on hook) twice; YO and draw through all 3 lps on hook.

3 dc tog: (YO, insert hook in next st and draw up a lp; YO and draw through first 2 lps on hook) 3 times; YO and draw through all 4 lps on hook.

2 hdc tog: (YO, insert hook in next st and draw up a lp) 2 times; YO and draw through all 5 lps on hook.

3 hdc tog: (YO, insert hook in next st and draw up a lp) 3 times; YO and draw through all 7 lps on hook.

Changing Colors: Colors are changed frequently, sometimes every row. To change colors, work last stitch of first color to last YO, then make the final YO with the new color. Unless otherwise stated, make color changes at the end of the row, on the stitch prior to the turning ch. To do this, read ahead to the next row and see what color is next. When making color changes, cut the first color and leave a 4" tail for weaving in later.

Note: The turning ch counts as a stitch on the following row throughout the pattern.

INSTRUCTIONS

Front Yoke

Starting at neckline with A, ch 65 (77).

Row 1 (right side): Sc in 2nd ch from hook and in next 30 (36) chs; 2 sc in next ch, ch 1, 2 sc in next ch; sc in next 30 (36) chs, ch 3, turn: 67 (79) sts, counting the ch-1 as a st.

Row 2: With B, dc to ch-1 sp, (2 dc, ch 1, 2 dc) in ch-1 sp; dc across, ch 3, turn: 71 (83) sts.

Row 3: With C, rep Row 2, but end with ch 2 (counts as hdc on following row), turn: 75 (87) sts.

Row 4: With D, hdc to ch-1 sp, (2 hdc, ch 1, 2 hdc) in ch-1 sp; hdc across, ch 3, turn: 79 (91) sts.

Row 5: With B, rep Row 2: 83 (95) sts.

Row 6: With C, dc to ch-1 sp, (2 dc, ch 1, 2 dc) in ch-1 sp; dc across, ch 2 (3), turn: 87 (99) sts.

For Size Large Only

Row 7: With B, rep Row 2: 103 sts.

Row 8: With C, rep Row 3: 107 sts.

For Both Sizes

Row 7 (9): With E, rep Row 4: 91 (111) sts.

Row 8 (10): With F, rep Row 3: 95 (115) sts.

Row 9 (11): With G, hdc to ch-1 sp, (2 hdc, ch 1, 2 hdc) in ch-1 sp; hdc across, ch 2, turn: 99 (119) sts.

Row 10 (12): With A, 3 hdc tog; hdc to ch-1 sp, (2 hdc, ch 1, 2 hdc) in ch-1 sp; hdc to last 4 sts; 3 hdc tog, hdc in tch; ch 3, turn.

Row 11 (13): With B, 3 dc tog; dc to ch-1 sp, (2 dc, ch 1, 2 dc) in ch-1 sp; dc to last 4 sts; 3 dc tog, dc in tch; ch 3, turn.

Row 12 (14): With C, 3 dc tog; dc to ch-1 sp, (2 dc, ch 1, 2 dc) in ch-1 sp; dc to last 4 sts; 3 dc tog, dc in tch; ch 2, turn.

Row 13 (15): With D, rep Row 10 (12).

Row 14 (16): With B, 3 dc tog; dc to ch-1 sp. (2 dc, ch 1, 2 dc) in ch-1 sp; dc to last 4 sts; 3 dc tog, dc in tch; ch 3 (2), turn.

For Size Large Only

Row 17: With D, 3 hdc tog; hdc to ch-1 sp, (2 hdc, ch 1, 2 hdc) in ch-1 sp; hdc to last 4 sts; 3 hdc tog; hdc in tch, ch 3, turn.

Row 18: With B, 3 dc tog; dc to ch-1 sp, (2 dc, ch 1, 2 dc) in ch-1 sp; dc to last 4 sts; 3 dc tog, dc in tch; ch 3, turn.

For Both Sizes

Row 15 (19): With C, rep Row 12 (14).

Row 16 (20): With D, 3 hdc tog, hdc to ch-1 sp, (2 hdc, ch 1, 2 hdc) in ch-1 sp; hdc to last 4 sts; 3 hdc tog, hdc in tch; ch 2, turn.

Row 17 (21): With E, 3 hdc tog; hdc to ch-1 sp, (2 hdc, ch 1, 2 hdc) in ch-1 sp; hdc to last 4 sts; 3 hdc tog, hdc in tch. Finish off; weave in ends.

Back Yoke

Rep Front Yoke.

Right Side Panel

Starting at underarm seam, with B, ch 34 (54).

Row 1 (right side): With B, dc in 4th ch from hook and in next 14 (24) chs; 2 dc in next ch, (ch 1, 2 dc) in same ch; dc in next 15 (25) chs; ch 3, turn: 35 (55) sts.

Row 2: With C, skip first st, 2 dc tog; dc to ch-1 sp, (2 dc, ch 1, 2 dc) in ch-1 sp; dc to last 3 sts; 2 dc tog, dc in tch, ch 2, turn: 37 (57) sts.

Row 3: With D, 2 hdc tog; hdc to ch-1 sp, (2 hdc, ch 1, 2 hdc) in ch-1 sp; hdc to last 3 sts; 2 hdc tog, hdc in tch; ch 3, turn: 39 (59) sts.

Row 4: With B, 2 dc tog; dc to ch-1 sp, (2 dc, ch 1, 2 dc) in ch-1 sp; dc to last 3 sts, 2 dc tog; dc in tch; ch 3, turn: 41 (61) sts.

Row 5: With C, dc to ch-1 sp (2 dc, ch 1, 2 dc) in ch-1 sp; dc across, ch 2, turn: 45 (65) sts.

Row 6: With D, rep Row 3: 47 (67) sts.

Row 7: With B, rep Row 4: 49 (69) sts.

Row 8: With C, rep Row 4: 51 (71) sts.

Row 9: With E, rep Row 2: 53 (73) sts.

Row 10: With F, hdc to ch-1 sp (2 hdc, ch 1, 2 hdc) in ch-1 sp; hdc across; ch 3, turn: 57 (77) sts.

Row 11: With E, rep Row 4: 59 (79) sts.

Row 12: With C, rep Row 4: 61 (81) sts.

Row 13: With B, rep Row 2: 63 (83) sts.

Row 14: With D, rep Row 3: 65 (85) sts.

Row 15: With C, dc to ch-1 sp, (2 dc, ch 1, 2 dc) in ch-1 sp; dc across; ch 3, turn: 69 (89) sts.

Row 16: With B, rep Row 2: 71 (91) sts.

Row 17: With D, rep Row 3: 73 (93) sts.

Row 18: With C, rep Row 4: 75 (95) sts.

Row 19: With E, rep Row 5: 79 (99) sts.

Row 20: With F, 2 hdc tog; hdc to ch-1 sp; (2 hdc, ch 1, 2 hdc) in ch-1 sp; hdc to last 3 sts; 2 hdc tog; hdc in tch: 81 (101) sts. Finish off; weave in ends.

Left Side Panel

Rep Right Side Panel.

Front Bottom Panel

Starting at hemline with C, ch 3 (counts as hdc and ch 1 on following row), turn.

Row 1 (right side): (2 hdc, ch 1, 3 hdc) in 3rd ch from hook; ch 2, turn: 7 sts.

Row 2: Hdc in first hdc; hdc in next 2 hdc, (2 hdc, ch 1, 2 hdc) in ch-1 sp, hdc in next 2 hdc: 2 hdc in tch, ch 2, turn: 13 sts.

Row 3: Hdc in next st; hdc to ch-1 sp, (2 hdc, ch 1, 2 hdc) in ch-1 sp; hdc to last 2 sts; 2 hdc in next st; hdc in tch, ch 2, turn: 19 sts.

Row 4: Hdc in next st; hdc to ch-1 sp, (2 hdc, ch 1, 2 hdc) in ch-1 sp; hdc to last 2 sts; 2 hdc in next st; hdc in tch, ch 3, turn: 25 sts.

Row 5: Dc in next st; dc to ch-1 sp, (2 dc, ch 1, 2 dc) in ch-1 sp; dc to last 2 sts; 2 dc in next st; dc in tch, ch 2, turn: 31 sts.

Row 6: With D, rep Row 4: 37 sts.

Row 7: With B, dc in next st; dc to ch-1 sp, (2 dc, ch 1, 2 dc) in ch-1 sp; dc to last 2 sts; 2 dc in next st, dc in tch; ch 3, turn: 43 sts.

Row 8: With C, rep Row 5: 49 sts.

Row 9: With D, rep Row 4: 55 sts.

Row 10: With B, rep Row 5: 61 sts.

Row 11: With C, rep Row 3: 67 sts. For size Small only, mark the hdc on each side of the ch-1 sp on Row 11.

For Size Large Only
Row 12: With D, rep Row 4: 73 sts.

Row 13: With B, rep Row 5: 79 sts.

Row 14: With C, rep Row 3: 85 sts. Mark the hdc on each side of the ch-1 sp on Row 14.

For Both Sizes
Note: *The remaining rows of the bottom panel form extensions on both sides of the triangle; these rows do not cross the increase point at the top of the panel. Work Rows 12 (15) through 16 (19) on both sides of the triangle.*

First Bottom Panel Extension

Row 12 (15): With D, 2 hdc in next st; hdc to marked st before ch-1 sp; hdc in marked st; ch 3, turn: 34 (43) sts.

Row 13 (16): With B, 2 dc in next st; dc to last 2 sts; 2 dc in next st; dc in tch, ch 2, turn: 36 (45) sts.

Row 14 (17): With A, 2 hdc in next st; hdc across; ch 2, turn: 37 (46) sts.

Row 15 (18): With G, 2 hdc in next st; hdc to last 2 sts; 2 hdc in next st; hdc in tch, ch3, turn: 39 (48) sts.

Row 16 (19): With E, 2 dc in next st; dc to last 2 sts; 2 dc in next st, dc in tch: 41 (50) sts. Finish off; weave in ends.

Second Bottom Panel Extension

Holding bottom panel with wrong side (right side) facing and top point of the triangle to the right, join D with sl st to the marked st left of the ch-1 sp of Row 11 (14).

Row 12 (15): With D, ch 2, hdc to last 2 sts; 2 hdc in next st, hdc in tch; ch 3, turn: 34 (43) sts.

Row 13 (16): With B, 2 dc in next st; dc to last 2 sts; 2 dc in next st, dc in tch; ch 2, turn: 36 (45) sts.

Row 14 (17): With A, hdc to last 2 sts; 2 hdc in next st; hdc in tch, ch 2, turn: 37 (46) sts.

Row 15 (18): With G, 2 hdc in next st; hdc to last 2 sts; 2 hdc in next st, hdc in tch; ch 3, turn: 39 (48) sts.

Row 16 (19): With E, 2 dc in next st; dc to last 2 sts; 2 dc in next st, dc in tch: 41 (50) sts. Finish off; weave in ends.

Back Bottom Panel

Rep Front Bottom Panel.

Sleeve (make 2)

Sleeve begins at the center top of the arm. Stitches are worked on both sides of the foundation chain so that each row of the sleeve is worked from armhole to wrist, across wrist, then from wrist back to arm-hole, with row ends forming armhole seam.

With G, ch 43 (46).

Row 1 (right side): Hdc in 2nd ch from hook (counts as 2 hdc); hdc in next 40 (43) chs, ch 4, do not turn; working in opposite side of foundation ch, hdc in next 42 (45) chs; ch 2, turn: 88 (94) sts.

Row 2: With A, 2 hdc tog in next 2 sts; dc in next 38 (41) sts, 2 hdc in next hdc; (ch 1, 4 hdc, ch 1) in ch-4 sp; 2 hdc in next hdc; dc in next 38 (41) sts; 2 hdc tog, hdc in tch; ch 3, turn: 90 (96) sts.

Row 3: With B, 3 dc tog; [dc to ch-1 sp, (2 dc, ch 1, 2 dc) in ch-1 sp] twice; dc to last 4 sts, 3 dc tog; dc in tch, ch 3, turn: 94 (100) sts.

Row 4: With C, 3 dc tog; [dc to ch-1 sp, (2 dc, ch 1, 2 dc) in ch-1 sp] twice; dc to last 4 sts; 3 dc tog; dc in tch; ch 2, turn: 98 (104) sts.

Row 5: With D, 3 hdc tog; [hdc to ch-1 sp, (2 hdc, ch 1, 2 hdc) in ch-1 sp] twice; hdc to last 4 sts; 3 hdc tog; hdc in tch, ch 3, turn: 102 (108) sts.

Row 6: With B, rep Row 3: 106 (112) sts.

Row 7: With C, 3 dc tog; [dc to ch-1 sp, (2 dc, ch 1, 2 dc) in ch-1 sp] twice; dc to last 4 sts; 3 dc tog; dc in tch, ch 2 (3), turn: 110 (116) sts.

For Size Large Only

Row 8: With B, rep Row 3: 120 sts.

Row 9: With C, rep Row 4: 124 sts.

For Both Sizes

Row 8 (10): With D, rep Row 5: 114 (128) sts.

Row 9 (11): With E, rep Row 4: 118 (132) sts.

Row 10 (12): With F, 3 hdc tog; [hdc to ch-1 sp; (2 hdc, ch 1, 2 hdc) in ch-1 sp] twice; hdc to last 4 sts; 3 hdc tog; hdc in tch; turn: 122 (136) sts.

Row 11 (13): Sl st in first st; change to E, ch 3 (counts as dc); 3 dc tog; [dc to ch-1 sp; (2 dc, ch 1, 2 dc) in ch-1 sp] twice; dc to last 4 sts; 3 dc tog; leaving tch unworked, ch 2, turn: 124 (138) sts.

Row 12 (14): With D, rep Row 5: 128 (142) sts.

Row 13 (15): With C, rep Row 3: 132 (146) sts.

For Size Large Only

Row 16: With B, rep Row 3: 150 sts.

Row 17: With F, rep Row 4: 154 sts.

Row 18: With E, rep Row 5: 158 sts.

Row 19: With D, rep Row 3: 162 sts.

Row 20: With C, rep Row 3: 166 sts.

Row 14 (21): With B, 3 dc tog; [dc to ch-1 sp; (2 dc, ch 1, 2 dc) in ch-1 sp] twice; dc to last 4 sts; 3 dc tog; dc in tch: 170 sts. Finish off; weave in ends.

Finishing

After weaving in all ends, mark right side of each piece. Hold both yokes with wrong sides tog and sew Row 1 through Row 8 (10) of Front Yoke to Row 1 through Row 8 (10) of Back Yoke for one shoulder seam. Rep on the opposite shoulder for other shoulder seam.

Hold Front Bottom Panel with wrong facing and Row 1 at the bottom, and hold Right Side Panel with wrong side facing and with Row 1 at the top; sew last row of one Front Bottom Panel extension to last row of Right Side Panel; seam will end at st prior to ch-1 sp on last row of Right Side Panel. Hold Left Side Panel with wrong facing and with Row 1 at the top; sew last row of other Front Bottom Panel extension to last row of Left Side Panel; seam will end at st prior to ch-1 sp on last row of Left Side Panel. Hold Back Bottom Panel with wrong side facing and Row 1 at the bottom; sew last row of one Back Bottom Panel extension to last row of Right Side Panel; seam will end at st prior to ch-1 sp on last row of Right Side Panel. Sew last row of other Back Bottom Panel extension to last row of Left Side Panel; seam will end at st prior to ch-1 sp on last row of Left Side Panel.

Sew yoke pieces to panels to form sweater body. With wrong sides both pieces facing, line up point of Front Yoke to point of Front Bottom Panel. Sew last row of Front Yoke to row ends of combined Front Bottom Panel and Side Panels. Line up point of Back Yoke to point of Back Bottom Panel. Sew last row of Back Yoke to row ends of combined Back Bottom Panel and Side Panels.

Sew underarm seams of sleeves. Fold Right Sleeve lengthwise with wrong side facing so that Row 1 runs along the top of the fold. Sew the last row together from row ends to ch-1 sps, leaving the sts between ch-1 sps free as wrist opening. Repeat this step for Left Sleeve. Sew sleeves into sweater body. Pin Right Sleeve to sweater body, matching colors carefully for first 7 row of sleeve. Repeat this step for Left Sleeve. Sew underarm seams.

#31 PLUM GRANNY RIPPLE

Designed by Janie Herrin

SIZE
46" x 70"

MATERIALS
Worsted weight yarn
   24 oz lt beige (MC)
   8 oz green (A)
   8 oz dk plum (B)
   15 oz variegated (C)

Note: Photographed model made with Red Heart® Super Saver® #329 Eggnog (MC), #661 Frosty Green (A), #533 Dark Plum (B), and #997 Sage Mary (C)

Size J (6 mm) crochet hook (or size required for gauge)

9 Bobby Pins

GAUGE
6 dc = 2"

Large Square = 10 $^1/_2$" x 10 $^1/_2$"

STITCH GUIDE
Front Post sc (FPsc): Insert hook from front to back to front around post (vertical bar) of specified st, YO and draw up a lp, YO and draw through 3 lps on hook: FPsc made

Loop (lp): To work lp, ch 10, sl st in 9th ch from hook, ch 1: lp made

Dc decrease (dcdec): Holding back last lp of each st on hook, dc in next 3 sts, YO, draw through all 4 lps on hook: dcdec made

INSTRUCTIONS

First Large Square (Square A)

With MC, starting with flower, ch 6, join with sl st to form a ring.

Rnd 1: Ch 1, in ring work (sc, ch 1, 3 dc, ch 1) 4 times, join with sl st in beg sc; ch 1, turn: 4 petals made.

Rnd 2: Working on wrong side, FPsc around next sc, (ch 3, FPsc around post of next sc) 3 times, ch 3, join in beg sc; ch 1, turn: 4 ch-3 lps.

Rnd 3: Sc in same st; *ch 1, in next lp work (3 dc, ch 1, sc, ch 1, 3 dc, ch 1), sc in next sc; rep from * around, join beg sc; ch 1, turn: 8 petals.

Rnd 4: Working on wrong side, sc around post of sc, (ch 3, sc around post of next sc) 7 times, ch 3, join in beg sc; finish off: 8 lps.

Rnd 5: With right side facing, working behind petals, join A with sl st in any ch-3 lp, ch 3, (2 dc, ch 2, 3 dc) all in same sp (beg corner made); * † ch 1, 3 dc in next ch-3 lp, ch 1, † in next lp work (3 dc, ch 2, 3 dc) for corner; rep from * 2 times more, then rep from † to † once, join in 3rd ch of beg ch-3.

Rnd 6: Sl st to ch-2 corner sp, ch 3, in same sp work (2 dc, ch 10, sc in 9th ch from hook: lp made, 3 dc), * † ch 1, (3 dc in next sp, ch 1) twice †; (3 dc, work lp as before, 3 dc) in next ch-2 corner sp; rep from * 2 times more then rep from † to † once, join with sl st to beg ch-3, finish off.

Rnd 7: Join MC with sl st in any corner sp to right of lp, ch 3, (2 dc in same sp, work lp, 3 dc to left of loop); * † ch 1, (3 dc in next sp, ch 1) 3 times †; in next corner sp work (3 dc to right of lp, work lp, 3 dc to left of lp); rep from * 2 times more then rep from † to † once, join with sl st in beg ch-3.

Rnd 8: Sl st to corner sp, ch 3, work (2 dc to right of lp, work lp, 3 dc to left of lp); * † ch 1, (3 dc in next sp, ch 1) 4 times †; in

next corner sp work (3 dc to right of lp, work lp, 3 dc to left of lp); rep from * 2 times more then rep from † to † once, join with sl st in beg ch-3; finish off.

Note: On the following rnd you will work 2 corner lps only, facing opposite ends from each other.

Rnd 9: Join C with sl st in any corner sp to right of lp; ch 3, 2 dc in same sp, ch 2, 3 dc to left of lp, *ch 1, (3 dc in next sp, ch 1) 5 times, in next corner sp work (3 dc to right of lp, work lp, 3 dc to left of lp), ch 1; (3 dc in next sp, ch 1) 5 times **, in next corner sp work (3 dc to right of lp, ch 2, 3 dc to left of lp); rep from * to ** once, join with sl st in beg ch-3; do not finish off: 84 dc, 4 corners, 2 with lps

Braid only the lps in the next corner and in opposite corner as follows: pull lp of Rnd 7 through lp of Rnd 6, pull lp of Rnd 8 through lp of Rnd 7; leave rem corners unbraided.

Rnd 10: Sl st to corner sp, ch 3, in same sp work [dc, then working in lp of Rnd 8 and in same ch-2 corner sp on Rnd 9 at the same time, work (dc, ch 2, dc), then work 2 dc in same corner sp of Rnd 9 only and to left of lp]; * ch 1, (3 dc in next sp, ch 1) 6 times, in next corner sp work (3 dc to right of lp, work lp, 3 dc to left of lp), ch 1, (3 dc in next sp, ch 1) 6 times **; in next ch-2 corner sp work [2 dc, working in lp of Rnd 8 and in same ch-2 corner sp on Rnd 9 at same time, work (dc, ch 2, dc), 2 dc in same corner sp to left of lp]; rep from * to ** once, join with sl st in beg ch-3; finish off: 96 dc, 4 corners, 2 with lps.

Second Large Square (Square B)

Make same as first sq through Rnd 4, change to B for Rnds 5 and 6, then continue through Rnd 10 same as before, joining one corner only to previous square as follows; in next ch-2 corner sp work [2 dc, working in lp of Rnd 8 and in same ch-2 corner sp on Rnd 9 at the same time, work (dc, ch 1, holding wrong sides tog, sc in corresponding corner sp of previous square, ch 1, dc in same sp as last dc made), 2 dc in same corner sp to left of lp]; joining made.

Following Fig below, make and join 3 more squares in same manner, alternating Squares A and B for a total of 5 squares, joining only at corners without lps.

Square C (make and join 8)

With B, ch 6, join to form ring.

Rnds 1 through 4: Rep rnds 1 thru 4 of First Square.

Rnd 5: With right side facing, working behind petals, join A with sl st in any lp, ch 3, in same sp work (2 dc, work lp, 3 dc); * ch 1, 3 dc in next lp, ch 1, in next lp work (3 dc, ch 2, 3 dc); rep from * around, ch 1, 3 dc in next lp, ch 1, join, finish off: 4 corners, 1 with lp.

Rnd 6: Skip corner with lp, join C with sl st in next ch-2 corner sp, ch 3, 2 dc in same sp,

ch 1, join small square between larger squares as follows: joining same as before, sc in 4th ch-1 sp from where 2 large squares meet, ch 1, 3 dc in same sp on small square, (sc in next sp on large square, 3 dc in next sp on small square) 3 times; to join corners, ch 1, sc in same sc where large squares meet, ch 1, 3 dc in same sp on small square; working across side, join to large square same as before until 3 dc in next corner are made; ch 1, sc in next sp on large square, ch 1, 3 dc in same sp on small square; ch 1, (3 dc in next sp, ch 1) twice, work corner with lp in next sp, ch 1, (3 dc in next sp, ch 1) twice, join: 4 corners, 3 which are joined and 1 with lp not joined)

Rep for a total of 4 small squares on each side between large squares (See Fig).

Ripples

Row 1: With right side facing, working across long edge on one side of joined squares strip, join MC with sl st in 14th dc from center point at end of strip, ch 3, (note: you will skip ch-1 sps across), dc in next 10 dc; *in corner work (2 dc, lp, 2 dc), dc in next 11 dc, skip next dc, skip joining, skip next dc, dc in next 11 dc; rep from * across until 9 corners (points) are made, dc in next 11 dc, ch 3, turn; leave rem sts unworked. You will have 6 lps across first point and 3 lps across next point alternately to be braided later.

Row 2: Working in BLO now and throughout unless otherwise stated, work dcdec over next 3 sts, dc in next 9 dc; *(2 dc, work lp, 2 dc) in corner, dc in next 10 dc, (work dcdec) twice, dc in next 10 dc; rep from * across, end with last point, dc in next 10 dc, work dcdec, ch 3, turn.

Rep Row 2 of Ripple for pattern, working 2 rows more with MC, change to C at end of last row, ch 3, turn; following color sequence, work a total of 17 rows.

Color Sequence

2 rows C

2 rows MC

2 rows A

2 rows B

2 rows A

3 rows MC

At end of last row, do not finish off.

Row 18: With MC, work dcdec, still working in BLO until otherwise stated, dc in next 9 dc; *2 dc to right of lp, ch 2, 2 dc to left of lp, dc in next 10 dc, (work dcdec) twice, dc in next 10 dc; rep from * across, work last point, dc in next 10 dc, work dcdec, changing to C, ch 3, turn.

To Braid Loops

With right side facing, working across ripple, beginning with first row of lps from point of first large square, bring all 22 lps to right side; working from center outward, insert 2nd lp into first lp, insert 3rd lp into 2nd lp, insert 4th lp into 3rd lp, continue in same manner until all 22 lps are braided, secure last lp with bobby pin.

Bring ALL lps to right side from point of next sq (19 lps), working from center outward, braid lps, secure last lp with bobby pin.

Rep as before until all peaks (points) are braided.

Row 19 (right side): with C, work dcdec, dc in next 9 dc; *in ch-2 sp work [dc, then working in last lp and in same ch 2 sp at the same time, work (dc, ch 2, dc), then dc in same corner sp only to left of lp], dc in next 10 dc, (work dcdec) twice, dc in next 10 dc; rep from * across, work last point, dc in next 10 dc, work dcdec. Finish off.

Rep ripple on opposite side of squares strip; at end of last row, do NOT finish off.

Edging

Ch 1, 2 sc in top of dec, working across top of afghan work (2 sc, ch 1) at end of each row across to center large square, sc in each dc and in each ch-1 sp to center ch-2 sp of point, 3 sc in point, sc in each dc and in each ch-1 sp to ripple, work across ripple same as before to corner.

Work 3 sc in corner, working in both lps now and throughout, working across long edge, sc in each dc to ch-2 sp, 3 sc in ch-2 sp (point); *sc in next 12 dc, skip both decs, sc in next 12 dc, work 3 sc in point; rep from * across, sc in last 12 dc, 3 sc in corner.

Rep around, ending with sc in same st as beg sc, join; ch 1, 3 sc in same st, sc in each sc around and in each ch-1 sp, working 3 sc in center sc at points and skipping 2 sts in valleys, end with sl st in beg sc. Finish off; weave in all ends.

#32 HARLEQUIN VEST

Designed by Noreen Crone-Findlay

Note: *Instructions are written for size Small; changes for sizes Medium and Large are in parentheses.*

SIZES	Small	Medium	Large
Body Bust Measurements	28" - 30"	32" - 36"	38" - 42"
Finished Bust Measurements	33"	38"	42"

Note: *To make vest longer, add motifs to rows 1, 2, 14 (16, 18) and 15 (17,19). To make vest shorter, remove motifs from rows 1, 2, 14 (16, 18) and 15 (17,19).*

MATERIALS

Sport weight yarn
   3 1/2 oz (3 1/2 oz, 5 1/4 oz) gold
   3 1/2 oz (3 1/2 oz, 5 1/4 oz) burgundy

Bulky weight eyelash yarn
   1 3/4 oz dark purple (for all sizes)

Note: *Photographed model made with Patons® Brilliant #3023 Golden Glow and #4430 Beautiful Burgundy, and Patons® Allure #4310 Amethyst*

Size K (6.5 mm) crochet hook

Size F (3.75 mm) crochet hook
   (or size required for gauge)

GAUGE

One motif worked with sport weight
   yarn and smaller hook = 2"
   (not counting picots)

STITCH GUIDE

Picot: Ch 3, sl st in top of last completed dc.

Motifs (all made with sport weight yarn and smaller hook):

Basic Motif (no joins): Ch 8; join with sl st to form a ring; ch 3 (counts as first dc), in ring work dc, picot, (2 dc, picot) 11 times; join with sl st in top of beg ch-3: 24 dc, 12 picots. Finish off, weave in ends.

Motif A: Ch 8; join with sl st to form a ring; ch 3 (counts as first dc); in ring work dc, picot (2 dc, picot) 9 times; (2 dc, ch 2; remove lp from hook, place hook through picot on last motif, draw lp through, ch 2; sl st in dc just made) twice, join in top of beg ch-3. Finish off; weave in ends.

Motif B: Ch 8: join with sl st to form a ring; ch 3 (counts as first dc); in ring work dc, picot (2 dc, picot) 9 times; (2 dc, ch 5; remove lp from hook, place hook through next available picot on motif in previous row, draw lp through, ch 5; sl st in dc just made) twice, join in top of beg ch-3. Finish off; weave in ends.

Motif C: Ch 8; join with sl st to form a ring; ch 3 (counts as first dc); in ring work dc, ch 2; remove lp from hook, place hook through 3rd picot from join of last motif to previous row, pull lp through, ch 2; sl st in dc just made; 2 dc, ch 2; remove lp from hook, place hook through 2nd picot from join, pull lp through, ch 2; sl st in dc just made; 2 dc, picot, 2 dc, ch 5; remove lp from hook, skipping next picot on corresponding motif on previous row, insert hook in next picot, pull lp through, ch 5; sl st in previous dc, 2 dc, ch 5; remove lp from hook, insert hook in next picot on corresponding motif, pull lp through, ch 5; sl st in previous dc, (2 dc, picot) 7 times, join in top of beg ch-3. Finish off; weave in ends.

Motif D: Ch 8: join with sl st to form a ring; ch 3 (counts as first dc); in ring work dc, ch 2; remove lp from hook, place hook through 3rd picot from join of last motif to previous row, pull lp through, ch 2; sl st in dc just made; 2 dc, ch 2; remove lp from hook, place hook through 2nd picot from join, pull lp through, ch 2; sl st in dc just made; 2 dc, picot, 2 dc, ch 2; remove lp from hook, skipping next picot on corresponding motif on previous row, insert hook in next picot, pull lp through, ch 2; sl st in previous dc, 2 dc, ch 2; remove lp from hook, insert hook in next picot on corresponding motif, pull lp through, ch 2; sl st in previous dc, (2 dc, picot) 7 times; join in top of beg ch-3 to join. Finish off; weave in ends.

INSTRUCTIONS

The Harlequin Vest is made of 15 (17, 19) rows of motifs in alternating gold and burgundy that are joined as the vest progresses. Motifs are joined vertically to create a row, and then following rows are joined horizontally to previous row.

Note: *There should always be one picot between joins.*

Row 1 (right side): 12 (13, 14) motifs

First Motif: Basic Motif, starting with gold yarn.

Remaining Motifs: Motif A, starting with burgundy yarn 11 (12, 13) times.

Row 2: 11 (12, 13) motifs.

First Motif: Motif B, starting with gold yarn. Join to second motif of Row 1.

Remaining Motifs: Motif C, starting with burgundy yarn, 6 (6, 6) times; Motif D 4 (5, 6) times.

Row 3: 6 motifs (all sizes).

First motif: Motif B, starting with gold yarn. Join to second motif of Row 2

Remaining motifs: Motif C, starting with burgundy yarn, 5 (5, 5) times.

Rows 4 (4 and 5), (4 to 6): 4 motifs in each row (all sizes)

First motif: Motif B, join to first motif of previous row. Alternate starting color for each row.

Remaining motifs: Motif C 3 (3, 3) times.

Row 5 (6, 7): 9 motifs (all sizes).

First motif: Motif B, join to first motif of previous row.

Remaining Motifs: Motif C 3 times; Motif A 5 times.

Row 6 (7, 8): 9 motifs (all sizes).

First motif: Motif B, join to first motif of previous row.

Remaining motifs: Motif C 3 times; Motif D 5 times.

Rows 7 to 9 (8 to 10, 9 to 11): 8 motifs (all sizes)

First motif: Motif B, join to first motif of previous row.

Remaining motifs: Motif C 7 times.

Row 10 (11, 12): 9 motifs (all sizes).

First motif: Motif B, join to first motif of previous row.

Remaining motifs: Motif C 7 times; Motif A one time.

Row 11 (12, 13): 9 motifs, all sizes.

First motif: Motif B. Join to first motif of previous row.

Remaining motifs: Motif C 8 times.

Rows 12 (13 to 14, 14 to 16): 4 motifs in each row, all sizes.

First motif: Motif B. Join to first motif of previous row.

Remaining motifs: Motif C 3 (3, 3) times.

Row 13 (15, 17): 6 motifs all sizes.

First motif: Basic Motif (no joins).

Remaining motifs: Motif C, joining to first motif of previous row; rep Motif C 3 (3, 3) times more, Motif A once.

Row 14 (16, 18): 11 (12, 13) motifs.

First motif: Basic Motif (no joins).

Remaining motifs: Join Motif C to first motif of previous row; rep Motif C 5 (5, 5) more times; Motif A 4 (5, 6) times.

Row 15 (17, 19): 12 (13, 14) motifs.

First motif: Basic Motif (no joins).

Remaining motifs: Join Motif C to first motif of previous row; rep Motif C 6 (6, 6) more times; Motif D 4 (5, 6) times.

Join Shoulders

With smaller hook and sport weight yarn, ch 8; join in first ch with sl st to form a ring; ch 3 (counts as first dc); dc, picot, (2 dc, picot) 3 times; 2 dc, ch 2; join to 2nd picot after join on last motif on row 5 (6, 7), ch 2; sl st in dc just made, 2 dc, ch 2; join to next picot, ch 2; sl st in dc just made; (2 dc, picot) 4 times, 2 dc, ch 2; join to 2nd picot after join on last motif on row 2, ch 2; sl st in dc just made, 2 dc, ch 2; join to next picot, ch 2; sl st in dc just made, sl st in top of beg ch 3 to join. Finish off.

With smaller hook and sport weight yarn, ch 8; join in first ch with sl st to form a ring; ch 3 (counts as first dc); dc, picot, (2 dc, picot) 3 times; 2 dc, ch 2; join to 3rd picot after join on last motif on row 6 (7, 8), ch 2; sl st in dc just made, 2 dc, ch 2; join to 2nd picot after join, ch 2; sl st in dc just made; 2 dc, picot, 2 dc, ch 2; join to 2nd picot after join on motif in next row, ch 2; sl st in dc just made, 2 dc, ch 2; join to next picot, ch 2; sl st in dc just made, 2 dc, picot, 2 dc, ch 2, join to 2nd picot after join of last motif on row 1 (1, 1), ch 2; sl st in dc just made, 2 dc, ch 2; join to next picot, ch 2; sl st in dc just made, sl st in top of beg ch 3 to join. Finish off.

Rep for other shoulder, joining row 14 (16, 18) to row 11 (12, 13) and row 15 (17, 19) to row 10 (11, 12).

Edging

Rnd 1: Start at lower edge of back center. With eyelash yarn and larger hook, join in picot with sl st, ch 1, sc in same picot; working loosely, sc in each picot around entire outer edge of vest, working ch 1 between motifs; join in beg sl st.

Rnd 2: Sl st in each sc and ch-1 sp. Finish off; weave in ends.

Armholes

With eyelash yarn and larger hook, join in picot at underarm with sl st, ch 1; sc in same picot; working loosely, sc in each picot around, working ch-1 between motifs; join in beg sl st. Finish off; weave in ends.

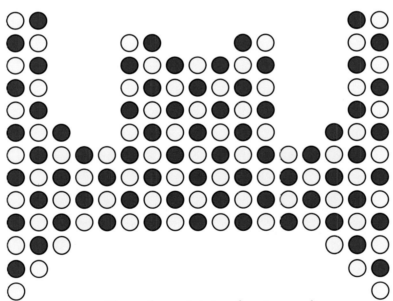

Note: Chart shows joining for size medium; for other sizes adjust joining per pattern.

SIZE
14" x 14"

MATERIALS
Size 10 cotton crochet thread
  150 yds white

Size 7 (1.65 mm) steel crochet
  hook (or size required for
  gauge)

GAUGE
10dc = 1

STITCH GUIDE

Long dc (Ldc): YO, insert hook in st indicated, YO and pull up a lp, YO and draw through first lp on hook; (YO and draw through 2 lps on hook) twice: Ldc made.

Block over Block (BL over BL): Ldc in next 3 Ldc.

Block over Space (BL over sp): 2 Ldc in next ch-2 sp, Ldc in next Ldc.

Space over Block (sp over BL): Ch 2, skip next 2 Ldc, Ldc in next Ldc.

Space over Space (sp over sp): Ch 2, Ldc in next Ldc.

Lacet: Ch 3, skip 2 sts, sc in next st, ch 3, Ldc in next Ldc.

Bar: Ch 5, Ldc in next Ldc.

INSTRUCTIONS

Ch 129.

Row 1 (right side): Ldc in 9th ch from hook; *ch 2, skip next 2 ch, Ldc in next ch; rep from * across, ch 5, turn: 41 ch-2 spaces.

Row 2: Ldc in next Ldc, (2 Ldc in next ch-2 sp, Ldc in next Ldc) 39 times, ch 2, Ldc in 3rd ch of turning ch-5; ch 5, turn: 39 blocks, 2 ch-2 spaces

Now begin following chart at Row 3. Read all odd-numbered rows (right side) from right to left; and all even-numbered rows from left to right. At end of last row of chart, finish off, weave in ends.

Block, using spray startch if desired.

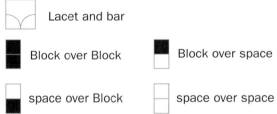

☐ Lacet and bar

■ Block over Block

▣ Block over space

▣ space over Block

☐ space over space

#34 MESH TUNIC

Note: Instructions are written for size Small; changes for sizes Medium and Large are in parentheses.

SIZES	Small	Medium	Large
Body Bust Measurements	30" - 32"	34" - 36"	38" - 40"
Finished Bust Measurements	36"	41"	46"

MATERIALS

Sport weight yarn
  15 $^3/_4$ (17 $^1/_2$, 19 $^1/_4$) oz apricot

Note: *Photographed model made with Patons® Grace #60603 Apricot*

Size D (3.25 mm) crochet hook
  (or size required for gauge)

GAUGE

6 ch-4 sps = 4"

12 ch-4 rows = 4 $^1/_2$"

PATTERN STITCHES

Shell: Work (3 dc, ch 1, 3 dc) all in specified st: shell made.

INSTRUCTIONS

Front

Ch 114 (130, 146).

Row 1 (right side): Sc in 2nd ch from hook; (ch 4, skip next 3 chs, sc in next ch) 8 (10, 12) times; *skip next 3 chs, shell in next ch, skip next 3 chs, sc in next ch*; (ch 4, skip next 3 chs, sc in next ch) 8 times; rep from * to * once; (ch 4, skip next 3 chs, sc in next ch) 8 (10, 12) times: 24 (28, 32) ch-4 sps and 2 shells; ch 6, turn.

Row 2: Sc in first ch-4 sp; (ch 4, sc in next ch-4 sp) 7 (9, 11) times; *ch 2, shell in ch-1 sp of next shell, ch 2, sc in next ch-4 sp*; (ch 4, sc in next ch-4 sp) 7 times; rep from * to * once; (ch 4, sc in next ch-4 sp) 7 (9, 11) times; ch 2, tr in last sc: 21 (25, 29) ch-4 sps, 2 shells, 5 ch-2 sps and 1 beg ch-6 sp; ch 1, turn.

Row 3: Sc in first tr; (ch 4, sc in next ch-4 sp) 7 (9, 11) times; *ch 4, sc in next ch-2 sp, shell in ch-1 sp of next shell, sc in next ch-2 sp*; (ch 4, sc in next ch-4 sp) 7 times; rep from * to * once; (ch 4, sc in next ch-4 sp) 7 (9, 11) times; ch 4, sc in 4th ch of turning ch-6: 24 (28, 32) ch-4 sps and 2 shells; ch 6, turn.

Rows 4 through 64 (66, 70): Rep Rows 2 and 3, 30 (31, 33) times more, then rep Row 2 until piece measures 24" (25", 26") ending by working a Row 2.

Row 65 (67, 71): Sc in first tr, (ch 4, sc in next ch-4 sp) 7 (9, 11) times; *ch 4, sc in next ch-2 sp, ch 4, sc in ch-1 sp of next shell, ch 4, sc in next ch-2 sp*; (ch 4, sc in next ch-4 sp) 7 times; rep from * to * once; (ch 4, sc in next ch-4 sp) 7 (9, 11) times; ch 4, sc in 4th ch of turning ch-6: 28 (32, 36) ch-4 sps; ch 6, turn.

Row 66 (68, 72): Sc in first ch-4 sp; (ch 4, sc in next ch-4 sp) 7 times; (ch 1, skip next sc, 3 sc in next ch-4 sp) 12 (16, 20) times; ch 1, sc in next ch-4 sp, (ch 4, sc in next ch-4 sp) 7 times; ch 2, tr in last sc: 14 ch-4 sps, 13 (17, 21) ch-1 sps, 52 (64, 76) sc, 1 beg ch-6 sp and 1 end ch-2 sp; ch 1, turn.

Row 67 (69, 73): Sc in first tr; (ch 4, sc in next ch-4 sp) 7 times; ch 4, sc in next ch-1 sp, (shell in next ch-1 sp, sc in next ch-1 sp) 6 (8, 10) times; (ch 4, sc in next ch-4 sp) 7 times; ch 4, sc in 4th ch of turning ch-6: 6 (8, 10) shells and 16 ch-4 sps. Finish off; weave in ends.

Back
Work same as Front.

Sleeves (make 2)
Ch 74 (82, 82).

Row 1 (right side): Sc in 2nd ch from hook, (ch 4, skip next 3 chs, sc in next ch) 8 (9, 9) times; skip next 3 chs, shell in next ch, skip next 3 chs, sc in next ch; (ch 4, skip next 3 chs, sc in next ch) 8 (9, 9) times: 16 (18, 18) ch-4 sps and 1 shell; ch 6, turn.

Row 2: Sc in first ch-4 sp, (ch 4, sc in next ch-4 sp) 7 (8, 8) times; ch 2, shell in ch-1 sp of next shell, ch 2, sc in next ch-4 sp; (ch 4, sc in next ch-4 sp) 7 (8, 8) times; ch 2, tr in last sc: 14 (16, 16) ch-4 sps, 1 shell, 3 ch-2 sps and 1 beg ch-6 sp; ch 1, turn.

Row 3: Sc in first tr, (ch 4, sc in next ch-4 sp) 7 (8, 8) times; ch 4, sc in next ch-2 sp, shell in ch-1 sp of next shell, sc in next ch-2 sp; (ch 4, sc in next ch-4 sp) 7 (8, 8) times; ch 4, sc in 4th ch of turning ch-6: 16 (18, 18) ch-4 sps and 1 shell; ch 6, turn.

Rows 4 through 8: Rep Rows 2 and 3 twice, then rep Row 2 until piece measures 3".

Row 9: Sc in first tr, ch 4, (sc, ch 4, sc) in first ch-4 sp; (ch 4, sc in next ch-4 sp) 6 (7, 7) times; ch 4, sc in next ch-2 sp, shell in ch-1 sp of next shell, sc in next ch-2 sp; (ch 4, sc in next ch-4 sp) 6 (7, 7) times; ch 4, (sc, ch 4, sc) in next ch-4 sp, ch 4, sc in 4th ch of turning ch-6: 18 (20, 20) ch-4 sps and 1 shell; ch 6, turn.

Row 10: Sc in first ch-4 sp, (ch 4, sc in next ch-4 sp) 8 (9, 9) times; ch 2, shell in ch-1 sp of next shell, ch 2, sc in next ch-4 sp; (ch 4, sc in next ch-4 sp) 8 (9, 9) times; ch 2, tr in last sc: 16 (18, 18) ch-4 sps, 1 shell, 3 ch-2 sps and 1 beg ch-6 sp; ch 1, turn.

Row 11: Sc in first tr, (ch 4, sc in next ch-4 sp) 8 (9, 9) times; ch 4, sc in next ch-2 sp, shell in ch-1 sp of next shell, sc in next ch-2 sp; (ch 4, sc in next ch-4 sp) 8 (9, 9) times; ch 4, sc in 4th ch of turning ch-6: 18 (20, 20) ch-4 sps and 1 shell; ch 6, turn.

Rows 12 through 14: Rep Rows 10 and 11 once, then rep Row 10 once more.

Row 15: Sc in first tr, ch 4, (sc, ch 4, sc) in first ch-4 sp; (ch 4, sc in next ch-4 sp) 7 (8, 8) times; ch 4, sc in next ch-2 sp, shell in ch-1 sp of next shell, sc in next ch-2 sp; (ch 4, sc in next ch-4 sp) 7 (8, 8) times; ch 4, (sc, ch 4, sc) in next ch-4 sp, ch 4, sc in 4th ch of turning ch-6: 20 (22, 22) ch-4 sps and 1 shell; ch 6, turn.

Row 16: Sc in first ch-4 sp, (ch 4, sc in next ch-4 sp) 9 (10, 10) times; ch 2, shell in ch-1 sp of next shell, ch 2, sc in next ch-4 sp; (ch 4, sc in next ch-4 sp) 9 (10, 10) times; ch 2, tr in last sc: 18 (20, 20) ch-4 sps, 1 shell, 3 ch-2 sps and 1 beg ch-6 sp; ch 1, turn.

Row 17: Sc in first tr, (ch 4, sc in next ch-4 sp) 9 (10, 10) times; ch 4, sc in next ch-2 sp, shell in ch-1 sp of next shell, sc in next ch-2 sp; (ch 4, sc in next ch-4 sp) 9 (10, 10) times; ch 4, sc in 4th ch of turning ch-6: 20 (22, 22) ch-4 sps and 1 shell; ch 6, turn.

Rows 18 through 20: Rep Rows 16 and 17 once, then rep Row 16 once more.

Row 21: Sc in first tr, ch 4, (sc, ch 4, sc) in first ch-4 sp; (ch 4, sc in next ch-4 sp) 8 (9, 9) times; ch 4, sc in next ch-2 sp, shell in ch-1 sp of next shell, sc in next ch-2 sp; (ch 4, sc in next ch-4 sp) 8 (9, 9) times; ch 4, (sc, ch 4, sc) in next ch-4 sp, ch 4, sc in 4th ch of turning ch-6: 22 (24, 24) ch-4 sps and 1 shell; ch 6, turn.

Row 22: Sc in first ch-4 sp, (ch 4, sc in next ch-4 sp) 10 (11, 11) times; ch 2, shell in ch-1 sp of next shell, ch 2, sc in next ch-4 sp; (ch 4, sc in next ch-4 sp) 10 (11, 11) times; ch 2, tr in last sc: 20 (22, 22) ch-4 sps, 1 shell, 3 ch-2 sps and 1 beg ch-6 sp; ch 1, turn.

Row 23: Sc in first tr, (ch 4, sc in next ch-4 sp) 10 (11, 11) times; ch 4, sc in next ch-2 sp, shell in ch-1 sp of next shell, sc in next ch-2 sp; (ch 4, sc in next ch-4 sp) 10 (11, 11) times; ch 4, sc in 4th ch of turning ch-6: 22 (24, 24) ch-4 sps and 1 shell; ch 6, turn.

Rows 24 through 26: Rep Rows 22 and 23 once, then rep Row 22 once more.

Row 27: Sc in first tr, ch 4, (sc, ch 4, sc) in first ch-4 sp; (ch 4, sc in next ch-4 sp) 9 (10, 10) times; ch 4, sc in next ch-2 sp, shell in ch-1 sp of next shell, sc in next ch-2 sp; (ch 4, sc in next ch-4 sp) 9 (10, 10) times; ch 4, (sc, ch 4, sc) in next ch-4 sp, ch 4, sc in 4th ch of turning ch-6: 24 (26, 26) ch-4 sps and 1 shell; ch 6, turn.

Row 28: Sc in first ch-4 sp, (ch 4, sc in next ch-4 sp) 11 (12, 12) times; ch 2, shell in ch-1 sp of next shell, ch 2, sc in next ch-4 sp; (ch 4, sc in next ch-4 sp) 11 (12, 12) times; ch 2, tr in last sc: 22 (24, 24) ch-4 sps, 1 shell, 3 ch-2 sps and 1 beg ch-6 sp; ch 1, turn.

Row 29: Sc in first tr, (ch 4, sc in next ch-4 sp) 11 (12, 12) times; ch 4, sc in next ch-2 sp, shell in ch-1 sp of next shell, sc in next ch-2 sp; (ch 4, sc in next ch-4 sp) 11 (12, 12) times; ch 4, sc in 4th ch of turning ch-6: 24 (26, 26) ch-4 sps and 1 shell; ch 6, turn.

Rows 30 through 32: Rep Rows 28 and 29 once, then rep Row 28 once more.

Row 33: Sc in first tr, ch 4, (sc, ch 4, sc) in first ch-4 sp; (ch 4, sc in next ch-4 sp) 10 (11, 11) times; ch 4, sc in next ch-2 sp, shell in ch-1 sp of next shell, sc in next ch-2 sp; (ch 4, sc in next ch-4 sp) 10 (11, 11) times; ch 4, (sc, ch 4, sc) in next ch-4 sp, ch 4, sc in 4th ch of turning ch-6: 26 (28, 28) ch-4 sps and 1 shell; ch 6, turn.

Row 34: Sc in first ch-4 sp, (ch 4, sc in next ch-4 sp) 12 (13, 13) times; ch 2, shell in ch-1 sp of next shell, ch 2, sc in next ch-4 sp; (ch 4, sc in next ch-4 sp) 12 (13, 13) times; ch 2, tr in last sc: 24 (26, 26) ch-4 sps, 1 shell, 3 ch-2 sps and 1 beg ch-6 sp; ch 1, turn.

Row 35: Sc in first tr, (ch 4, sc in next ch-4 sp) 12 (13, 13) times; ch 4, sc in next ch-2 sp, shell in ch-1 sp of next shell, sc in next ch-2 sp; (ch 4, sc in next ch-4 sp) 12 (13, 13) times; ch 4, sc in 4th ch of turning ch-6: 26 (28, 28) ch-4 sps and 1 shell; ch 6, turn.

Rows 36 through 48 (50, 54): Rep Rows 34 and 35 six (seven, nine) times more, then rep Row 34 once more. Note: Sleeve should measure 18" (19", 20") long. Adjust rows as necessary to achieve desired length of sleeve, ending by working a wrong-side row. Finish off; weave in ends.

Finishing

Pin garment pieces to measurements given in diagrams. Steam lightly and cover with a damp cloth, leaving to dry.

Front and Back Bottom Edging

Row 1: Hold piece with wrong side facing and beg ch at top; join yarn with sl st in free lp of same ch as first sc on Row 1, ch 1, sc in same sp as joining; *3 sc in next ch-3 sp (3

skipped chs on Row 1), ch 1, skip next sc; rep from * to last ch-3 sp; 3 sc in last ch-3 sp, sc in free lp of last ch: 86 (98, 110) sc and 27 (31, 35) ch-1 sps; ch 1, turn.

Row 2: Sc in first sc, *shell in next ch-1 sp, sc in next ch-1 sp; rep from * across, ending with sc in last sc: 14 (16, 18) shells. Finish off; weave in ends.

Sleeve Bottom Edging

Row 1: Work same as Front and Back Bottom Edging Row 1: 56 (62, 62) sc and 17 (19, 19) ch-1 sps; ch 1, turn.

Row 2: Work same as Front and Back Edging Row 2: 9 (10, 10) shells. Finish off; weave in ends.

Joining Shoulders

Place Front and Back with right sides together. Working through both thicknesses, join with sl st in sc at edge of last row, ch 1, sc in same st, ch 1, sc in next ch-4 sp, (ch 3, sc in next ch-4 sp) 7 times, ch 1, sc in next sc. Finish off; weave in ends. Rep for other shoulder.

Joining Sleeves

Place markers on Front and Back side edges 9" (9 1/2", 9 1/2") down from shoulder seams. Working through both thicknesses with right sides tog, join top edge of sleeves to Front and Back between markers working (sc, ch 1) along seams.

Side and Sleeve Seams

Place Front and Back with right sides tog. Working through both thicknesses, join side and sleeve seams working (sc, ch 1) along seams.

#35 BUCKET BAG

Designed by Linda W. Cyr for Lion Brand®

SIZE

6 1/2" x 10 1/2"

MATERIALS

Super bulky weight yarn
 6 oz off-white

Note: Photographed model made with Lion Brand® Wool-Ease® Thick & Quick® #4099 Fisherman

Stitch marker or piece of contrast yarn

Size K (6.5 mm) crochet hook (or size required for gauge)

GAUGE

8 sc = 3"

INSTRUCTIONS

Starting at bottom, ch 2; 6 sc in 2nd ch from hook; do not join, work in continuous rnds; mark beg of rnds.

Rnd 1: 2 sc in each sc: 12 sc.

Rnd 2: 2 sc in first sc; sc in next sc; *2 sc in next sc, sc in next sc; rep from * 4 more times: 18 sc.

Rnd 3: 2 sc in first sc; sc in next 2 sc; *2 sc in next sc, sc in next 2 sc; rep from * 4 more times: 24 sc.

Rnd 4: 2 sc in first sc, sc in next 3 sc; *2 sc in next sc, sc in next 3 sc; rep from * 4 more times: 30 sc.

Rnd 5: 2 sc in first sc, sc in next 4 sc; *2 sc in next sc, sc in next 4 sc; rep from * 4 more times: 36 sc.

Rnd 6: 2 sc in first sc, sc in next 5 sc; *2 sc in next sc, sc in next 5 sc; rep from * 4 more times: 42 sc.

Rnd 7: 2 sc in first sc, sc in next 6 sc; *2 sc in next sc, sc in next 6 sc; rep from * 4 more times: 48 sc.

Rnd 8: Sc in each sc.

Rnd 9 through 14: Rep Rnd 8.

Rnd 15: Sc in first 4 sc; *Cluster Fan in next sc, sc in next 7 sc; rep from * 4 more times, Cluster Fan, sc in next 3 sc.

Cluster Fan: This is a group of 5 long lps worked in rnds below the working rnd. Be sure to work these lps loosely and draw them up to the height of the working rnd; if worked too tightly the lps will draw up the fabric. (See photo.)

Step 1: Using next sc as the reference point, count 2 sts to the right, and two rnds below, insert hook in this sp and draw a long lp up to working row: 2 lps on hook.

Step 2: Count 1 st to the right and 3 rnds below, insert hook in this sp and draw a long lp up to working row: 3 lps on hook.

Step 3: Count 4 rnds directly below reference point sc, insert hook and draw up a lp to working row: 4 lps on hook.

Step 4: Count 1 st to left and 3 rnds below, insert hook and draw up a lp: 5 lps on hook.

Step 5: Count 2 sts to left and 2 rnds below, insert hook and draw up a lp: 6 lps on hook; YO and draw through all 6 lps: Cluster Fan made.

Reference point sc behind Cluster Fan is left unworked.

Rnd 16 through 18: Rep Rnd 8.

Rnd 19: Sc in first 7 sc; *Cluster Fan, sc in next 7 sc; rep from * 4 more times, Cluster Fan.

Rep Rnd 8 until piece measure 6" from top of last Cluster Fan rnd.

Strap

Ch 70, skip 24 sc; join in 25th sc at top edge of bag on opposite side.

Rnd 1: 69 sc along strap ch; skip last strap ch; working along top edge of bag, sc in next 4 sc, sl st in next 16 sc, sc in next 4 sc.

Rnd 2: Skip first sc of strap, sc in next 67 sc in strap sc; skip last strap sc; working along top edge of bag, sc in next 3 sc, sl st in next 18 sc, sc in next 3 sc.

Rnd 3: Skip first sc of strap, sc in next 65 sc in strap sc; skip last strap sc; working along top edge of bag, sc in next 2 sc, sl st in next 20 sc, sc in next 2 sc.

Rnd 4: Skip first sc of strap, sc in next 63 sc in strap sc; skip last strap sc; and working along top edge of bag, sc in next sc, sl st in next 22 sc, sc in next sc; join in first sc. Finish off.

Join yarn in first unused lp of strap ch. Sc in 69 unused lps, skip last lp; working along top edge of bag, sc in next 4 sc, sl st in next 16 sc, sc in next 4 sc.

Rep Rnds 2 through 4 to complete Strap.

Fold Strap in half to the inside. Sew with an overcast st leaving approximately 2" free on each end. Lightly steam block if desired.

#36 MAGNIFICENT IN MESH

Designed by Valentina Devine

Note: *Instructions are written for size Small; changes for sizes Medium and Large are in parentheses*

SIZE	Small	Medium	Large
Body Bust Measurments	32" - 34"	36" - 38"	40" - 42"
Finished Bust Measurements	36 1/2"	41 1/4"	46"
Length: 26"			

MATERIALS

Heavy worsted weight cotton yarn
  28 (30, 32) oz tan

Note: *Photographed model made with Henry's Attic Inca Cotton Ecru*

Size J (6 mm) crochet hook
  (or size required for gauge)

Four 3/4" x 1 1/2" buttons

GAUGE

7 dc and 7 ch-1 sps = 4 1/4"

7 rows = 4"

INSTRUCTIONS

Back

Starting at bottom, ch 62 (70, 78).

Row 1 (right side): Sc in 2nd ch from hook, sc in next ch and in each ch across: 61 (69, 77) sc; ch 4 (counts as dc and ch-1 sp on next row now and throughout), turn.

Row 2: Skip first 2 sc, dc in next sc; *ch 1, skip next sc, dc in next sc; rep from * across: 31 (35, 39) dc and 30 (34, 38) ch-1 sps; ch 4, turn.

Row 3: Skip first ch, dc in next dc; *ch 1, skip next ch, dc in next dc; rep from * across, working last dc in 3rd ch of turning ch-4; ch 4, turn.

Rep Row 3 until piece measures about 25". At end of last row, do not ch 4. Finish off; weave in ends.

Front (make 2)

Starting at bottom, ch 32 (36, 40).

Row 1 (right side): Sc in 2nd ch from hook, sc in next ch and in each ch across: 31 (35, 39) sc; ch 4, turn.

Row 2: Rep Row 2 of back: 16 (18, 20) dc and 15 (17, 19) ch-1 sps.

Row 3: Rep Row 3 of back.

Rep Row 3 until piece measures same as back. At end of last row, do not ch 4. Finish off; weave in ends.

Starting at sides, sew shoulder seams through 12 (13, 14) ch-1 sps. Starting at bottom edge, sew side seams leaving top 14 ch-1 sps open for sleeves.

Sleeve (make 2)

Ch 38.

Row 1 (wrong side): Sc in 2nd ch from hook, sc in next ch and in each ch across: 37 sc; ch 4, turn.

Row 2: Rep Row 2 of back: 19 dc and 18 ch-1 sps.

Row 3: Rep Row 3 of back.

Rows 4 through 29: Rep Row 3 of back 26 times more. At end of Row 29, do not ch 4. Finish off; weave in ends.

Sew first and last row of sleeve together. Sew sleeve to side edge in sleeve opening.

Sleeve Edging

Rnd 1: With right side facing, join with sc in sleeve joining, work sc in edge of Row 1 and 2 sc in edge of each row around: 58 sc; join with sl st in first sc. Ch 1, turn.

Rnd 2: Work lp st in same st as joining and in each sc around: 58 lp sts; join with sl st in first lp st. Ch 1, do not turn.

Rnd 3: Work lp st in same st as joining and in each lp st around: 58 lp sts; join with sl st in first lp st. Ch 1, do not turn.

Rnd 4: Rep Rnd 3. At end of row, ch 1, turn.

Rnd 5: Work rev sc in each st around: 58 rev sc; join with sl st in first rev sc. Finish off; weave in ends.

Collar

Row 1: With wrong side facing, join with sc in edge of Row 27 on left front, sc in same sp, 2 sc in edge of next row and in edge of each row around to Row 27 on right front, working 4 sc in top corner sp on left and right front; ch 1, turn.

Row 2: Work lp st in each sc across. Finish off; weave in ends.

Row 3: With right side facing, join with sl st in 2nd lp st on last row, ch 1, work lp st in same st as joining, work lp st in each lp st across to last lp st, leaving last lp st unworked. Finish off; weave in ends.

Row 4: Rep Row 3.

Edging

With right side facing, join with sc in edge of Row 26 on left front, sc in same sp, 2 sc in edge of next row and in edge of each row down to Row 26. Finish off; weave in ends. With right side facing, join with sc in edge of Row 2 on right front, sc in same sp, 2 sc in edge of next row and in edge of each row up to Row 26; ch 1, work rev sc in each st down right front edge around bottom edge, up left front edge, and edges of collar; join with sl st in first rev sc. Finish off; weave in ends.

Drawstring

Make a chain about 60" (65", 70") long, or to desired length, sl st in each ch across. Finish off; weave in ends. Weave through squares in waist area. Tie knot in each end.

Sew buttons to left front edge at desired intervals.

#37 A LITTLE SOMETHING

Note: *Instructions are written for size X-Small; with changes sizes Small, Medium and Large are in parentheses. Garment stretches to fit snugly.*

SIZES	X-Small	Small	Medium	Large
Body Bust Measurements	32"	34"	36"	38"

MATERIALS

Size 5 crochet cotton
  100 (100, 100, 100) grams lilac

Note: *Photographed models made with Twilleys Lyscordet #81 Lilac*

Stitch markers

Size C (2.75 mm) crochet hook

SIze D (3.25 mm) crochet hook
  (or size required for gauge)

GAUGE

16 dcDec = 4" with larger hook in
  Double Decrease pattern

STITCH GUIDE

Double Decrease (dcDec): For first decrease of row: YO, draw up lp in first st, YO, draw through 2 lps on hook, YO, draw up lp in next st, YO, draw through 2 lps on hook, YO, draw through 3 lps on hook.

For following decreases: YO, draw up lp in same st as last insertion, YO, draw through 2 lps on hook, YO, draw up lp in next st, YO, draw through 2 lps on hook, YO, draw through 3 lps on hook.

2dcCl: YO, insert hook in specified st and draw up lp, YO, draw through 2 lps on hook, insert hook in same st and draw up lp, YO, draw through 2 lps on hook, YO, draw through 3 lps on hook: 2dcCl made.

Dc2tog: [YO, draw up lp in next st, YO, draw through 2 lps on hook] 2 times, YO, draw through all 3 lps on hook: dc2tog made.

Dc3tog: [YO, draw up lp in next st, YO, draw through 2 lps on hook] 3 times, YO, draw through all 4 lps on hook: dc3tog made.

Double Decrease Pattern: Ch 3, dcDec over first 2 sts, dcDec across, working last insertion in 3rd ch of beg ch-3 of previous row, turn:

Designed by Susan Lowman

SIZE

Place Mat: 11" x 15 $\frac{1}{2}$"

Coaster: 4" square

Napkin Ring: 3" wide x 5 $\frac{1}{2}$" in circumference

Potholder: 7" square

MATERIALS

Worsted weight cotton yarn
  188 yds multicolor
  68 yds tea rose
  50 yds lt blue
  45 yds ecru
  11 yds rose
  4 yds lt green

Note: Photographed models made with Lily Sugar 'n Cream #130 Shaded Pastel, #42 Tea Rose, #26 Light Blue, #1004 Soft Ecru, #79 Dusty Rose and #55 Light Green

Size I (5.5 mm) crochet hook (or size required for gauge)

GAUGE

8 dc = 2"

7 dc rows = 3"

PLACE MAT

INSTRUCTIONS

Square
(make 3 multicolor and 3 tea rose)
With appropriate color, ch 17.

Row 1 (right side): Dc in 3rd ch from hook and in each rem ch: 15 dc and one beg ch-2 sp; ch 2, turn.

Row 2: Skip first dc, (FPdc in next 2 dc, BPdc in next 2 dc) 3 times, FPdc in next 2 dc, dc in next ch: 8 FPdc, 6 BPdc, 1 dc and one beg ch-2 sp; ch 2, turn.

Rows 3 through 9: Rep Row 2 seven times more. At end of Row 9, do not ch 2. Finish off and weave in ends.

Square Edging

Rnd 1: With right side facing, join lt blue with sc in last dc on Row 9, 2 sc in same dc, FP sc around post of same dc; (2 sc in next ch-2 sp, FPsc around post of next dc) 4 times, 3 sc in free lp of next ch of beg ch, sc in free lp of next 13 chs, 3 sc in free lp of last ch; (sc in next ch-2 sp, 2 FP sc around post of next dc) 4 times, sc in next ch-2 sp, 3 sc in first FPdc on Row 9, sc in next 13 sts, changing to ecru in last sc. Finish off lt blue; weave in ends.

Rnd 2: Sc in next sc, (3 sc in next sc, sc in next 15 sc) 3 times, 3 sc in next sc, sc in next 14 sc; join with sl st in beg sc. Finish off; weave in ends.

Assembly

With right sides facing, arrange squares into 2 rows of 3 squares each, alternating square colors. Whip stitch squares together.

Edging

Rnd 1: With right side facing, join ecru with sc in middle sc (corner sc) of 3 sc at top left corner, 2 sc in same sc; *sc in next 17 sc, sc dec in corner sc of same square and corner sc of next square, sc in next 17 sc, 3 sc in next corner sc, (sc in next 17 sc; sc dec in corner sc of same square and corner sc of next square) 2 times, sc in next 17 sc*, 3 sc in next corner sc; rep from * to * once, changing to lt blue in last sc. Finish off ecru.

Rnd 2: Sc in next sc, *3 sc in next corner sc, sc in next 37 sc, 3 sc in next corner sc*, sc in next 55 sc; rep from * to * once; sc in next 54 sc, changing to multicolor in last sc. Finish off lt blue.

Rnd 3: Sc in next 2 sc, *2 sc in next corner sc, sc in next 39 sc, 2 sc in next corner sc*, sc in next 57 sc; rep from * to * once; sc in next 55 sc; join with sl st in beg sc. Finish off; weave in ends.

COASTER

INSTRUCTIONS

With multicolor yarn, ch 13.

Row 1 (wrong side): Dc in 3rd ch from hook and in each rem ch: 11 dc and one beg ch-2 sp; ch 2, turn.

Row 2: Skip first dc, (FPdc in next 2 dc, BPdc in next 2 dc) 2 times, FPdc in next 2 dc, dc in next ch: 6 FPdc, 4 BPdc, 1 dc and one beg ch-2 sp; ch 2, turn.

Rows 3 through 6: Rep Row 2 four times more. At end of Row 6, do not ch 2. Finish off and weave in ends.

Edging

Rnd 1: With right side facing, join lt blue with sc in free lp of 11th ch of beg ch-13, 2 sc in same ch, sc in free lp of next 9 chs, 3 sc in free lp of last ch; *(sc around post of next dc, 2 sc in next ch-2 sp) 3 times*; 3 sc in first FPdc on Row 6, sc in next 9 sts, 3 sc in last dc; rep from * to * once, changing to multicolor in last sc. Finish off lt blue.

Rnd 2: Sc in next sc, (2 sc in next sc, sc in next 11 sc) 3 times, 2 sc in next sc, sc in next 10 sc; join with sl st in beg sc. Finish off and weave in ends.

NAPKIN RING

INSTRUCTIONS

With multicolor yarn, ch 19, join with sl st to form a ring.

Row 1 (right side): Ch 3 (counts as dc), dc in each ch around: 19 dc; join with sl st in 3rd ch of beg ch-3.

Row 2: Ch 2, (FPdc in next 2 dc, BPdc in next 2 dc) 4 times, FPdc in next 2 dc*: 10 FPdc, 8 BPdc and one beg ch-2 sp; join with sl st in 2nd ch of beg ch-2.

Row 3: Ch 2, (BPdc in next 2 dc, FPdc in next 2 dc) 4 times, BPdc in next 2 dc: 10 BPdc, 8 FPdc and one beg ch-2 sp; join with sl st in 2nd ch of beg ch-2.

Row 4: Rep Row 2 through *, sc in 2nd ch of beg ch-2, changing to lt blue. Do not finish off multicolor.

Top Edging

Row 1: Sc in next 18 sts, sc in next sc, changing to blue. Finish off multicolor.

Row 2: Sc in next 19 sc; join with sl st in beg sc. Finish off; weave in ends.

Bottom Edging

Row 1: With right side facing, join lt blue with sc in free lp of 19th ch on Row 1, sc in free lp of next 17 chs, sc in free lp of beg ch, changing to multicolor. Finish off lt blue.

Row 2: Sc in next 19 sc; join with sl st in beg sc. Finish off; weave in ends.

POTHOLDER

INSTRUCTIONS

With multicolor, ch 25.

Row 1 (wrong side): Dc in 3rd ch from hook and in each rem ch: 23 dc and one beg ch-2 sp; ch 2, turn.

Row 2: Skip first dc, (FPdc in next 2 dc, BPdc in next 2 dc) 5 times, FPdc in next 2 dc, dc in next ch: 12 FPdc, 10 BPdc, 1 dc and one beg ch-2 sp; ch 2, turn.

Rows 3 through 14: Rep Row 2 twelve times more. At end of Row 14, do not ch 2. Finish off and weave in ends.

Edging

Rnd 1: With right side facing, join lt blue with sc in last dc on Row 14, 2 sc in same dc, FP sc around post of same dc, *2 sc in next ch-2 sp, (FPsc around post of next dc, 2 sc in next ch-2 sp) 6 times*; 3 sc in free lp of next ch (where first dc on Row 1 was worked), sc in free lp of next 21 chs, 3 sc in free lp of last ch, FPsc around post of next dc; rep from * to * once; 3 sc in first FPdc on Row 14, sc in next 21 sts, changing to multicolor in last sc. Finish off lt blue.

Rnd 2: Sc in next sc, (2 sc in next sc, sc in next 23 sc) 3 times, 2 sc in next sc, sc in next 22 sc, sl st in next 3 sc, ch 9 for loop; join with sl st in same sc as last sl st. Finish off and weave in ends.

Flower and Leaf (make 4)

Petals

With rose, ch 5, join with sl st to form a ring.

Rnd 1: Ch 2, dc in same ch as joining, ch 2, sl st in same ch; (*sl st in next ch, ch 2, dc in same ch, ch 2*, sl st in same ch) 3 times; rep from * to * once; join with sl st in free lp of same ch, changing to multicolor: 5 petals. Finish off rose; weave in ends.

Center

Ch 2, hdc in same free lp as last sl st, (2 hdc in free lp of next ch) 4 times: 10 hdc; join with sl st in 2nd ch of beg ch-2. Finish off, leaving a 12" end for sewing

Leaf

With lt green, ch 3, (dc, tr, ch 1, dc, ch 2, sl st) in 3rd ch from hook. Finish off, leaving a 10" end for sewing.

Sew flower and leaf to top left corner of place mat and coaster, to front of napkin ring and to top left corner of potholder next to lp.

#42 FOUR-WAY PONCHO

Designed by Ruthie Marks

SIZE
24" long x 21" wide
   (including fringe)

MATERIALS
Super bulky yarn
   6 oz white with black
   6 oz black with white

Worsted weight yarn
   3 yds black

Note: *Photographed model made with TLC® Macaroon™ #9317 Granite and #9318 Salt & Pepper*

Size L (8 mm) crochet hook
   (or size required for gauge)

GAUGE
8 tr plus 8 chs = 6 ^{1}/$_2$"

2 sc rows plus 2 tr rows = 3 ^{1}/$_4$"

INSTRUCTIONS

White Side

Using white with black, ch 58.

Row 1 (wrong side): Sc in 2nd ch from hook and in each ch across: 57 sc; ch 1, turn.

Row 2 (right side): Sc in first st and in each st across; ch 1, turn.

Row 3: Sc in first st and in each st across; ch 5 (counts as tr and ch-1 sp on next row), turn.

Row 4: Skip first 2 sts, tr in next st; *ch 1, skip next st, tr in next st; rep from * across: 29 tr and 28 ch-1 sps; ch 1, turn.

Row 5: Sc in first tr; *sc in next ch-1 sp, sc in next tr; rep from * across to last 2 sts; sc in turning ch-5 sp, sc in 4th ch of turning ch: 57 sc; ch 5 (counts as tr and ch-1 sp on next row), turn.

Rows 6 through 23: Rep Rows 4 and 5 nine times more. At end of Row 23, ch 1 instead of ch 5.

Row 24: Rep Row 2.

Row 25: Sc in first st and in each st across. Finish off; weave in ends.

Black Side

Using black with white, ch 58.

Rows 1 through 25: Rep Rows 1 through 25 on white side.

Assembly

With black, sew sc rows on one short edge of white and black sides together. Leave other edge open.

Shoulder Seam

With black worsted weight yarn, sew white and black sides together through unused lps of foundation chs, starting at open edge and ending halfway between edges.

Fringe

Following fringe instructions on page 255, cut strands of bulky yarns 8" long. Remove white strand from black with white and black strand from white with black. Knot 2 strands black on white side and 2 strands white on black side in every other st on Row 25.

#43 AWESOME BLOSSOM

Designed by Myra Wood

For the experienced crocheter

SIZE
Fits up to 21" head

MATERIALS
Worsted weight yarn
  1 ¹/₂ oz white (A)
  1 ¹/₂ oz cream (B)
  1 ¹/₂ oz gold (C)
  1 ¹/₂ oz medium rose (D)
  1 ¹/₂ oz dark rose (E)
  1 ¹/₂ oz medium green (F)

Stitch markers or contrast yarn

Size H (5 mm) crochet hook
  (or size required for gauge)

GAUGE
14 sc = 4"

2 sc tog: Draw up a lp in each of next 2 sts; YO and draw through all 3 lps on hook: decrease made.

To change colors: work new color in ch indicated, cut old color leaving 4" tail to weave in.

Note: Hat, which begins at crown and is worked towards the brim, consists of petal rounds, followed by one or more base rounds. When working a round following a petal round, work behind the petals and into the stitches of the round made before the petal round. Do not turn rounds.

INSTRUCTIONS

With A, ch 5; join with sl st to form a ring.

Rnd 1 (right side): Ch 2, 12 hdc in ring; join with sl st in front lp of first hdc; mark back lp of first hdc: 12 hdc.

Rnd 2: * Ch 4, sc in 2nd ch from hook, sc in next ch, hdc in next ch (petal made); skip next sc, sl st in front lp of next sc; rep from * 5 more times, ending last rep join with sl st in ch at base of first petal; ch 1: 6 petals.

Rnd 3: Beg with marked st and working in back lp of Rnd 1 sts with petals attached, and in both lps of remaining Rnd 1 sts, * (2 sc in next hdc); rep from * around; join with sl st in beg sc: 24 sc.

Rnd 4: Sc in each sc around, join; mark back lp of first sc of this rnd.

Rnd 5: * Ch 5, sc in 2nd ch from hook, sc in next ch, (hdc in next ch) 2 times (petal made); skip 2 sc, sl st in front lp of next sc; rep from * 7 more times, ending last rep skip rem sc, sl st in ch at base of first petal; ch 1: 8 petals.

Note: On all rnds following a petal rnd, work in back lp of sts with petals attached, and in both lps of rem sts.

Rnd 6: Beginning with marked st of Rnd 4, *(sc in next sc) 2 times, (2 sc in next sc); rep from * around, join; ch 1: 32 sc.

Rnd 7: Rep Rnd 4.

Rnd 8: * † Ch 5, sc in 2nd ch from hook, sc in next ch; (hdc in next ch) 2 times (petal made) †; skip 2 sc, sl st in front lp of next sc; rep from * 7 more times; rep from † to † once; skip 3 sc, sl st in front lp of next sc; rep from † to † once, skip rem sc, sl st in ch at base of first petal; ch 1: 10 petals.

Rnd 9: Beg with marked st of Rnd 7, *(sc in next sc) 3 times, 2 sc in next sc; rep from * around, join; change to B, ch 1: 40 sc.

Rnd 10: Rep Rnd 4.

Rnd 11: * Ch 6, sc in 2nd ch from hook, sc in next ch, (hdc in next ch) 2 times, dc in next ch (petal made); skip 2 sc, sl st in front lp of next sc; rep from * 12 more times, ending last rep skip rem sc, sl st in ch at base of first petal; ch 1: 13 petals.

Beg with marked st of Rnd 10, *(sc in next sc) 4 times, 2 sc in next sc; rep from * around, join, ch 1: 48 sc.

Rnd 13: Rep Rnd 4.

Rnd 14: * Ch 7, sc in 2nd ch from hook, sc in next ch, (hdc in next ch) 2 times, (dc in next ch) 2 times (petal made); skip 2 sc, sl st in front lp of next sc; rep from * 15 more times, ending last rep skip rem sc, sl st in ch at base of first petal; ch 1: 16 petals.

Rnd 15: Beg with marked st of Rnd 13, *(sc in next sc) 5 times, 2 sc in next sc; rep from * around, join; change to C, ch 1: 56 sc.

Rnd 16: Rep Rnd 4.

Rnd 17: * † Ch 7, sc in 2nd ch from hook, sc in next ch, (hdc in next ch) 2 times, (dc in next ch) 2 times (petal made) †; skip 2 sc, sl st in front lp of next sc; rep from * 15 more times; rep from † to †, skip 3 sc, sl st in front lp of next sc; rep from † to †, skip rem sc, sl st in ch at base of first petal; ch 1: 18 petals.

Rnd 18: Beg with marked st of Rnd 16, *(sc in next sc) 6 times, 2 sc in next sc; rep from * around, join, ch 1: 64 sc.

Rnd 19: Rep Rnd 4.

Rnd 20: * Ch 7, sc in 2nd ch from hook, sc in next ch, (hdc in next ch) 2 times, (dc in next ch) 2 times (petal made); skip 2 sc, sl st in front lp of next sc; rep from * 20 more times ending last rep skip rem sc, sl st in ch at base of first petal; ch 1: 21 petals.

Rnd 21: Beg with marked st of Rnd 19, *(sc in next sc) 7 times, 2 sc in next sc; rep from * around, join; change to D, ch 1: 72 sc.

Rnd 22: Rep Rnd 4.

Rnd 23: * Ch 8, sc in 2nd ch from hook, (sc in next ch) 2 times, (hdc in next ch) 2 times, (dc in next ch) 2 times (petal made); skip 2 sc, sl st in front lp of next sc; rep from * 23 more times ending last rep skip rem sc, sl st in ch at base of first petal; ch 1: 24 petals.

Rnd 24: Beg with marked st of Rnd 22, *(sc in next sc) 8 times, 2 sc in next sc; rep from * around, join; change to E, ch 1: 80 sc.

Rnd 25: Rep Rnd 4.

Rnd 26: * † Ch 8, sc in 2nd ch from hook, (sc in next ch) 2 times, (hdc in next ch) 2 times, (dc in next ch) 2 times (petal made) †; skip 2 sc, sl st in front lp of next sc; rep from * 23 more times; rep from † to † once. Skip 3 sc, sl st in front lp of next sc; rep from † to † once, skip rem sc, sl st in ch at base of first petal; ch 1: 26 petals.

Rnd 27: Beg with marked st of Rnd 25, *(sc in next sc) 8 times, 2 sc tog; rep from * around, join; ch 1: 72 sc.

Rnd 28: Rep Rnd 4.

Rnd 29: * Ch 9, sc in 2nd ch from hook, (sc in next ch) 3 times, (hdc in next ch) 2 times, (dc in next ch) 2 times (petal made); skip 2 sc, sl st in front lp of next sc; rep from * 23 more times, ending last rep skip rem sc, sl st in ch at base of first petal; ch 1: 24 petals.

Rnd 30: Beg with marked of Rnd 28; sc in each sc around; join; change to F, ch 1: 72 sc.

Rnd 31: Rep Rnd 4.

Rnd 32: Rep Rnd 29.

Rnd 33: Beg with marked st of Rnd 31, sc in each sc around, join; ch 1: 72 sc.

Rnds 34 through 36: Sc in each sc around; join, ch 1. At end of last rnd, do not ch 1. Finish off; weave in all ends.

#44 PATCHWORK TOTE

Designed by Patons Design Staff

SIZE:
13" wide x 18" high

MATERIALS
Bulky weight yarn
- 1 ¼ oz plum (A)
- 1 ¼ oz red (B)
- 1 ¼ oz green (C)
- 1 ½ oz gold (D)
- 5 oz brown (E)

Note: Photographed model made with Patons® Shetland Chunky #3405 Deep Plum, #3532 Deep Red, #3242 Saget Green, #3608 Nugget Gold and #3031 Earthy Brown

Size J (6 mm) crochet hook
(or size required for gauge)

Toggle for fastening

GAUGE
13 sc = 4"

14 sc rows = 4"

STITCH GUIDE

Sc decrease (sc dec): (Insert hook in next st and draw up a lp) twice, YO and draw through all 3 lps on hook: sc dec made.

Reverse sc (rev sc): Ch 1; *Insert hook in st to the right of last st, YO and draw up a lp, YO and draw through 2 lps on hook*; rep from * to * for rev sc.

To change color: Work st until 2 lps rem on hook, drop old color, pick up new color and draw through both lps on hook, cut dropped color.

INSTRUCTIONS

Front
With red, ch 44.

Row 1 (right side): Sc in 2nd ch from hook, sc in next 9 chs, changing to brown in last sc; sc in next 23 chs, changing to plum in last sc; with plum, sc in next 10 chs: 43 sc; ch 1, turn.

Row 2: Sc in first 2 sc; (ch 1, skip next sc, sc in next sc) 4 times, changing to brown in last sc; with brown, (ch 1, skip next sc, sc in next sc) 11 times, changing to red in last sc; with red, (ch 1, skip next sc, sc in next sc) 5 times, sc in last sc: 23 sc and 20 ch-1 sps; ch 1, turn.

#45 SWEET SUMMER SUIT

Designed by Angela Best

Note: *Instructions are written for size X-Small; changes for sizes Small and Medium are in parentheses.*

SIZES	X-Small	Small	Medium
Top (cup size)	A	B	C
Skirt			
Body Hip Measurements	28" - 30"	32" - 34"	36" - 38"
Finished Hip Measurments	28 1/2"	32 3/4"	37"

MATERIALS

Worsted weight cotton/acrylic yarn
8 3/4 (10 1/2, 12 1/4) oz coral

Note: *Photographed model made with Needful Yarns Kim #552*

Size H (5 mm) hook (or size required for gauge)

1 mm clear round or flat elastic, optional

Washable glue, optional

GAUGE

15 sc = 4"

8 sc shells = 4"

16 sc shell rows = 4"

INSTRUCTIONS

Top Cups (make 2)

Ch 10.

Row 1: Sc in 2nd ch from hook and in next 7 chs, 3 sc in last ch, working in free lps on other side of ch, sc in next 8 chs: 19 sc; ch 1, turn.

Row 2: Sc shell in first sc; *skip next sc, sc shell in next sc*; rep from * to * 3 times more; sc shell inc in next sc, sc shell in next sc; rep from * to * 4 times more: 10 sc shells and 1 sc shell inc; ch 1, turn.

Row 3: Sc shell in ch-1 sp of first sc shell, sc shell in ch-1 sp of each sc shell around and in each ch-1 sp of sc shell inc at center of previous row: 12 sc shells; ch 1, turn.

Row 4: Sc shell in ch-1 sp of first sc shell, sc shell in ch-1 sp of next 4 sc shells, sc shell inc in ch-1 sp of next 2 sc shells, sc shell in ch-1 sp of next 5 sc shells: 10 sc shells and 2 sc shell inc; ch 1, turn.

Row 5: Rep Row 3: 14 sc shells.

For Size X-Small Only

Row 6: Sc shell in ch-1 sp of first sc shell, sc shell in ch-1 sp of next 6 sc shells, sc shell inc in ch-1 sp of next sc shell, sc shell in ch-1 sp of next 6 sc shells: 13 sc shells and 1 sc shell inc; ch 1, turn.

Row 7: Rep Row 3: 15 sc shells; ch 1, turn.

For Size Small Only

Row 6: Sc shell in ch-1 sp of first sc shell, sc shell in ch-1 sp of next 5 sc shells, sc shell inc in ch-1 sp of next 2 sc shells, sc shell in ch-1 sp of next 6 sc shells: 12 sc shells and 2 sc shell inc; ch 1, turn.

Row 7: Rep Row 3: 16 sc shells.

Row 8: Sc shell in ch-1 sp of first sc shell, sc shell in ch-1 sp of next 7 sc shells, sc shell inc in ch-1 sp of next sc shell, sc shell in ch-1 sp of next 7 sc shells: 15 sc shells and 1 sc shell inc; ch 1, turn.

For Size Medium Only

Rows 6 through 8: Rep Rows 6 through 8 on medium.

Row 9: Rep Row 3: 17 sc shells.

Edging (all sizes)

Rnd 1: Sc in ch-1 sp of first sc shell; *dc shell in next ch-1 sp of next sc shell or sc shell inc, sc in next ch-1 sp of next sc shell or sc shell inc; rep from * around; work (dc shell, sc) 3 (3, 4) times evenly spaced across bottom edge, ending with sl st around post of first sc: 10 (11, 12) dc shells and 9 (10, 11) sc. Do not turn.

For First Cup Only

Row 2: Ch 3, dc shell in ch-1 sp of first dc shell; *dc around post of next sc, dc shell in ch-1 sp of next dc shell; rep from * around; join with sl st in 3rd ch of beg ch-3. Finish off; weave in ends.

For Second Cup Only

Row 2: Ch 3, dc shell in ch-1 sp of first dc shell, dc around post of next sc; *dc shell in ch-1 sp of next dc shell, dc around post of next sc*; rep from * to * 4 (5, 5) times more; 3 dc in ch-1 sp of next dc shell, ch 1, sl st in ch-1 sp of first dc shell on Rnd 2 of first cup, 3 dc in same ch-1 sp on second cup, dc around post of next sc, sl st in 3rd ch of beg ch-3 on Row 2 of first cup; rep from * to * 2 (2, 3) times more; dc shell in ch-1 sp of last dc shell, join with sl st in 3rd ch of beg ch-3. Finish off; weave in ends.

Neck Ties (make 2)

Join with sl st in ch-1 sp in shell at top of cup on sizes x-small and medium and in dc at top of cup on size small, make a chain about 21" long or to desired length. Finish off; weave in ends. Tie knot in loose end of chain close to end.

Tie Strap

Make a chain about 60" (64", 68") long, or to desired length. Finish off; weave in ends. Weave strap through bottom shell row on cups and center strap at center of cups. Tie knot in each end of chain close to end.

Bottom Front

Starting at crotch, ch 8 (10, 12).

Row 1 (right side): Sc in 2nd ch from hook and in each ch across: 7 (9, 11) sc; ch 1, turn.

Row 2: Sc shell in first sc; *skip next sc, sc shell in next sc; rep from * across: 4 (5, 6) sc shells; ch 1, turn.

Row 3: Sc shell in ch-1 sp of each sc shell across; ch 1, turn.

Rows 4 through 6: Rep Row 3 three times more.

Row 7: Sc shell inc in ch-1 sp of first sc shell, sc shell in ch-1 sp of each sc shell across to last sc shell, sc shell inc in ch-1 sp of last sc shell: 2 (3, 4) sc shells and 2 sc shell inc; ch 1, turn.

Rows 8 through 13: Rep Row 3 six times more: 6 (7, 8) sc shells.

Row 14: Rep Row 7: 4 (5, 6) sc shells and 2 sc shell inc.

Rows 15 through 19: Rep Row 3 five times more: 8 (9, 10) sc shells.

Row 20: Rep Row 7: 6 (7, 8) sc shells and 2 sc shell inc.

Rows 21 through 25: Rep Row 3 five times more: 10 (11, 12) sc shells. At end of Row 25, do not ch 1. Finish off; weave in ends.

Bottom Back

Row 1 (right side): With right side facing and foundation ch at top, join with sc through last sc st on Row 1 of bottom front, sc through each sc st across row: 7 (9, 11) sc; ch 1, turn.

Row 2: Rep Row 2 of bottom front: 4 (5, 6) sc shells.

Rows 3 through 12: Rep Row 3 of bottom front 10 times.

Row 13: Rep Row 7 of bottom front: 2 (3, 4) sc shells and 2 sc shell inc.

Rows 14 through 21: Rep Row 3 of bottom front 8 times more: 6 (7, 8) sc shells.

Row 22: Rep Row 7 of bottom front: 4 (5, 6) sc shells and 2 sc shell inc.

Rows 23 through 27: Rep Row 3 of bottom front 5 times more: 8 (9, 10) sc shells.

Row 28: Rep Row 7 of bottom front: 6 (7, 8) sc shells and 2 sc shell inc.

Rows 29 through 33: Rep Row 3 of bottom front 5 times more: 10 (11, 12) sc shells.

Row 34: Rep Row 7 of bottom front: 8 (9, 10) sc shells and 2 sc shell inc.

Rows 35 through 37: Rep Row 3 of bottom front 3 times more: 12 (13, 14) sc shells.

Row 38: Rep Row 7 of bottom front: 10 (11, 12) sc shells and 2 sc shell inc.

Rows 39 through 42: Rep Row 3 of bottom front 4 times more: 14 (15, 16) sc shells.

Joining Band

Rnd 1: *Sc in ch-1 sp of first sc shell, ch 1*; rep from * to * across Row 42 of bottom back, ending with sc in ch-1 sp of last sc shell; ch 30 (36, 42); rep from * to * across bottom front, ending with sc in ch-1 sp of last sc shell; ch 30 (36, 42): 24 (26, 28) sc, 22 (24, 26) ch-1 sps and 60 (72, 84) chs; join with sl st in first sc; ch 1, turn.

Rnd 2: Sc in same sc as joining, sc in each sc and in each ch around: 106 (122, 138) sc; join with sl st in first sc. Do not turn.

Rnd 3: Ch 1, sc in same sc as joining, sc in each sc around; join with sl st in first sc; ch 1, turn.

Rnd 4: Sc in back lp of same sc as joining, sc in back lp of each sc around; join with sl st in first sc. Do not turn.

Rnd 5: Ch 1, sc in same sc as joining, sc in each sc around; join with sl st in first sc. Do not turn.

Rnd 6: Ch 1, sc in same sc as joining; *ch 1, skip next sc, sc in next sc; rep from * around to last sc; ch 1, skip last sc, join with sl st in first sc: 53 (61, 69) sc and 53 (61, 69) ch-1 sps. Do not turn.

Rnd 7: Rep Rnd 5 working in each sc and ch-1 sp. Finish off; weave in ends.

Skirt

Rnd 1 (wrong side): With right side facing, join with sc in first sc on Rnd 4 of joining band working in front lp of Rnd 4 sc; *ch 5, skip next 2 sc, sc in next sc; rep from * around to last 3 (4, 2) sc; ch 2, skip last 3 (4, 2) sc, dc in first sc to form last ch-5 sp: 35 (40, 46) ch-5 sps. Do not turn.

Rnd 2: Ch 1, sc around post of dc; *ch 5, sc in next ch-5 sp; rep from * around, ending with ch 2, dc in first sc. Do not turn.

Rnds 3 through 20: Rep Row 2 eighteen times more. At end of Row 20, ch 1, turn.

Rnd 21: Sc in ch-2 sp, dc shell in next sc; *sc in next ch-5 sp, dc shell in next sc; rep from * around: 35 (40, 46) dc shells; join with sl st in first sc. Finish off; weave in ends.

Make a chain about 46" (50", 54") long, or to desired length. Finish off; weave in ends. Weave chain through ch-1 sps on Rnd 6 of joining band, starting and ending at center of bottom front. Tie knot in each end of chain close to end.

Leg Edging

With wrong side facing, join with sc in free lp of first ch of ch-30 on Rnd 1 of joining band, sc in next 29 free lps of ch-30, sc in edge of each row of bottom front and back, join with sl st in first sc. Finish off; weave in ends. Rep leg edging on second leg opening. Note: If desired, work sc sts over elastic. Tie ends of elastic together. Apply glue to knot and allow to dry.

#46 ROSE GARDEN

Designed by Carol Carlile and Carole Sullivan

SIZE
50" x 66" including border

MATERIALS
Worsted weight yarn
  27 oz oatmeal
  12 oz dk green
  5 oz green
  5 oz lt yellow
  5 oz lt rose
  5 oz med rose
  5 oz dk rose

Note: *Photographed model made with Patons® Canadiana #105 Oatmeal, #054 Dk Juniper (dk green), #052 Juniper (green), #169 Lt Yellow, #133 Lt Rosewood. #135 Med Rosewood and #136 Dk Rosewood*

Size H (5 mm) crochet hook
  (or size required for gauge)

GAUGE
12 dc = 2 $\frac{1}{2}$"
Flower Motif = 5 $\frac{1}{2}$"

INSTRUCTIONS

Flower Motif

Make 20 with lt rose and dk juniper (Motif A on chart)

Make 20 with med rose and dk juniper (Motif B on chart)

Make 21 with dk rose and dk juniper (Motif C on chart)

Make 24 with lt yellow and juniper (Motif D on chart)

With first color, ch 5, join with sl st to form a ring.

Rnd 1: Ch 3 (counts as a dc); in ring work: dc, ch 2; (2 dc, ch 2) five times, join with sl st in 3rd ch of beg ch-3.

Rnd 2: Sl st between beg ch-3 and next dc, ch 3; in next ch-2 sp work (3 dc, ch 2, 3 dc): petal made; * ch 3, sl st between next 2 dc, ch 3; in next ch-2 sp work (3 dc, ch 2, 3 dc) for petal; rep from * around, ch 3, join with sl st in beg sl st; finish off first color: 6 petals made.

Rnd 3: Working behind Row 2, join 2nd color with sl st in first dc of any 2-dc group of Rnd 1, ch 3 (counts as a dc), dc in same st, 2 dc in next dc; *ch 2, 2 dc in each of next 2 dc, rep from * around, ch 2, join in 3rd ch of beg ch-3: 24 dc and 6 ch-2 sps.

Rnd 4: Ch 3, *dc in each dc to next ch-2 sp (3 dc, ch 2, 3 dc) in sp; rep from * around, join with sl st in 3rd ch of beg ch-3, finish off 2nd color.

Rnd 5: Join oatmeal with sl st in any ch-2 sp, ch 3, (dc, ch 2, 2 dc) in same sp; *dc in each dc to next ch-2 sp, in sp work (2 dc, ch 2, 2 dc); rep from * around, join in 3rd ch of beg ch-3. Finish off; weave in ends.

Half Motif (make 14)
(Motif E on chart)

With oatmeal, ch 5, join with sl st to form a ring.

Rnd 1: Ch 3 (counts as a dc), in ring work (2 dc, ch 2, 2 dc, ch 2, 3 dc); ch 3, turn.

Rnd 2: Dc in same st as turning ch, (2 dc in each of next 2 dc, ch 2) twice; 2 dc in each of next 2 dc; 2 dc in 3rd ch of turning ch; ch 3, turn: 16 dc and 2 ch-2 sps.

Rnd 3: Dc in same st as turning ch; *dc in each dc to next ch-2 sp, in sp work (2 dc, ch 2, 2 dc); rep from * once; dc in each dc to turning ch, 2 dc in 3rd ch of turning ch; ch 3, turn: 26 dc.

Rnd 4: Rep Rnd 3, but at end do not work turning ch: 36 dc. Finish off; weave in ends.

Plain Motif (make 12)
(Motif F on chart)

With oatmeal, ch 5, join with sl st to form a ring.

Rnd 1: Ch 3 (counts as a dc), dc in ring; (ch 2, 2 dc in ring) 5 times, ch 2, join in 3rd ch of beg ch.

Rnd 2: Ch 3, dc in same st; 2 dc in next dc; * ch 2, 2 dc in each of next 2 dc; rep from * around, ch 2, join in 3rd ch of beg ch: 24 dc and 6 ch-2 sps.

Rnd 3: Ch 3, *dc in each dc to next ch-2 sp; in sp work (2 dc, ch 2, 2 dc); rep from * around join in 3rd ch of beg ch-3: 48 dc.

Rnd 4: Rep Row 3, but do not work turning ch: 72 dc, Finish off; weave in ends.

Assembly

Follow arrangement chart. To join motifs, hold two with right sides tog and sew with overcast or whip st through outer lps only, carefully matching sts and placing an extra st in corner sps. Begin joining in rows in same manner, starting at top of chart with a row of 7 Motifs with a Half Motif at each end.

Edging

Hold afghan with right side facing you and one short edge at top. Join oatmeal in corner st of half motif at upper right.

Rnd 1: Ch 1, sc in same st; sc evenly around entire outer edge of afghan, working 3 sc in outer corners and points; join in beg sc.

Rnd 2: Ch 1, sc in each sc around, join. Finish off; weave in ends.

#47 QUILT BLOCK PILLOW

Designed by Susan Lowman

FRONT

BACK

SIZE
14" square plus 3" ruffle

MATERIALS
Worsted weight yarn
  7 ¹/₂ oz tan (A)
  2 ¹/₂ oz B (B)
  2 ¹/₂ oz C (C)

Note: Photographed model made with TLC® Heathers #2441 A (A), #2470 B (B) and #2452 C(C)

14" pillow

Size G (4 mm) crochet hook
  (or size required for gauge)

GAUGE
One square = 3 ¹/₂" x 3 ¹/₂"

STITCH GUIDE
To change color: Drop old color, pick up new color and work specified sts, cut dropped color, leaving a 6" end (unless another length is specified).

INSTRUCTIONS

Solid Color Motif
(make 4 for pillow front)

With A, ch 4, join with sl st to form a ring.

Rnd 1: Ch 3, 2 dc in ring; (ch 2, 3 dc in ring) 3 times, ch 1; join with sc in 3rd ch of beg ch-3.

Rnd 2: Ch 3, 2 dc over sc; [ch 1, (3 dc, ch 2, 3 dc) in next ch-2 sp] 3 times, ch 1, 3 dc in next ch sp; ch 1, join with sc in 3rd ch of beg ch-3.

Rnd 3: Ch 3, 2 dc around sc; [*ch 1, 3 dc in next ch-1 sp, ch 1*; (3 dc, ch 2, 3 dc) in next ch-2 sp] 3 times; rep from * to * once; 3 dc in next ch-1 sp, ch 2, join with sl st in 3rd ch of beg ch-3. Finish off, leaving an 18" end.

Two-Color Square

Square 1: Make 4 with A for first color, C for second color.

Square 2: Make 4 with A for first color and B for second color

Square 3: Make 4 with B for first color and C for second color

Square 4: Make 8 with A for first color and C for second color

Square 5: Make 8 with A for first color and B for second color.

With first color, ch 4, join with sl st to form a ring.

Rnd 1: Ch 3, (2 dc, ch 2, 3 dc) in ring; drop first color; with second color, ch 2, (3 dc, ch 2, 3 dc) in ring; drop second color; with first color, ch 1, join with sc in 3rd ch of beg ch-3.

Rnd 2: Ch 3, 2 dc around sc, ch 1; (3 dc, ch 2, 3 dc) in ch-2 sp, ch 1, 3 dc in next ch-2 sp, drop first color; with second color, ch 2, 3 dc in same ch-2 sp, ch 1, (3 dc, ch 2, 3 dc) in next ch-2 sp, ch 1, 3 dc in next ch sp, drop second color; with first color, ch 1, join with sc in 3rd ch of beg ch-3.

Rnd 3: Ch 3, 2 dc around sc, ch 1, 3 dc in next ch-1 sp, ch 1; (3 dc, ch 2, 3 dc) in next ch-2 sp, ch 1, 3 dc in next ch-1 sp, ch 1, 3 dc in next ch-2 sp; cut first color (leave an 18" end); with second color (leave an 18" end), ch 2, 3 dc in same ch-2 sp, ch 1, 3 dc in next ch-1 sp; ch 1, (3 dc, ch 2, 3 dc) in next ch-2 sp, ch 1; 3 dc in next ch-1 sp, ch 1, 3 dc in next ch sp; cut second color (leave an 18" end); with first color (leave an 18" end), ch 2, join with sl st in 3rd ch of beg ch-3. Finish off, leaving an 18" end.

Assembly

Arrange squares for front section following diagram; with 18" ends, sew squares into rows, then sew rows together. Rep for back section. Weave in any yarn ends not used for sewing.

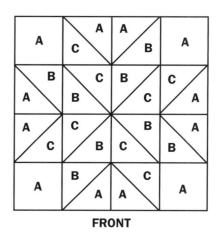

FRONT

BACK

Ruffle

Rnd 1: With wrong sides of front and back sections together, working through both layers, join A with sc in any corner ch, sc in each ch and dc around 3 sides, insert pillow form, sc in rem chs and dc: 208 sc; join with sl st in first sc.

Rnd 2: Ch 3, 2 dc in same sc; [*(ch 1, skip next sc, 3 dc in next sc) 12 times; ch 1, skip next 2 sc, 3 dc in next sc; (ch 1, skip next sc, 3 dc in next sc) 12 times*, ch 2, 3 dc in next sc] 3 times; rep from * to * once; join with dc in 3rd ch of beg ch-3.

Rnd 3: Sl st around post of joining dc, ch 3, 2 dc around same dc; [*(ch 1, 3 dc in next ch-1 sp) 25 times, ch 1*; (3 dc, ch 2, 3 dc) in next ch-2 sp] 3 times; rep from * to * once, 3 dc in sp before joining dc; join with dc in 3rd ch of beg ch-3.

Rnd 4: Sl st over post of joining dc, ch 3, 2 dc over same dc; [*(ch 1, 3 dc in next ch-1 sp) 26 times, ch 1*; (3 dc, ch 2, 3 dc) in next ch-2 sp] 3 times; rep from * to * once, 3 dc in sp before joining dc; join with dc in 3rd ch of beg ch-3.

Rnd 5: Sl st over post of joining dc, ch 4, (tr, ch 1, dc) over same dc; [*ch 1, (dc, ch 1, tr, ch 1, dc) in next ch-1 sp] 27 times, ch 1**; (dc, ch 1, tr, ch 1, dc, ch 2, dc, ch 1, tr, ch 1, dc) in next ch-2 sp, rep from * twice, rep from * to ** once; (dc, ch 1, tr, ch 1, dc, ch 2) in sp before joining dc; join with sl st in 3rd ch of beg ch-4. Finish off; weave in ends.

Cording

Cut four 3-yd pieces each of C and B. Hold one piece of each color together as a unit and tie a knot in each end. Slip one end over a chair or door knob. Stand far away and twist other end about 50 times. Bring ends together and allow yarn to twist on itself. Rep with other 3 lengths. Weave cords through sc on Rnd 1 of ruffle on front side, starting at one corner and working toward next corner, one cord per side, in and out of each sc in which a dc has been worked. Tie ends into bows at each corner. Tie a new knot at appropriate length and trim off excess. Make 4 more cords in same manner with 2 yd- lengths of C and B. Tie bows around previous cords in corners on back of pillow. Tie a new knot at appropriate length and trim off excess.

#48 SIMPLY SHRUG

Designed by C. Yvette Holmes

SIZE
23 ¹/₂" wide x 40 ¹/₂" long

MATERIALS
DK weight yarn
  750 yds tan

Eyelash yarn
  609 yds tan

Note: Photographed model made with Plymouth Encore DK #1415 and Trendsetter Antico #117

Size H (5 mm) crochet hook

Size I (5.5 mm) crochet hook (or size required for gauge)

Stitch markers

GAUGE
14 hdc = 4" with I hook and both yarns held together

9 hdc rows = 4"

STITCH GUIDE
Sc decrease (sc dec): (Insert hook in next st and draw up a lp) twice, YO and draw through all 3 lps on hook: sc dec made.

INSTRUCTIONS

With H hook and DK yarn, ch 33.

Row 1 (right side): Sc in 2nd ch from hook and in each ch across: 32 sc; ch 1, turn.

Row 2: With both yarns held together, sc in first st and in each st across; ch 1, turn.

Rows 3 through 6: Sc in both lps of first st, sc in back lp of next st and in back lp of each st across to last st, sc in both lps of last st; ch 1, turn.

Note: Work in both lps of first and last sts and in back lp of each st between first and last sts on Rows 7 through 94.

Row 7: Sc in first st, 2 sc in next st, sc in next st and in each st to last 2 sts, 2 sc in next st, sc in last st: 34 sc; ch 1, turn.

Row 8: Sc in first st and in each st across; ch 1, turn.

Rows 9 through 21: Rep Rows 7 and 8 six times more, then rep Row 7 once more. At end of Row 21: 48 sc; ch 2 (counts as hdc on next row now and throughout), turn. Place markers in first and last sts on Row 21.

Row 22: With I hook, hdc in next st and in each st across: 48 hdc; ch 2, turn.

Row 23 through 73: Rep Row 22 fifty one times more. At end of Row 73, ch 1, turn.

Row 74: With H hook, sc in first st and in each st across: 48 sc; ch 1, turn. Place markers in first and last sts.

Row 75: Sc in first st, sc dec in next 2 sts, sc in next st and in each st across to last 3 sts, sc dec in next 2 sts, sc in last st: 46 sc; ch 1, turn.

Row 76: Sc in first st and in each st across; ch 1, turn.

Row 77 through 90: Rep Rows 75 and 76 seven times more. At end of Row 90: 32 sc.

Rows 91 through 94: Rep Row 76 four times more.

Row 95: With DK yarn only, sc in both lps of first st and in both lps of each st across; ch 1, do not turn.

Border

Sc in edge of each row across to foundation ch, ch 1, sc in free lps of foundation ch, ch 1, sc in other edge of each row across to Row 95, ch 1, sc in each sc across Row 95; join with sl st in first sc. Finish off; weave in ends.

Sleeve Seams

Fold in half lengthwise with right sides together, matching markers. Seam along edge between Row 1 and markers on Row 21. Seam along edge between Row 95 and markers on Row 74.

Collar/Edging

Rnd 1: With right side facing and I hook, join DK yarn with sc in sc on border at either sleeve seam, sc in each sc across border to other sleeve seam, sc in each sc across border to first sleeve seam, increasing or decreasing sts as necessary to achieve a multiple of 5; join with sl st in first sc.

Rnd 2: Ch 3, (2 dc, ch 2, 3 dc) in same st; *skip next 4 sts, (3 dc, ch 2, 3 dc) in next st; rep from * around; join with sl st in 3rd ch of beg ch-3.

Rnd 3: With both yarns held together, sl st in next 2 dc and in ch sp, ch 3, (3 dc, ch 2, 4 dc) in same sp; *(4 dc, ch 2, 4 dc) in next ch sp; rep from * around; join with sl st in 3rd ch of beg ch-3.

Rnd 4: Rep Rnd 3.

Rnd 5: With DK yarn only, rep Rnd 3. Finish off; weave in ends.

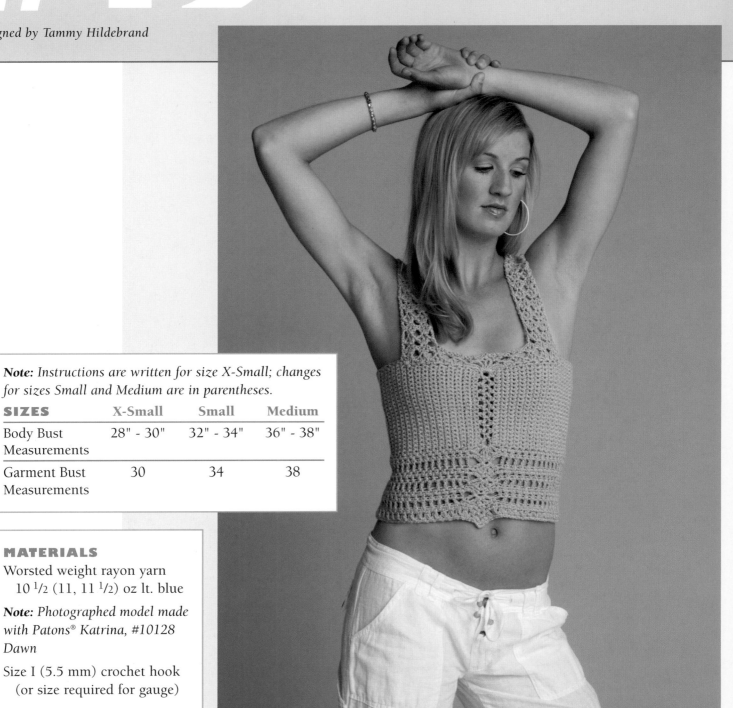

Note: *Instructions are written for size X-Small; changes for sizes Small and Medium are in parentheses.*

SIZES	X-Small	Small	Medium
Body Bust Measurements	28" - 30"	32" - 34"	36" - 38"
Garment Bust Measurements	30	34	38

MATERIALS

Worsted weight rayon yarn
  10 ½ (11, 11 ½) oz lt. blue

Note: *Photographed model made with Patons® Katrina, #10128 Dawn*

Size I (5.5 mm) crochet hook
  (or size required for gauge)

GAUGE

16 sc = 4"

18 sc rows = 4"

INSTRUCTIONS

Back and Right Front

Starting at left side, ch 26.

Row 1 (right side): Sc in 2nd ch from hook and in each ch across: 25 sc; ch 1, turn.

Rows 2 through 77 (89, 101): Sc in first sc and in each sc across; ch 1, turn.

Row 78 (90, 102): Skip first sc, sc in next sc and in each sc across: 24 sc; ch 1, turn.

Row 79 (91, 103): Sc in first sc and in each sc across to last sc: 23 sc; ch 1, turn, leaving last sc unworked.

Rows 80 (92, 104) through 96 (108, 124): Sc in first sc and in each sc across; ch 1, turn.

Row 97 (109, 125): Sc in first sc; *ch 3, skip next sc, sc in next sc; rep from * across: 12 sc and 11 ch-3 sps. Finish off; weave in ends.

Left Front

Row 1: With right side facing, working in free lps of starting ch, join with sc in first ch, sc in next ch and in each ch across: 25 sc; ch 1, turn.

Rows 2 through 11 (15, 15): Sc in first sc and in each sc across; ch 1, turn.

Row 12 (16, 16): Sc in first sc and in each sc across to last sc: 24 sc; ch 1, turn, leaving last sc unworked.

Row 13 (17, 17): Skip first sc, sc in next sc and in each sc across: 23 sc; ch 1, turn.

Rows 14 (18, 18) through 30 (34, 38): Sc in first sc and in each sc across; ch 1, turn.

Row 31 (35, 39): Sc in first sc; *ch 1, sl st in corresponding ch-3 sp on Row 97 (109, 125), ch 1, skip next sc, sc in next sc; rep from * across: 12 sc and 11 joined ch sps. Finish off; weave in ends.

Bottom Skirting

Rnd 1: With right side facing, working in edges of rows without decreases, join with sl st in edge of last joined ch sp on Row 31 (35, 39) of left front, ch 5 (counts as tr and ch-1 sp), (tr, ch 1) 3 times in same ch sp, tr in same ch sp, skip next 2 sc rows, sc in edge of next row; *ch 1, skip next row, sc in edge of next row*; rep from * to * across to foundation ch; ch 1, skip next row, sc in edge of foundation ch; rep from * to * around to last 2 sc rows: 62 (70, 80) sc, 5 tr and 65 (73, 83) ch-1 sps; skip last 2 sc rows, join with sl st in 4th ch of beg ch-5.

Rnd 2: Ch 1, sc in same ch as joining, sc in next ch-1 sp, sc in next tr, sc in next ch-1 sp, ch 2, sc in next tr, (sc in next ch-1 sp, sc in next tr) twice, dc in next ch-1 sp and in each ch-1 sp around: 61 (69, 79) dc, 9 sc and 1 ch-2 sp; join with sl st in beg sc.

Rnd 3: Sl st in next 3 sc and in ch-2 sp, ch 4 (counts as dc and ch-1 sp), (dc, ch 1) 3 times in same ch sp, dc in same ch sp, skip next 5 sc, tr in next dc and in each dc around: 61 (69, 79) tr, 5 dc and 4 ch-1 sps; join with sl st in 3rd ch of beg ch-4.

Rnd 4: Ch 1, sc in same ch as joining, (skip next ch-1 sp, sc in next dc) twice, ch 2, sc in same dc as last sc, (skip next ch-1 sp, sc in next dc) twice; skip next tr; *ch 1, sc in next tr; rep from * around; ch 1: 66 (74, 84) sc, 61 (69, 79) ch-1 sps and 1 ch-2 sp; join with sl st in beg sc.

Rnd 5: Sl st in next 2 sc and in ch-2 sp, ch 4 (counts as dc and ch-1 sp), (dc, ch 1) 3 times in same ch sp, dc in same ch sp, skip next 3 sc, dc in next ch-1 sp and in each ch-1 sp around: 66 (74, 84) dc and 4 ch-1 sps; join with sl st in 3rd ch of beg ch-4.

Rnd 6: Ch 1, sc in same ch as joining, (sc in next ch-1 sp, sc in next dc) 4 times, tr in next dc and in each dc around: 61 (69, 79) tr and 9 sc; join with sl st in beg sc.

Rnd 7: Ch 1, sc in same sc as joining, (ch 1, skip next sc, sc in next sc) twice, ch 2, sc in same sc as last sc, (ch 1, skip next sc, sc in next sc) twice; skip next tr; *ch 1, sc in next tr; rep from * around; ch 1: 66 (74, 84) sc, 65 (73, 83) ch-1 sps and 1 ch-2 sp; join with sl st in beg sc.

Rnd 8: Sl st in next 2 ch-1 sps and in ch-2 sp, ch 4 (counts as dc and ch-1 sp), (dc, ch 1) 3 times in same ch sp, dc in same ch sp, skip next 3 sc, dc in next ch-1 sp and in each of next 60 (68, 78) ch-1 sps: 66 (74, 84) dc and 4 ch-1 sps; join with sl st in 3rd ch of beg ch-4.

Rnd 9: Rep Rnd 6.

For Sizes Small and Medium Only
Rnds 10 through 12 (15): Rep Rnds 7 through 9 one (two) times more.

For All Sizes
Rnd 10 (13, 16): Rep Rnd 7.

Rnd 11 (14, 17): Sl st in next ch-1 sp, ch 1, sc in same sp, ch 3, sc in next ch-1 sp, ch 3, (sc, ch 3, sc) in next ch-2 sp; *ch 3, sc in next ch-1 sp; rep from * around; ch 3: 66 (74, 84) sc and 66 (74, 84) ch-3 sps; join with sl st in beg sc.

Rnd 12 (15, 18): Sl st in next ch-3 sp, ch 1, sc in same ch sp, ch 1, sc in next ch-3 sp, ch 1, (sc, ch 3, sc) in next ch-3 sp; *ch 1, sc in next ch-3 sp; rep from * around; ch 1: 67 (75, 85) sc, 66 (74, 84) ch-1 sps and 1 ch-3 sp; join with sl st in beg sc. Finish off; weave in ends.

Top Edging

Row 1: With right side facing, working in edges of rows on top edge of front and back, join with sl st in edge of first joined ch sp on Row 31 (35, 39) on left front, sc in edge of next row; *ch 1, skip next row, sc in edge of next row*; rep from * to * across to foundation ch; ch 1, skip next row, sc in edge of foundation ch; rep from * to * across: 64 (72, 82) sc and 63 (71, 81) ch-1 sps; sl st in same sp as beg sl st. Finish off; weave in ends.

Row 2: With right side facing, join with sc in 10th (10th, 12th) ch-1 sp before center on top of left front; *shell in next ch-1 sp, sc in next ch-1 sp; rep from * 3 (3, 4) times more; skip next ch-1 sp, (tr, ch 1) 4 times in same sp as beg and end sl sts on Row 1, tr in same sp, skip next ch-1 sp; **sc in next ch-1 sp, shell in next ch-1 sp; rep from ** 3 (3, 4) times more; sc in next ch-1 sp: 5 tr, 4 ch-1 sps, 10 (10, 12) sc and 8 (8, 10) shells; ch 3 (counts as dc on next row now and through-out), turn.

Row 3: Shell in center dc of next 4 shells, (dc, ch 1, dc) in next ch-1 sp, skip next tr and next ch-1 sp, (sc, ch 3, sc) in next tr, skip next ch-1 sp and next tr, (dc, ch 1, dc) in next ch-1 sp, shell in center dc of next 4 shells, dc in beg sc on Row 2: 8 (8, 10) shells, 6 dc, 2 sc, 2 ch-1 sps and 1 ch-3 sp; ch 3, turn. Do not finish off.

First Strap

Row 1: Shell in center dc of next 2 shells, dc in center dc of next shell: 2 shells and 2 dc; ch 3, turn.

Row 2: Shell in center dc of next 2 shells, dc in 3rd ch of turning ch-3; ch 3, turn.

Rows 3 through 21: Rep Row 2 nineteen times more, or to desired length. Finish off, leaving a long length for sewing.

Second Strap

Row 1: With right side facing, join with sl st in center dc of 3rd shell on Row 3 of top edging, ch 3 (counts as dc), shell in center dc of next 2 shells, dc in 3rd ch of turning ch-3: 2 shells and 2 dc; ch 3, turn.

Rows 2 through 21: Rep Row 2 of first strap twenty times more, or to desired length. Finish off, leaving a long length for sewing.

With right sides together, stitch Row 21 of each strap to top edge of back where desired.

Note: *Instructions are given for Single bed coverlet; changes for larger sizes are in parentheses.*

SIZES

Single bed coverlet: 72" x 105"

Double bed coverlet: 83" x 105"

Queen bed coverlet: 94" x 105"

King bed coverlet: 105" x 116"

Square toss pillow: 15" x 15"

Round toss pillow: 10" diameter

MATERIALS

Size 10 bedspread weight cotton

Coverlet:
    41(48, 53, 66) 325-yd balls natural (A)
    10 (12, 12, 14) 150-yd balls pink (B)
    5 (5, 7, 7) 150-yd balls green (C)

Pillows (for both):
    4 balls natural (A)
    3 balls pink (B)
    3 balls green (C)

Note: *Photographed models made with J&P Coats® Knit-Cro-Sheen® #62 Natural, #35 Almond Pink and #179 Spruce*

Natural color sewing thread

Sewing needle

12" x 12" square pillow form (for square pillow)

8" round pillow form (for round pillow)

1 ½ yds ⅛" wide ribbon (for square pillow)

½ yd ⅛" wide ribbon (for round pillow)

Size 6 (1.8 mm) steel crochet hook (or size required for gauge)

GAUGE

Finished Square = 5 ½" x 5 ½"

Rnds 1 through 5 of Popcorn Square or Rnds 1 through 7 of Flower Square = 2 ¾" x 2 ¾".

STITCH GUIDE

Popcorn (PC): Ch 1, 5 dc in next st; remove hook from lp, insert hook from front to back through ch-1 sp and into dropped lp, draw lp through sp: PC made.

Beginning Triple Crochet Cluster (beg trCL): Ch 4; * YO twice, insert hook in specified st and draw up a lp; (YO and draw through first 2 lps on hook) 2 times; rep from * once, YO and draw through all 3 lps on hook: beg trCL made.

Triple Crochet Cluster (trCL): *YO twice, insert hook in specified st and draw up a lp; (YO and draw through first 2 lps on hook) 2 times; rep from * 2 more times, YO and draw through all 4 lps on hook: trCL made.

Picot: Ch 3, sl st in side lp (upper left side) of dc just made: picot made.

Double Triple Crochet (dtr): YO 3 times; insert hook in specified st or sp, YO and draw up a lp; (YO and draw through first 2 lps on hook) 4 times: dtr made

Double Triple Cluster (dtrCL): *YO three times, insert hook in specified st or sp and draw up a lp, (YO and draw through first 2 lps) 3 times; rep from * once, YO and draw through 3 rem lps: dtrCL made.

COVERLET

INSTRUCTIONS

Note: *Join with a sl st unless otherwise specified.*

Popcorn Square
make 124 (143, 162, 200)
With Color A, ch 7; join to form a ring.

Rnd 1: Ch 1, 16 sc in ring; join in first sc.

Rnd 2: Ch 4 (counts as a dc and ch-1 sp), dc in same sc as joining, PC in next sc; *(dc, ch 1, dc) in next sc, PC in next sc; rep from * 7 times more, join in 3rd ch of beg ch-4: 8 PC.

Rnd 3: Sl st into next ch-1 sp, ch 6 (counts as dc and ch-3 sp), dc in same sp: first corner made; * ch 1, 2 dc in next dc, skip PC, dc in next dc, dc in ch-1 sp; dc in next dc, skip PC, 2 dc in next dc, ch 1 **; in next ch-1 sp work (dc, ch 3, dc) for corner; rep from * around, ending last rep at **; join in 3rd ch of beg ch-6.

Rnd 4: Sl st in next 2 chs, ch 6, dc in last sl st; *ch 1, skip next dc, 2 dc in next ch-1 sp, dc in next 7 dc, 2 dc in next ch-1 sp, ch 1, skip next dc **; in 2nd ch of next ch-3 sp work (dc, ch 3, dc): corner made; rep from * around, ending last rep at **; join in 3rd ch of beg ch-6.

Rnd 5: Sl st in next 2 chs, ch 6, dc in last sl st; *ch 1, skip next dc, 2 dc in next ch-1 sp, dc in next 11 dc, 2 dc in next ch-1 sp, ch 1, skip next dc **, work corner as before; rep from * around, ending last rep at **; join in 3rd ch of beg ch -6.

Rnd 6: Sl st in next 2 chs, ch 6, dc in last sl st; *ch 1, dc in next dc, PC in next ch-1 sp, dc in next 15 dc, PC in next ch-1 sp, dc in next dc, ch 1 **; work corner; rep from * around, ending at **; join in 3rd ch of beg ch-6.

Rnd 7: Sl st in next 2 chs, ch 6, dc in last sl st; *(ch 1, skip next ch or st, dc in next dc) 3 times, PC in next dc, dc in next 11 dc, PC in next dc; (dc in next dc, ch 1, skip next ch or st) 3 times **; work corner; rep from * around, ending at **; join in 3rd ch of beg ch-6.

Rnd 8: Sl st in next 2 chs, ch 6, dc in last sl st; *(ch 1, skip next ch or st, dc in next dc) 5 times, PC in next dc, dc in next 7 dc, PC in next dc; (dc in next dc, ch 1, skip next ch or st) 5 times **, work corner; rep from * around, ending at **; join in 3rd ch of beg ch-6.

Rnd 9: Sl st in next 2 chs, ch 6, dc in last sl st; *(ch 1, skip next ch or st, dc in next dc) 7 times, PC in next dc, dc in next 3 dc, PC in next dc; (dc in next dc, ch 1, skip next ch or st) 7 times **; work corner; rep from * around, ending at **; join in 3rd ch of beg ch-6.

Rnd 10: Ch 3; *in next ch-3 sp work (PC, ch 7, PC), dc in next dc, (ch 1, skip next ch or st, dc in next dc) 8 times, PC in next dc; (dc in next dc, ch 1, skip next ch or st) 8 times **, dc in next dc; rep from * around, ending at **; join in 2nd ch of beg ch 3. Finish off; weave in ends.

Flower Square
make 123 (142, 161, 199)
Note: Weave in yarn ends as you finish off a color.

With Color B, ch 5; join to form a ring.

Rnd 1: Ch 1, 8 sc in ring; join in first sc.

Rnd 2: Ch 5 (counts as a dc and ch-2 sp), (dc in next sc, ch 2) 7 times; join in 3rd ch of beg ch 5: 8 ch-2 sps.

Rnd 3: Ch 1; *in next ch-2 sp work petal of (sc, hdc, 3 dc, hdc, sc, ch 1); rep from * 7 times more; join in beg ch 1: 8 petals made.

Rnd 4: Working behind petals, ch 1, sc in top of joining of Rnd 2, (ch 4, sc in next dc of Rnd 2) 7 times, ch 4: 8 ch-4 sps; join in beg sc.

Rnd 5: Ch 1; *in next ch-4 sp work petal of (sc, hdc, dc, 3 tr, dc, hdc, sc); rep from * 7 times more, join in beg sc: 8 petals. Finish off.

Note: See Stitch Guide for instructions on working trCL sts in following row.

Rnd 6: Join Color C in center tr of any petal made in Rnd 5; in same tr work (beg trCL, ch 4, trCL, ch 4, trCL); *ch 3, sc in center tr of next petal, ch 3 **; in center tr of next petal work (trCL, ch 4, trCL, ch 4, trCL); rep from * around, end at **; join in beg trCL. Finish off.

Rnd 7: Join Color A in tip of middle trCL of any corner; ch 1, 2 sc in same trCL; *5 sc in next ch-4 sp, 4 sc in next ch-3 sp, sc in next sc, 4 sc in next ch-3 sp, 5 sc in next ch-4 sp **; 3 sc in tip of next trCL; rep from * around, end at **; sc in same trCL as first 2 sc; join in first sc.

Rnd 8: Ch 6, dc in same sc; *ch 1, skip next sc, dc in next sc; PC in next sc, dc in next 15 sc, PC in next sc; dc in next sc, ch 1, skip next sc **; in next sc work (dc, ch 3, dc); rep from * around, end at **; join in 3rd ch of beg ch-6.

Rnds 9 through 12: Work same as Popcorn Square Rnds 7 through 10. Finish off; weave in ends.

Joining

Using Color A, sew squares tog as follows:

For single size, 19 rows of 13 squares

For double size, 19 rows of 15 squares

For queen size, 19 rows of 17 squares

For king size, 21 rows of 19 squares

Alternate Popcorn and Flower Squares, with a Popcorn Square in each corner.

Edging

With right side facing, join Color A in any st, ch 3, dc in each sp or st evenly around, working 3 dc in each outer corner; join in 3rd ch of beg ch 3. Finish off; weave in ends

SQUARE PILLOW

INSTRUCTIONS

Pillow Back

Make 4 Popcorn Squares and sew together in a square.

Pillow Back Edging

Rnd 1: Join Color A in PC before corner sp, ch 3; ***7 dc in ch-7 sp, dc in PC, *(2 dc in next ch-1 sp) 8 times, 2 dc in PC, (2 dc in next ch-1 sp) 8 times **; dc in PC, 3 dc in next ch-3 sp, dc in seam, 3 dc in next ch-3 sp, dc in PC; rep from * to ** to next corner; dc in PC; rep from *** around, end at **; join in 3rd ch of beg ch-3. Finish off; weave in ends.

Pillow Front

Make 4 Flower Squares; sew tog.

Rnd 1: Rep Rnd 1 of Pillow Back Edging; do not fasten off.

Hold front and back pieces with wrong sides tog. Working through both layers and matching each st, join thread in corresponding st of Pillow Front.

Rnd 2: Ch 1, sc in first 4 sts, 3 sc in next st, (sc in each st to next corner, 3 sc in 4th dc of corner 7-dc group) 3 times, sc in next 5 sts; now working only in sts of front (to leave an opening for pillow form), sc in each st to end; join in first sc.

Rnd 3: Sl st in next sc, ch 4, skip first 2 sc, dc in next sc, ch 1, skip next sc; * in corner sc work (dc, ch 1) 3 times, skip next sc; (dc in next sc, ch 1, skip next sc) around to next corner; rep from * around, work last side as before, join in 3rd ch of beg ch-4.

Rnd 4: Ch 3, dc in first ch-4 sp; *PC in next dc, dc in next sp **; dc in next dc, dc in next ch-1 sp; rep from * around, end at **; join in 3rd ch of beg ch-3. Finish off.

Rnd 5: Join Color B in any st; ch 1, sc in each st around, working 3 sc in corner PC; join in beg ch-1. Finish off.

Rnd 6: Join Color C in any st; ch 1, sc in each sc around, working 3 sc in each corner sc; join in beg ch-1. Finish off.

Rnd 7 (ruffle): Join Color A in any sc, ch 4 (counts as a dc and ch-1 sp); *dc in next sc, ch 1; rep from * around; join in 3rd ch of beg ch-4.

Rnds 8 and 9: Ch 5 (counts as a dc and ch-2 sp); * dc in next dc, ch 2; rep from * around; join in 3rd ch of beg ch-5.

Rnd 10: In first ch-2 sp work (sl st, ch 3, 2 dc); * in next ch-2 sp work 2 dc and picot (see Stitch Guide), 3 dc in next ch-2 sp; rep from * around, ending (2 dc, picot, 3 dc) in last sp; join in 3rd ch of beg ch-3. Finish off; weave in all ends

Finishing

Insert pillow form. Weave ribbon through dcs of Rnd 3; tack ends to wrong side of Pillow Front. Sew seam closed.

ROUND PILLOW

INSTRUCTIONS

Note: Weave in yarn ends as you finish a color.

Pillow Front Flower Ring

First Flower: Work Flower Square Rnds 1 through 5. Finish off.

Second Flower: Work Flower Square Rnds 1 through 4.

Rnd 5: Ch 1, in first ch-4 sp work (sc, hdc, dc, 2 tr); remove hook from lp and insert hook from the right side into center tr of any petal on First Flower, insert hook in dropped lp and draw through: petal joined; in same ch-4 sp work (tr, dc, hdc, sc); work and join next petal of First Flower in the same manner; complete remaining 6 petals as for First Flower. Finish off.

Third through Fifth Flowers

Work as for Second Flower, joining two petals of each new flower to previous flower as before.

Sixth Flower

Work as for Second Flower, but join two petals to Fifth Flower, work 3 petals, join 2 petals to First Flower to complete circle, work last petal. Finish off.

Center Flower

Rnds 1 through 5: Work Flower Square Rnds 1 through 5. Finish off.

Rnd 6 (join to Flower Ring): Join Color C in center tr of any petal made in Rnd 5, work beg trCL in same tr, ch 7; insert hook between 2 joined petals at inner edge of Flower Ring, draw thread through: center join made; ch 7, trCL in same st as beg trCl; * ch 3, join to middle tr of next free petal on Flower Ring, ch 3, sl st in top of last trCL **; in center tr of next petal of Center Flower work (trCl, ch 7, center join, ch 7, trCL); rep from * around, end at **; join in beg trCl. Finish off; weave in ends.

Pillow Front Edging

Rnd 1: Join Color C in middle tr of first free petal of any flower on outer edge of Flower Ring; ch 1, sc in same tr; *(ch 7, sc in center tr of next petal) twice, ch 7; dtrCL (see Stitch Guide) in next st; ch 7 **; sc in center tr of next free petal; rep from * around, end at **; join in first sc.

Rnd 2: Sl st in next 2 chs, ch 1, in next ch-7 sp work (sc, ch 3, sc); *ch 5, in next ch-7 sp work (sc, ch 3, sc); rep from * around; ch 5, join in first sc.

Rnd 3: Sl st into ch-3 sp; in same ch-3 sp work [ch 3, 3 dc, ch 3, sl st in side lp of last dc (picot made), 3 dc]; sc in next ch-5 sp, in next ch-3 sp work (4 dc, picot, 3 dc), sc *in next ch-5 sp; rep from * around; join in top of first ch-3: 32 shells. Finish off; weave in ends.

Pillow Back Edging

Rnd 1: With right side facing and holding shells forward, join Color C in any ch-7 sp of Rnd 1 of Front edging between the sc under the shell; ch 1, sc in same sp; *ch 7, sc in next ch-7 sp between sc under shell; rep from * around; ending ch 4, tr in beg sc.

Rnds 2 and 3: *Ch 7, sc in next ch-7 sp; rep from * around, ending ch 4, tr in joining tr.

Rnds 4 through 8: *Ch 5, sc in next ch-4 sp; rep from around ending ch 2, tr in joining. Finish off; weave in ends

Finishing

Insert pillow form. Weave ribbon through sps of Rnd 8 and draw up to hold pillow form in place, knot; Tie ends in a bow.

DRAWSTRING TOP

Note: *Instructions are written for Size X-Small; changes for Small, Medium and Large are in parentheses.*

SIZES	X-Small	Small	Medium	Large
Body Bust Measurements	32"	34"	36"	38"
Finished Bust Measurements	34"	36"	38"	40"

MATERIALS

Fingering weight yarn
   200 (200, 225, 225) grams gunmetal grey
   50 (50, 50, 50) grams black
   50 (50, 50, 50) grams cream.

Note: *Photographed model made with Twilleys Goldfingering #57 gunmetal; and Twilleys Silky #79 black, and #11 cream*

2 large beads or cord ends.

Size C (2.75 mm) crochet hook

Size E (3.50 mm) crochet hook (or size required for gauge)

GAUGE

21 sts = 4" with larger hook, measured over Stripe Pattern

Note: *Check gauge by working 12 rows of Stripe Pattern (below), beginning with ch 22.*

STITCH GUIDE

Sc3tog: Draw up a lp in each of next 3 sts, YO and draw through all 4 lps on hook: sc3tog made.

Sc2tog: Draw up a lp in each of next 2 sts; YO and draw through all 3 lps on hook: sc2tog made

INSTRUCTIONS

Stripe Pattern

In sc:

4 rows grey

2 rows black

4 rows grey

2 rows cream.

Rep these 12 rows in sequence for stripe pattern throughout

Bodice

Note: *When changing colors, work to last step of last st of row, complete the st in the new color; finish off first color. Colors may be loosely stranded up side edge of work.*

Back

First Half of Bodice

With larger hook and grey, ch 2.

Row 1: 3 sc in 2nd ch from hook, turn.

Row 2: 2 sc in first sc, sc in next sc, 2 sc in last sc, ch 1, turn: 5 sc.

Row 3: 2 sc in first sc, sc in each sc to last sc, 2 sc in last sc, ch 1, turn: 7 sc.

Row 4: Rep Row 3: 9 sc.

Change to black.

Rows 5 and 6: Rep Row 3: 13 sc.

Change to grey.

Rows 7 through 10: Rep Row 3: 21 sc.

Change to cream.

Rows 11 and 12: Rep Row 3 twice: 25 sc.

Continue in Stripe Pattern as established.

Rows 13 through 16 (18, 20, 22): Rep Row 3: 33 (37, 41, 45) sc.

Shape Armhole

Armhole Row 1: 2 sc in first sc, sc in each sc to last 2 sc, sc2tog over last 2 sc, ch 1, turn.

Armhole Row 2: Sc in first sc, sc in each sc to last sc, 2 sc in last sc, ch 1, turn: 34 (38, 42, 46) sc, 18 (20, 22, 24) rows.

Rep Armhole Rows 1 and 2 five more times: 39 (43, 47, 51) sc, 28 (30, 32, 34) rows.

Armhole Row 3: 2 sc in first sc, sc in each sc across, ch 1, turn: 40 (44, 48, 52) sc.

Armhole Row 4: Sc in each sc to last sc, 2 sc in last sc, ch 1, turn: 41 (45, 49, 53) sc, 30 (32, 34, 36) rows.

Rep Armhole Rows 3 and 4 twice: 45 (49, 53, 57) sc, 34 (36, 38, 40) rows.

Shape Center

Front Row 1: Sc2tog over first 2 sc, sc in each sc across, ch 1, turn: 44 (48, 52, 56) sc.

Front Row 2: Sc in each sc to last 2 sc, sc2tog over last 2 sc, ch 1, turn: 43 (47, 51, 55) sc.

Front Row 3: Sc2tog over first 2 sc, sc in each sc across, ch 1, turn: 42 (46, 50, 54) sc.

Front Row 4: Sc in each sc across, ch 1, turn: 42 (46, 50, 54) sc, 38 (40, 42, 44) rows.

Rep Front Rows 1 through 4 four more times: 30 (34, 38, 42) sc, 54 (56, 58, 60) rows.

Shape Top

Top Row 1: Sc2tog over first 2 sc, sc in each sc to last 2 sc, sc2tog over last 2 sc, ch 1, turn: 28 (32, 36, 40) sc.

Top Row 2: Sc in each sc across, ch 1, turn: 28 (32, 36, 40) sc, 56 (58, 60, 62) rows.

Top Rows 3 and 4: Rep Top Rows 1 and 2: 26 (30, 34, 38) sc, 58 (60, 62, 64) rows.

Top Rows 5 through 7: Rep Top Row 1: 20 (24, 28, 32) sc.

Top Row 8: Rep Top Row 2: 20 (24, 28, 32) sc, 62 (64, 66, 68) rows.

Rep Top Rows 5 through 8 three (three, four, five) more times: 2 (6, 4, 2) sc, 74 (76, 82, 88) rows.

For Size Small Only
Work Top Rows 5 and 6 once more.

For Size Medium Only
Work Top Rows 1 and 2 once more.

For All Sizes
You should have 2 sc remaining, 74 (78, 84, 88) rows. X-Small size should end with 2 rows of grey. Small size should end with 2 rows of black. Medium size should end with 2 rows of cream. Large size should end with 4 rows of grey.

Last Row: Using same color as last row, work ch 1, sc2tog over last 2 sc. Finish off; weave in ends.

Second Half of Bodice

Rows 1 through 16 (18, 20, 22): Work as for First Half of Bodice Rows 1 through 16 (18, 20, 22).

Shape Armhole

Armhole Row 1: Sc2tog over first 2 sc, sc in each sc to last sc, 2 sc in last sc, ch 1, turn.

Armhole Row 2: 2 sc in first sc, sc in each sc across, ch 1, turn: 34 (38, 42, 46) sc, 18 (20, 22, 24) rows.

Rep Armhole Rows 1 and 2 five more times: 39 (43, 47, 51) sc, 28 (30, 32, 34) rows.

Armhole Row 3: Sc in each sc to last sc, 2 sc in last sc, ch 1, turn: 40 (44, 48, 52) sc.

Armhole Row 4: 2 sc in first sc, sc in each sc across, ch 1, turn: 41 (45, 49, 53) sc, 30 (32, 34, 36) rows.

Rep Armhole Rows 3 and 4 twice: 45 (49, 53, 57) sc, 34 (36, 38, 40) rows.

Shape Center

Center Row 1: Sc in each sc to last 2 sc, sc2tog over last 2 sc, ch 1, turn: 44 (48, 52, 56) sc.

Center Row 2: Sc2tog over first 2 sc, sc in each sc across, ch 1, turn: 43 (47, 51, 55) sc.

Center Row 3: Sc in each sc to last 2 sc, sc2tog over last 2 sc, ch 1, turn: 42 (46, 50, 54) sc.

Center Row 4: Sc in each sc across, ch 1, turn: 42 (46, 50, 54) sc, 38 (40, 42, 44) rows.

Rep Center Rows 1 through 4 four more times: 30 (34, 38, 42) sc, 54 (56, 58, 60) rows.

Shape Top

Work as for First Half of Bodice - Shape Top.

Lower Body

Sew two halves of bodice together at center seam, matching stripes. With right side of work facing, using larger hook, join grey to base chain at corner of bodice.

Row 1: Work 78 (84, 90, 96) sc evenly along lower edge of bodice (about 7 sc in side edge of every 6 rows), ch 1, turn.

Row 2: Sc in first sc, sc in each sc across, ch 3, turn.

Row 3 (eyelet row): Skip first 2 sc; * dc in next 2 sc, ch 1, skip 1 sc; rep from * across, ending with dc in last sc, ch 1, turn: 26 (28, 30, 32) eyelets.

Row 4: Sc in first dc; * sc in ch-1 sp, sc in next 2 dc; rep from * across; ending with sc under ch-3, sc in 2nd ch of ch-3, ch 1, turn.

Row 5: Sc in first sc, sc in each sc across, ch 2, turn.

Row 6: Skip first sc, dc in each sc across, ch 2, turn.

Row 7: Skip first dc, dc in each dc across, dc in 2nd ch of ch-2, ch 2, turn.

Row 8: Dc in first dc, dc in each dc across, 2 dc in 2nd ch of ch-2, ch 2, turn: 80 (86, 92, 98) sts.

Rows 9 through 17: Rep Row 7.

Row 18: Rep Row 8: 82 (88, 94, 100) sts.

Rep Rows 9 through 18 once more: 84 (90, 96, 102) sts.

Rep Row 7 until length measures 10 (10 1/2, 11, 11 1/2) inches from lower edge of bodice, or length required. Finish off; weave in ends.

Front

First Half of Bodice

Work as for Back - First Half of Bodice through Shape Center: 54 (56, 68, 60) rows. Finish off; weave in ends.

Second Half of Bodice

Work as for Back - Second Half of Bodice through Shape Center: 54 (56, 68, 60) rows total. Finish off; weave in ends.

Lower Body

Work as for Back - Lower Body.

Finishing

Sew side seams.

Lower Border

With right side of work facing, using smaller hook, join grey at base of one side seam.

Round 1: Ch 1, sc in first dc, sc in each dc around; ending with sl st in first sc of round. Finish off.

First Strap

With right side of work facing, using smaller hook, join grey to point at top of right side of Front. Ch 42 (44, 46, 48); without twisting chs, join with sl st in top right corner of Back; check for correct length of strap; if necessary, pull out ch and work again with more or fewer chs, then proceed to Rnd 1.

Rnd 1: Sc in side edge of every row around armhole edge, ending with sl st in first ch made at point of Front.

Rnd 2: Ch 1, sc in each ch and sc around, working sc3tog at underarm seam and ending with sl st in first sc of rnd. Finish off.

With right side facing, join black to top of sc3tog at underarm.

Rnd 3: Ch 1, skip 1 sc, sc in each sc around; ending with sc2tog, sl st under ch-1 at beg of rnd.

Rnd 4: Sl st in each st to end. Finish off.

Second Strap

Beginning at top left corner of Back, work to match First Strap.

Neck Border

With right side of work facing, using smaller hook, join grey at center back neck.

Rnd 1: Ch 1, sc in side edge of each row to base of strap; sc3tog at corner; sc in base of each ch along strap; sc in side edge of each row to center front; sc3tog at center front; sc in side edge of each row to base of next strap; sc in base of each ch along strap ending with sc3tog at corner; sc in side edge of each row ending with sl st in first sc of rnd.

Rnd 2: Ch 1, sc in first sc, sc in each sc around, working sc3tog at each back corner and at center front, ending with sl st in first sc of rnd.

Change to black.

Rnd 3: Rep Rnd 2.

Rnd 4: Sl st in each st around. Finish off; weave in ends.

Drawstring

Cut four 3 1/2 yd lengths of black. Tie a knot at one end and attach to a fixed point (e.g. a doorknob), then hold the length taut and twist the free end between your fingers, over and over, until the length is very tightly twisted. Bring the two ends together and tie them with an overhand knot, allowing the cord to twist around itself. With a small crochet hook pull the smooth (not cut) end through one bead and push the bead down to the knot. Beginning and ending at center front, thread smooth end of cord through row of eyelets. Thread on 2nd bead and tie an overhand knot. Trim thread ends 1 inch below knots to form tassels.

DIAGONAL STRIPE TOP

Note: Instructions are written for size X-Small; changes for sizes Small, Medium and Large are in parentheses.

SIZE	X-Small	Small	Medium	Large
Body Bust Measurements	32"	34"	36"	38"
Finished Bust Measurements	34"	36"	38"	40"

MATERIALS

Fingering weight yarn

    100 (100, 125, 150) grams wine

    25 (25, 50, 50) grams pink

    25 (25, 50, 50) grams black.

Note: *Photographed model made with Twilleys Goldfingering #58 wine, #59 pink, and #31 black*

Size D (3.25 mm) crochet hook

Size E (3.5 mm) crochet hook (or size required for gauge)

GAUGE

22 dc = 4"with larger hook

11 dc rows = 4" with larger hoook

STITCH GUIDE:

Dc2tog: [YO, draw up lp in next st, YO, draw through first 2 lps on hook] 2 times; YO, draw through all 3 lps on hook: dc2tog made.

Dc3tog: [YO, draw up lp in next st or sp, YO, draw through first 2 lps on hook] 3 times; YO, draw through all 4 lps on hook: dc3tog made.

Sc3tog: Draw up a lp in each of next 3 sts, YO and draw through all 4 lps on hook: sc3tog made.

INSTRUCTIONS

Stripe Pattern

3 rows wine

1 row pink

1 row black

Rep these 5 rows in sequence for pattern

Note: *When changing colors, work to last step of last st of row, complete last st with new color; finish off first color. Colors may be loosely carried up side edges of work.*

143

Back

With larger hook and wine, ch 106 (112, 118, 124) loosely.

Row 1 (right side): Dc in 4th ch from hook and in next 48 (51, 54, 57) chs; ch 1, skip 1 ch, dc3tog over next 3 chs; ch 1, skip 1 ch, dc in next 48 (51, 54, 57) chs; 2 dc in last ch, ch 3, turn: 50 (53, 56, 59) dc at each side of center 3 sts, counting beg 3 skipped chs as a dc.

Row 2: Dc in first dc (inc made), dc each dc to dc before center 3 sts; ch 1, skip 1 dc, dc3tog over next ch-1 sp, top of dc3tog and following ch-1 sp; ch 1, skip 1 dc; dc in each dc across; ending with 2 dc in top of tch (inc made); ch 3, turn.

Row 3 (decrease row): Skip first dc, dc in each dc to dc before center 3 sts; ch 1, skip 1 dc, dc3tog over next ch-1 sp, top of dc3tog and following ch-1 sp; ch 1, skip 1 dc, dc in each dc across, ending with dc in tch; ch 3, turn: 49 (52, 55, 58) dc at each side of center 3 sts.

Note: *Remember to maintain color sequence throughout pattern.*

Row 4: Rep Row 2.

Rows 5 through 10: Rep Rows 2 through 4 twice: 47 (50, 53, 56) dc at each side of center 3 sts.

Rows 11 and 12: Rep Row 2.

Row 13: 2 dc in first dc; dc in each dc to dc before center 3 sts; ch 1, skip 1 dc; dc3tog over next ch-1 sp, top of dc3tog and following ch-1 sp; ch 1, skip 1 dc; dc in each dc across, ending with 2 dc in last dc and 2 dc in top of turning ch; ch 3, turn: 48 (51, 54, 57) dc at each side of center 3 sts.

Row 14: Rep Row 2.

Rows 15 through 22: Rep Rows 13 and 14 four times: 52 (55, 58, 61) dc at each side of center 3 sts.

Rows 23 through 24 (24, 28, 28): Rep Row 2.

Note: *Sizes X-Small and Small should end with one row of pink; sizes Medium and Large sizes should end with 3 rows of wine.*

Shape Armholes

Row 1: Skip next dc, dc2tog over next 2 dc, work in pattern as established to last 2 dc and ch-3, dc3tog over last 2 dc and 3rd ch of tch, ch 3, turn.

Row 2: Skip the dc3tog; dc2tog over next 2 dc, work in pattern as established to last 4 sts, dc3tog over last 2 dc and dc2tog, turn, do not work in tch: 46 (49, 52, 55) sts at each side of center 3 sts, NOT counting first ch-3.

Rows 3 through 9 (9, 10, 10): Rep Row 2: 25(28, 28, 31) sts at each side of center 3 sts: 33 (33, 38, 38) rows total, ending with 3 rows of wine. Finish off; weave in ends.

Front

Work same as Back.

Finishing

Sew side seams, matching stripes.

Lower Border

With right side facing and beg ch at top, with smaller hook join wine at bottom of one side seam.

Rnd 1: Ch 1; (sc in unused lp of each ch to center ch, 3 sc in center ch, sc in unused lp of each ch to 2 chs before side seam, sc3tog over next 3 chs) twice; join with sl st in first sc of rnd.

Rnd 2: Ch 1; (sc in each sc to center sc, 3 sc in center sc, sc in each sc to sc before sc3tog, sc3tog over next 3 sts) twice; join. Finish off; weave in ends.

First Strap and Armhole Border

With right side of work facing, using smaller hook, join wine at top right point of Back; ch 50 (55, 60, 65) for strap; without twisting chs, join with sl st in top left point of Front.

Lay work flat and measure armhole depth, placing ruler in a straight line down from middle of strap to beg of armhole shaping. Armhole depth should measure 7 ¹/₂" (8", 8", 8 ¹/₂"). If necessary rework the ch with more or fewer chains. When length is correct, continue with Rnd 1.

Rnd 1: Ch 1, 3 sc in side edge of every row around armhole edge to base of ch; sc in each ch along strap, join with sl st in beg ch-1 at point of Front.

Rnd 2: Ch 1, sc in each sc to underarm seam, sc3tog at seam, sc in each sc around, ending with sl st in ch-1 at beg of round. Finish off; weave in ends.

Second Strap and Armhole Border

Beginning at top right point of Front, and joining to top left point of Back, work to match First Strap.

Neck Border

With right side of work facing, using smaller hook, join wine at top right of Back, in 3rd dc from base of strap.

Rnd 1: Ch 1, (sc in each dc to center, sc3tog at center, sc in each dc to base of strap, sc3tog, sc in base of each ch to end of strap, sc3tog) twice; sc in next dc, sl st in ch-1 at beg of rnd.

Rnd 2: Ch 1, sc in each sc and sc3tog at center back, center front and each end of straps, ending with sl st in ch-1 at beg of rnd. Finish off; weave in all yarn ends.

#55 STRIPES ON PARADE

Designed by Janie Herrin

SIZE
52" x 62"

MATERIALS
Worsted weight yarn
  10 oz black (A)
  10 oz blue (B)
  10 oz lt blue (C)
  10 oz lt raspberry (D)
  10 oz aran (E)
Size H (5 mm) crochet hook
  (or size required for gauge)

GAUGE
One block = 8" x 8"
  (before edging)

INSTRUCTIONS

Block A (make 12)
Rows 1 through 6: Use B

Rows 7 through 12: Use C

Rows 13 through 19: Use B

Block B (make 9)
Rows 1 through 6: Use C

Rows 6 through 12: Use B

Rows 7 through 19: Use C

Block C (make 12)
Rows 1 through 6: Use D

Rows 6 through 12: Use E

Rows 13 through 19: Use D

Block D (make 9)
Rows 1 through 6: Use E

Rows 7 through 13: Use D

Rows 14 through 19: Use E

Block Instructions
Following color sequences as above, with first color, ch 30 loosely.

To Change Color: With first color, YO, insert hook in st specified and draw up a lp (3 lps on hook); with new color, YO and draw through all 3 lps on hook.

Placement Chart for Blocks

A	A	A	A	A	A
C	B	B	B	B	B
C	D	A	A	A	A
C	D	C	B	B	B
C	D	C	D	A	A
C	D	C	D	C	B
C	D	C	D	C	D

Row 1 (right side): Sc in 2nd ch from hook and in each rem ch, ch 2, turn: 29 sc.

Note: Do not count turning ch-2 as first hdc on following rows; work hdc in first st at beg of each row.

Row 2: Hdc in first st; *ch 1, skip next st, hdc in next st; rep from * across, ch 2, turn: 14 ch-1 sps.

Row 3: Hdc in first st, hdc in each ch-1 sp and in each hdc across, ch 2, turn: 29 hdc.

Row 4: Hdc in first st; *ch 1, skip next sc, hdc in next st; rep from * across, ch 2, turn.

Rows 5 through 6: Rep Rows 3 and 4; at end of Row 6, change color, ch 2, turn.

Rows 7 through 12: With new color rep Rows 3 and 4; at end of Row 12, change color, ch 2, turn.

Rows 13 through 18: With new color rep Rows 3 and 4; at end of last row, ch 1, turn.

Row 19: Sc in first st, sc in each ch-1 sp and in each hdc across: 29 sc. Finish off, weave in ends.

Assembly
(edging for first square only)

Beginning with one Block A, with right side facing, join A with sc in first st at upper right corner, ch 3, sc in same st (corner made); *ch 3, skip 3 sts, (sc in next st, ch 3, skip next 2 sts) 8 times; work corner in corner st, ch 3, working across side, skip first hdc row, sc in end st of next hdc row,

Note: Read chart from right to left, and from top to bottom.

(ch 3, skip next row, sc in end st of next row) across, ch 3, skip last hdc row, work corner in corner (9 lps made across side excluding corners); rep from * once ending with sl st in beg sc. Finish off; weave in all ends.

Note: Arrange Blocks A and B with stripes in horizontal position and Blocks C and D in vertical position. (see photo)

Following Placement Chart, work edging in same manner as first block, joining 6 vertical strips of 7 squares each as follows: holding blocks with wrong sides facing, omit center ch of ch-3 lps and replace with sc in corresponding lp of prev square. When working into corner sp that has been previously joined, work into first joining sc.

Border

Rnd 1: With right side facing, join A with sc in any outer corner sp, ch 3, sc in same sp; *(ch 3, sc in next sp) 9 times, ch 3, sc in sp between joinings; rep from * around working (sc, ch 3, sc) in each corner sp, end with ch 3, sl st in beg sc.

Rnd 2: Sl st in corner sp, ch 1, (sc, ch 2, sc, ch 1) in same sp and in each sp around, sl st in beg sc. Finish off; weave in ends.

#56 & 57 CUTE COMBO

Designed by Nazanin S. Fard

148

JACKET

INSTRUCTIONS

Note: Garment is worked in one piece to armholes.

Starting at bottom edge ch 181 (201, 221).

Row 1: Dc in 3rd ch from hook and in each rem ch: 180 (200, 220) dc, counting first 2 skipped chs as a st; ch 3 (counts as first dc of following row), turn.

Row 2: *FPdc around next dc, BPdc around next dc; rep from * to last dc; dc in last dc (skipped chs); ch 3, turn.

Row 3: *Fpdc around next BPdc, PBdc around next FPdc; rep from * across, dc in last dc; ch 3, turn.

Rows 4 and 5: Rep Row 3.

Row 6: *FPdc around next BPdc, BPdc around next FPdc; rep from * across, turn (do not chain).

Row 7 (Patt Row): Ch 2 (counts as first hdc); *sl st in next st, hdc in next st; rep from * across to last st, sl st in last st; turn.

Rep Patt Row until back measures 15" (15 1/2", 16").

Right Front

Row 1 (right side): Work in patt as established across 36 (40, 44) sts; leave rem sts unworked; mark this row as right side, turn.

Row 2: Work even in patt to last 2 sts, skip next st, sl st in last st; turn: one st decreased: 35 (39, 44) sts.

Row 3: Work even in patt as established.

Rep Rows 2 and 3 until 20 (22, 24) sts rem.

Work even in patt until piece measures 25" (26", 27"). Finish off; weave in ends.

Left Front

Row 1: With right side facing you, skip next 108 (120, 132) sts for back, join yarn with sl st in next st, ch 2 (counts as first hdc of row, work even in patt as established across, ending at center front; ch 1; turn: 36 (40, 44) sts.

Row 2: Sl st in first st, skip next st (decrease made); work in patt as established across: 35 (39, 43) sts.

Row 3: Work even in patt across.

Rep Rows 2 and 3 until 20 (22, 24) sts rem.

Work even in patt until piece measures 25" (26', 27"). Finish off; weave in ends.

Back

Row 1: With right side facing you, skip 20 sts from inner edge of right front for armhole; join yarn with sl st in next st, ch 2 (counts as first hdc), work in patt across 67 (79, 91) more sts: 68 (80, 92) sts; turn, leaving rem sts unworked for armhole.

Work even in patt until back measures 25" (26", 27"). Finish off; weave in ends.

Sleeve (make 2)

Ch 45 (49, 53).

Row 1: Dc in 3rd ch from hook and in each rem ch: 44 (48, 52) dc, counting first 2 skipped chs as a st; ch 3, turn.

Row 2: *FPdc around next dc, BPdc around next dc; rep from * across, dc in last dc, ch 3, turn.

Row 3: *FPdc around next BPdc, BPdc around next FPdc; rep from * across, dc in last dc; ch 3, turn.

Row 4: *FPdc around next BPdc, BPdc around next FPdc; rep from * across, turn (do not chain).

Row 5 (increase row): Work Pattern Row across, working a Dbl inc (see Stitch Guide) 3 times evenly spaced: 50 (54, 58) sts.

Row 6: Work in patt across, working the added sts into the pattern.

Rows 7 through 9: Work even in patt.

Row 10: Work in patt, working a Dbl inc at beg and end of row: 4 sts added.

Rep Rows 6 through 10 until there are 86 (90, 94) sts.

Work even in patt until sleeve measures 18" (19", 19 1/2"). Finish off; weave in all ends.

Finishing

Sew shoulder seams.

Front Edging

Row 1: With right side of work facing, join yarn with sl st at bottom edge of right front; ch 1; sc in same st; work sc evenly across right front, neckline, and left front, adjusting sts as needed to keep work flat; at bottom of left front, ch 1, turn.

Row 2: Sc evenly around, again adjusting sts to keep work flat; ch 1; turn.

Place work on a flat surface and measure for 6 buttons evenly spaced on left front edging, placing top button at beg of neckline shaping and bottom button 3/4" up from bottom edge. Mark button placement.

Row 3 (buttonhole row): Sc evenly around, working buttonholes opposite buttons as follows: for each buttonhole, ch 2, skip next 2 sc, continue in sc to next buttonhole; continue in sc around, ch 1, turn.

Row 4: Sc in each sc around, working 2 sc in each ch-2 sp; and end of row, do not ch or turn.

Row 5: Work Rev sc around. Finish off; weave in all ends.

Finishing

Mark center of sleeve top and pin to shoulder seam; sew top of sleeve into armhole, with straight rows of sleeve sides across underarms. Sew sleeve seam.

Sew buttons opposite buttonholes.

TOP

INSTRUCTIONS

Back

With larger hook, ch 81 (89, 97).

Row 1: Dc in 3rd ch from hook and in each rem ch: 80 (88, 96) dc, counting first 2 skipped chs as a st; ch 3 (counts as first dc of following row), turn.

Row 2: *FPdc around next dc, BPdc around next dc; rep from * to last dc (skipped chs), dc in last dc, ch 3; turn.

Row 3: *FPdc around next BPdc, BPdc around next FPdc; rep from * across, dc in last dc; ch 3, turn.

Rows 4 and 5: Rep Row 3.

Row 6: *FPdc around next BPdc, BPdc around next FPdc; rep from * across, turn (do not chain).

Row 7 (Patt Row): Ch 2 (counts as first hdc); *sl st in next st, hdc in next stitch; rep from * across to last st, sl st in last st; turn.

Rep Patt Row until back measures 14" (15", 15"). At end of last row, ch 1; turn.

Armhole Shaping

Row 1 (right side): Sl st in first 11 sts; ch 2 (counts as hdc), sl st in next st; *hdc in next st, sl st in next st; rep from * to last 10 sts, turn, tleaving rem sts unworked: 60 (68, 76) sts.

Work even in patt as established until piece measures 23" (24", 25"); mark last row worked for wrong side; turn.

Shoulder Shaping

Row 1 (right shoulder): Work even in pattern as established over first 20 (22, 24) sts, turn, leaving rem sts unworked. Work even on 20 (22, 24) sts for 1". Finish off.

Row 1 (left shoulder): With right side facing, skip next 20 (24, 28) sts for neck, join yarn with sl st in next stitch, ch 2 (counts as a hdc), work in patt across, turn.

Work even in pattern as established for 1". Finish off; weave in all ends.

Front

Work same as back, including armhole shaping, until piece measures 18" for all sizes; mark last row worked as wrong side; turn.

Left Shoulder

Row 1 (right side): Work even across 23 (27, 31) sts, ch 1; turn, leaving rem sts unworked.

Row 2: Sl st in next st (dec made); work in patt across, turn.

Row 3: Work even in patt, turn.

Rep Rows 2 and 3 until 20 (22, 24) sts rem.

Work even in pattern as established until front measures 23" (24", 25"). Finish off; weave in ends.

Right Shoulder

With right side facing, skip next 14 sts for center neck; join yarn with sl st in next st.

Row 1: Ch 2 (counts as first hdc); work even in patt across, ch 1, turn

Row 2: Sl st in next st (dec made), work in patt across, ch 1, turn

Row 3: Work even in patt, turn.

Rep Rows 2 and 3 until 20 (22, 24) stitches rem.

Work even in pattern as established until front measures 23" (24", 25"). Finish off; weave in ends.

Finishing

Sew side and shoulder seams.

Armhole Finishing

Rnd 1: With smaller hook and right side facing, join yarn with sl st at underarm side seam, ch 1, sc in same st; sc evenly around armhole opening, adjusting sts as needed to keep work flat; join with sl st in beg sc.

Rnds 2 through 4: Ch 1, sc in same st and in each st around, join.

Rnd 5: Work Rev sc in each st around; join. Finish off; weave in ends.

Neckline Finishing

Rnd 1: With smaller hook and right side facing, join yarn with sl st in any st at center back, ch 1, sc in same st; sc evenly around neck opening, adjusting sts as needed to keep work flat; join with sl st in beg sc.

Rnd 2: Work Rev sc in each st around, join. Finish off; weave in all ends.

#58 SNOWFLAKE EARRING

Designed by Janie Herrin

SIZE
2 ¹/₄" diameter

MATERIALS
Size 10 crochet cotton
 white

Note: Photographed model made with Royale Classic Crochet Thread #201 White

Size 10 (1.3 mm) steel crochet hook (or size required for gauge)

2 Fishhook earring wires

GAUGE
20 dc = 2"

STITCH GUIDE
Triple Picot (trP): Ch 7, sl st in 4th ch from hook; (ch 4, sl st in 4th ch from hook) twice, sl st in 4th ch of beg ch-7, ch 3: trP made.

INSTRUCTIONS
(make 2)

Ch 5; join with sl st to form a ring.

Rnd 1: Ch 1, (sc in ring, ch 1) 6 times, join with sl st in beg sc: 6 ch-1 sps.

Rnd 2: Sl st in next sp, ch 1, in same sp and in each sp around work (sc, ch 1) twice; join in beg sc: 12 ch-1 sps.

Rnd 3: Sl st in next sp, ch 1, sc in same sp; *trP, sc in next ch-1 sp; rep from * around, skip last ch-1 sp, join in beg sc. Finish off; weave in ends.

Finishing
Starch if desired; attach center picot of any trP group to earring.

PRETTY POSIES

Designed by Edie Eckman

MATERIALS

Sport weight yarn
  11 $\frac{1}{4}$ (12 $\frac{1}{2}$, 15, 17 $\frac{1}{2}$) oz blue
  2 $\frac{1}{2}$ oz yellow
  $\frac{1}{4}$ oz pink
  $\frac{1}{4}$ oz orange
  $\frac{1}{2}$ oz green

Note: *Photographed model made with
Lion Brand® MicroSpun, #148
Turquoise, #158 Buttercup, #146
Fuchsia, #186 Mango and #194 Lime*

Size I (5.5 mm) crochet hook (or size
  required for gauge)

Stitch markers

Five buttons, $\frac{5}{8}$" diameter

GAUGE

12 hdc = 4"

12 hdc rows = 4"

Note: *Instructions are written for size 4; changes for sizes 6, 8 and 10
are in parentheses.*

CARDIGAN SIZES	4	6	8	10
Body Chest Measurements	23"	25"	26 $\frac{1}{2}$"	28"
Finished Chest Measurements	25 $\frac{1}{2}$"	27 $\frac{1}{2}$"	29"	30 $\frac{1}{2}$"
CAP SIZES				
Finished Circumference	16"	16"	18"	18"

CARDIGAN

INSTRUCTIONS

Back

Starting at bottom, with blue, ch 42 (45, 46, 49).

Row 1 (right side): Hdc in 3rd ch from hook (skipped chs count as hdc), hdc in next ch and in each ch across: 41 (44, 45, 48) hdc; ch 2 (counts as hdc on next row now and throughout), turn.

Row 2: Hdc in next hdc and in each hdc across; ch 2, turn.

Rep Row 2 until piece measures about 7 1/2" (8 1/2", 9 1/2", 10 1/2"), ending by working a wrong side row. At end of last row: ch 1, turn.

Armhole Shaping

Row 1: Skip first st, sl st in next 3 (3, 3, 4) sts, ch 2 (counts as hdc), hdc in next hdc and in each hdc to last 3 (3, 3, 4) sts, leaving last 3 (3, 3, 4) sts unworked: 35 (38, 39, 40) hdc; ch 2, turn.

Row 2: Hdc in next hdc and in each hdc across; ch 2, turn.

Rep Row 2 until back measures 14" (15 1/2", 17", 18 1/2") from beg. At end of last row, do not ch 2. Finish off; weave in ends.

Left Front

Starting at bottom, with blue, ch 21 (22, 24, 25).

Row 1 (right side): Hdc in 3rd ch from hook (skipped chs count as hdc), hdc in next ch and in each ch across: 20 (21, 23, 24) hdc; ch 2 (counts as hdc on next row now and throughout), turn.

Row 2: Hdc in next hdc and in each hdc across; ch 2, turn.

Rep Row 2 until piece measures about 7 1/2" (8 1/2", 9 1/2", 10 1/2"), ending by working a wrong side row. At end of last row: ch 1, turn.

Armhole Shaping

Row 1: Skip first hdc, sl st in next 3 hdc, ch 2 (counts as hdc), hdc in next hdc and in each hdc across: 17 (18, 20, 21) hdc; ch 2, turn.

Row 2: Hdc in next hdc and in each hdc across; ch 2, turn.

Rep Row 2 until piece measures about 12 1/2" (14", 15 1/2", 16 1/2") from beg, ending by working a wrong side row.

Neck Shaping

Row 1: Hdc in next hdc and in each hdc across to last 6 (7, 8, 9) sts, leaving last 6 (7, 8, 9) sts unworked: 11 (11, 12, 12) hdc; ch 2, turn.

Row 2: Hdc dec in next 2 hdc, hdc in next hdc and in each hdc across: 10 (10, 11, 11) hdc; ch 2, turn.

Row 3: Hdc in next hdc and in each hdc across to last st, leaving last st unworked: 9 (9, 10, 10) hdc; ch 2, turn.

Row 4: Rep Row 2: 8 (8, 9, 9) hdc; ch 2, turn.

Row 5: Hdc in next hdc and in each hdc across; ch 2, turn.

Rep Row 5 until piece measures about 14" (15 1/2", 17", 18 1/2") from beg. At end of last row, do not ch 2. Finish off; weave in ends.

Right Front
Starting at bottom, with blue, ch 21 (22, 24, 25).

Rows 1 and 2: Rep Rows 1 and 2 on Left Front.

Rep Row 2 on Left Front until piece measures about 7 1/2" (8 1/2", 9 1/2" 10 1/2"), ending by working a wrong side row; ch 2 (counts as hdc on next row now and throughout), turn.

Armhole Shaping
Row 1: Hdc in next hdc and in each hdc across to last 3 sts, leaving last 3 sts unworked: 17 (18, 20, 21) hdc; ch 2, turn.

Row 2: Hdc in next hdc and in each hdc across; ch 2, turn.

Rep Row 2 until piece measures about 12 1/2" (14", 15 1/2", 16 1/2") from beg, ending by working a wrong side row. At end of last row, ch 1, turn.

Neck Shaping
Row 1: Skip first hdc, sl st in next 6 (7, 8, 9) hdc, ch 2 (counts as hdc), hdc in next hdc and in each hdc across: 11 (11, 12, 12) hdc; ch 2, turn.

Row 2: Hdc in next hdc and in each hdc across to last 2 sts, hdc dec in last 2 sts: 10 (10, 11, 11) hdc; ch 1, turn.

Row 3: Skip first hdc, sl st in next hdc, ch 2 (counts as hdc), hdc in next hdc and in each hdc across: 9 (9, 10, 10) hdc; ch 2, turn.

Row 4: Rep Row 2: 8 (8, 9, 9) hdc; ch 2, turn.

Row 5: Hdc in next hdc and in each hdc across; ch 2, turn.

Rep Row 5 until piece measures about 14" (15 1/2", 17", 18 1/2") from beg. At end of last row, do not ch 2. Finish off; weave in ends.

Sleeves (make 2)
Starting at bottom, with blue, ch 23 (26, 26, 27).

Row 1 (right side): Hdc in 3rd ch from hook (skipped chs count as hdc), hdc in next ch and in each ch across: 22 (25, 25, 26) hdc; ch 2 (counts as hdc on next row now and throughout), turn.

Row 2: Hdc in next hdc and in each hdc across; ch 2, turn.

Row 3: Hdc in first hdc, hdc in next hdc and in each hdc across to last st, 2 hdc in last st: 24 (27, 27, 28) hdc; ch 2, turn.

Rows 4 through 6: Rep Row 2.

Rep Rows 3 through 6 8 (8, 5, 6) times more. At end of last row: 40 (43, 37, 40) hdc.

For Sizes 8 and 10 Only
Row 7: Rep Row 3: 39 (42) hdc; ch 2, turn.

Rows 8 and 9: Rep Row 2.

Rep Rows 7 through 9 four times more. At end of last row: 47 (50) hdc.

For All Sizes

Rep Row 2 until sleeve measures about 13 ½" (14 ½", 15 ½", 16 ½"), or to desired length. At end of last row, do not ch 2. Finish off; weave in ends.

Finishing

Sew shoulder seams. Sew sleeves to front and back with center of sleeves at shoulder seams. Sew side and sleeve seams.

Sleeve border

With right side facing, join yellow with sc in free lp of first ch on bottom edge of sleeve, work rev sc in free lp of each ch around bottom edge of sleeve; join with sl st in first sc. Finish off; weave in ends. Rep on second sleeve.

Sweater border

Place 5 markers for buttonholes along right front center edge of sweater, with top and bottom markers ½" from neck and bottom edge and other 3 markers evenly spaced between top and bottom markers.

Row 1: With right side facing, join blue with sc in beg edge of Row 1 on Right Front, sc evenly up Right Front edge, 3 sc in corner st at beg of right neck shaping, sc evenly around neck, 3 sc in corner st at beg of left neck shaping, sc evenly down Left Front edge to bottom corner; ch 1, turn.

Row 2: Sc in first sc and in each sc around, working 3 sc in corner st at beg of right and left neck shapings and making buttonholes with (ch 1, skip next sc, sc in next sc) at each marker. Finish off; weave in ends.

Row 3: With right side facing, join yellow with sc in free lp of ch at bottom corner of Right Front, work rev sc in free lp of each ch around entire bottom edge and in each sc up Left Front edge, around neck and down Right Front edge; join with sl st in first rev sc. Finish off; weave in ends.

Sew buttons to Left Front center edge on Row 2 of border, aligning with buttonholes on Right Front edge.

Flowers and Leaves

Make a variety of flowers and leaves. Sew onto sweater following photograph, or as desired.

Pink Flower

With pink, ch 14.

Row 1: 2 sc in 2nd ch from hook and in each ch across: 26 sc. Finish off, leaving 9" end for sewing. Roll into spiral shape and tack base of flower.

Yellow Flower

With yellow, ch 4; join with sl st to form a ring.

Rnd 1: Ch 7; *sc in ring, ch 6; rep from * 6 times more; join with sl st in first ch of beg ch-7. Finish off, leaving 9" end for sewing.

Orange Flower

With orange, ch 4; join with sl st to form a ring.

Rnd 1: Ch 4, dc in ring, ch 3, *sc in ring, ch 3, dc in ring, ch 3; rep from * 3 times more; join with sl st in first ch of beg ch-4. Finish off, leaving 9" end for sewing.

Leaf Pair #1

With green, ch 9.

Row 1: Sl st in 2nd ch from hook, sc in next ch, hdc in next 3 chs, sc in next ch, sl st in last 2 chs; ch 11, sl st in 2nd ch from hook and next ch, sc in next ch, hdc in next 3 chs, sc in next ch, sl st in next 2 chs, leaving one ch unworked in center. Finish off, leaving 9" end for sewing.

Leaf Pair #2
With green, ch 7.

Row 1: Sc in 2nd ch from hook, hdc in next ch, dc in next 2 chs, hdc in next ch, sc in next sc; ch 9, sc in 2nd ch from hook and in next ch, hdc in next ch, dc in next ch, hdc in next ch, sc in next ch, leaving 2 chs unworked in center. Finish off, leaving 9" end for sewing.

Leaf Pair #3
With green, ch 7.

Row 1: Sc in 2nd ch from hook, dc in next ch, tr in next ch, dc in next ch, hdc in next ch, sc in last ch; ch 9, hdc in 3rd ch from hook, dc in next ch, tr in next ch, dc in next ch, hdc in next ch, sc in next ch, leaving one ch unworked in center. Finish off, leaving 9" end for sewing.

CAP

INSTRUCTIONS

With blue, ch 4; join with sl st to form a ring.

Rnd 1 (right side): Ch 2 (counts as hdc now and throughout), 7 hdc in ring: 8 hdc; join with sl st in 2nd ch of beg ch-2.

Rnd 2: Ch 2, hdc in same ch as joining, 2 hdc in next hdc and in each hdc around: 16 hdc; join as before.

Rnd 3: Ch 2, 2 hdc in next hdc, *hdc in next hdc, 2 hdc in next hdc; rep from * around: 24 hdc; join.

Rnd 4: Ch 2, hdc in next hdc, 2 hdc in next hdc; *hdc in next 2 hdc, 2 hdc in next hdc; rep from * around: 32 hdc; join.

Rnd 5: Ch 2, hdc in next hdc and in each hdc around; join.

Rnd 6: Ch 2, hdc in same ch as joining, hdc in next 3 hdc; *2 hdc in next hdc, hdc in next 3 hdc; rep from * around: 40 hdc; join.

Rnd 7: Rep Rnd 5.

Rnd 8: Ch 2, hdc in next 3 hdc, 2 hdc in next hdc; *hdc in next 4 hdc, 2 hdc in next hdc; rep from * around: 48 hdc; join.

For Sizes 8 and 10 Only
Rnd 9: Rep Rnd 5.

Rnd 10: Ch 2, hdc in same ch as joining, hdc in next 7 hdc; *2 hdc in next hdc, hdc in next 7 hdc; rep from * around: 54 hdc; join.

For All Sizes
Rep Rnd 5 until cap measures 5" (5 1/2") from center to last rnd, or to desired length. Do not finish off.

Increase Rnd: Ch 2, 2 hdc in same ch as joining; *3 hdc in next hdc; rep from * around; join. Finish off; weave in ends.

With right side facing, join yellow with sc in any hdc on increase rnd, work rev sc around entire edge; join with sl st in first rev sc. Finish off; weave in ends.

Make flowers and leaves following instructions. Sew onto cap following photograph, or as desired.

#61 ASYMMETRICAL PONCHO

Designed by Marty Miller

Note: *Instructions are written for size Small; changes for sizes Medium and Large are in parentheses.*

SIZES	Small	Medium	Large
Body bust Measurements	32" - 34"	36" - 38"	40" - 42"

MATERIALS

Cotton boucle, Eyelash and Metallic yarn blended 366 (427, 488) yds

Note: *Photographed model made with Ironstone Yarns Pizzazz, #21*

Size L (8 mm) crochet hook (or size required for gauge)

GAUGE

3 ch-5 sps = 5"

Note: *This poncho is stretchy, so an accurate row gauge is not possible.*

INSTRUCTIONS

Ch 50 (54, 58).

Row 1: Sc in 6th ch from hook; *ch 5, skip next 3 chs, sc in next ch; rep from * across: 12 (13, 14) ch-5 sps; ch 5, turn.

Row 2: Sc in first ch-5 sp; *ch 5, sc in next ch-5 sp; rep from * across: 12 (13, 14) ch-5 sps; ch 5, turn.

Rows 3 through 71 (73, 75): Rep Row 2 sixty nine (71, 73) times more, or until piece measures about 60" (63", 66") without stretching. At end of last row, do not ch 5. Do not finish off.

Finishing

Fold piece in half lengthwise. Working through both layers and starting at corner, work 3 sc in each of next 23 (24, 25) ch-5 sps along side edge, stopping about 11" from folded edge for neck opening, sc in next ch-5 sp through both layers, work 2 sc in same ch-5 sp through front layer only, work 3 sc in each of rem ch-5 sps through front layer only around neck edge, join with sl st in last sc worked through both layers. Finish off; weave in ends.

#62 TEXAS ROSES

Designed by Janie Herrin

SIZE
39" x 52"before border

MATERIALS
Worsted weight yarn
  24 oz pale yellow
  16 oz mint green
  16 oz white

Note: Photographed model made with Red Heart® Super Saver®, #322 Pale Yellow, #364 Lt Mint, and #311 White

Size H (5 mm) crochet hook (or size
  required for gauge)

GAUGE
7 dc = 2"

10-rnd square = 6 ¹/₂" x 6 ¹/₂"

block (4 squares joined) = 13" x 13"

INSTRUCTIONS

Block (make 12)
Note: Four joined squares form one Block

First Square

With yellow, ch 5, join with sl st to form a ring.

Rnd 1: Ch 1; in ring work (sc, ch 3) 8 times, join with sl st in beg sc: 8 ch-3 lps.

Rnd 2: Sl st in next ch-3 lp, ch 1, (sc, 2 dc, sc: petal made) in same lp; * (sc, 2 dc, sc) in next lp, rep from * around, join in beg sc: 8 petals.

Rnd 3: Ch 1, working behind petals of Rnd 2, sc from front to back to front around post of sc on Rnd 1, ch 3; *sc around post of next sc on Rnd 1, ch 3; rep from * around, join: 8 ch-3 lps.

Rnd 4: Sl st in next lp, ch 1, (sc, 4 dc, sc) in same lp; *(sc, 4 dc, sc) in next lp; rep from * around, join.

Rnd 5: Ch 1,* working behind petals, work sc around post of next sc on Rnd 3, ch 4; rep from * around, join: 8 ch-4 lps.

Rnd 6: Sl st in next lp, ch 1; (sc, 6 dc, sc) in same lp and in each rem lp around; join: 8 petals.

Rnd 7: Ch 1, *working behind petals, work sc around post of next sc on Rnd 5, ch 5; rep from * around, join: 8 ch-5 lps. Finish off yellow.

Rnd 8: Join mint with sl st in any ch-5 lp, in

same lp work beg trCL, (ch 2, trCL) 3 times in same lp (first corner made); *ch 2, in next lp work (trCL, ch 2) twice; in next lp work (trCL, ch 2) 4 times (corner made); rep from * around to first corner, join in top of beg trCL. Finish off mint.

Rnd 9: Join white with sc in center ch-2 of any corner sp; (ch 3, sc) in same sp; *(ch 3, sc in next sp) 5 times; ch 3, in next sp work (sc, ch 3, sc); rep from * around, ending with ch 1, hdc in beg sc to form last sp: 28 ch-3 sps.

Rnd 10: * (Sc, ch 3, sc) in next ch-3 sp, ch 3; (sc in next sp, ch 3) 6 times; rep from * around, join. Finish off; weave in all ends.

Second Square

Work as for First Square through Rnd 9.

Rnd 10: Work as for First Square until 3 sides are worked, ending at corner; holding two squares with wrong sides tog and working through corresponding lp in both squares, ch 3, sc in same lp; *ch 3, sc in next lp, working again through both squares; ch 3, sc in next lp of both squares along side to beg corner, join. Finish off.

Third Square

Work as for First Square through Rnd 9.

Rnd 10: Work as above, joining one of the first two squares on one side.

Fourth Square

Work as for First Square through Rnd 9.

Rnd 10: Work as above, joining to the first three square on two sides.

These four joined squares form one Block.

Block Edging

Hold Block with right side facing; join white with sc in any outer corner ch-3 sp, 2 sc in same sp; *2 sc in each ch-3 sp to next corner, 3 sc in corner; rep from * twice, 2 dc in each rem ch-3 sp, join to beg sc. Finish off.

Joining

Hold blocks with right sides tog; with white, and sewing through outer lps only, carefully match sts and corners. Join in four rows of three blocks each.

Border

Rnd 1: With right side facing you, join white with sc in corner sp at top right, work 2 more sc in same sp; work sc evenly around, adjusting sts to keep work flat, and working 3 sc in each corner sp, join. Finish off white.

Rnd 2: Join green with sl st in center sc of 3-sc corner group at top right; ch 1, 3 hdc in same st; hdc in each st around, adjusting sts to keep work flat, and working 3 hdc in each corner; join in beg hdc.

Rnd 3: Sl st into next hdc, ch 1, 3 sc in same st; work sc evenly around, adjusting sts to keep work flat, and working 3 sc in each corner; join with sc in first sc.

Rnd 4: *Ch 3, sk next 2 sc, sc in next sc; rep from * around, join. Finish off; weave in all ends.

#63 TINY BUBBLES JACKET

Designed by Laura Gebhardt

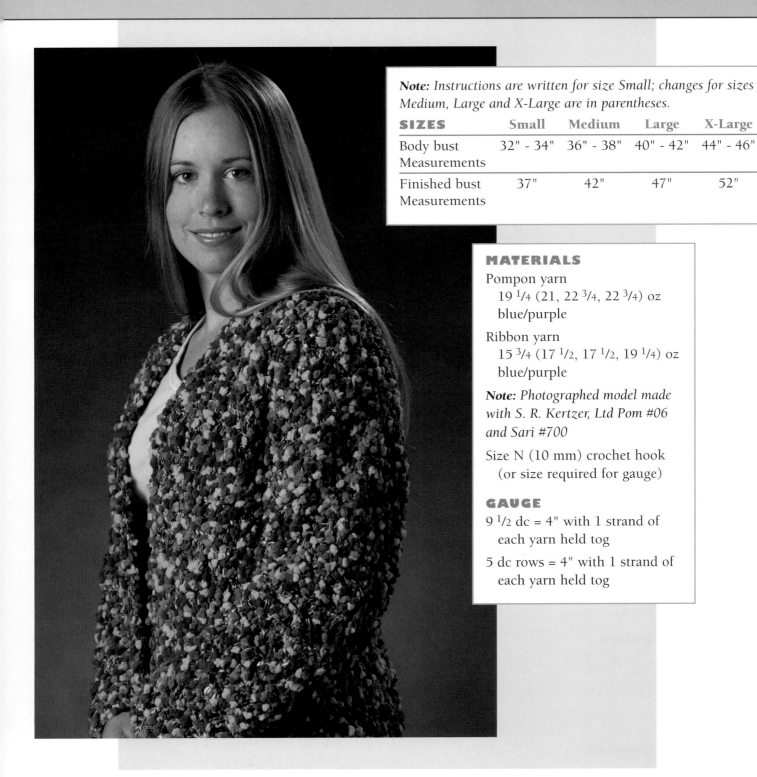

Note: *Instructions are written for size Small; changes for sizes Medium, Large and X-Large are in parentheses.*

SIZES	Small	Medium	Large	X-Large
Body bust Measurements	32" - 34"	36" - 38"	40" - 42"	44" - 46"
Finished bust Measurements	37"	42"	47"	52"

MATERIALS

Pompon yarn
  19 1/4 (21, 22 3/4, 22 3/4) oz
  blue/purple

Ribbon yarn
  15 3/4 (17 1/2, 17 1/2, 19 1/4) oz
  blue/purple

Note: *Photographed model made with S. R. Kertzer, Ltd Pom #06 and Sari #700*

Size N (10 mm) crochet hook
  (or size required for gauge)

GAUGE

9 1/2 dc = 4" with 1 strand of
  each yarn held tog

5 dc rows = 4" with 1 strand of
  each yarn held tog

INSTRUCTIONS

Note: Entire jacket is worked holding 1 strand of each yarn together.

Back

Ch 46 (52, 58, 64).

Row 1 (right side): Dc in 4th ch from hook and in each ch across: 44 (50, 56, 62) dc; ch 3 (counts as dc on next row now and throughout), turn.

Row 2: Dc in next st and in each st across; ch 3, turn.

Rep Row 2 until piece measures about 13" (14', 14", 16"), ending by working a wrong side row. At end of last row, do not ch 3.

Armhole Shaping

Row 1: Sl st in first 7 (8, 9, 10) sts, ch 3 (counts as dc), dc in next st and in each st across to last 6 (7, 8, 9) sts: 32 (36, 40, 44) dc; ch 3, turn.

Row 2: Dc in next st and in each st across; ch 3, turn.

Rep Row 2 until armhole measures about 9" (10", 11", 11"), ending by working a wrong side row. At end of last row, do not ch 3. Finish off; weave in ends.

Left Front

Ch 24 (27, 30, 33).

Row 1 (right side): Dc in 4th ch from hook and in each ch across: 22 (25, 28, 31) dc; ch 3, turn.

Row 2: Dc in next st and in each st across; ch 3, turn.

Rep Row 2 until piece measures about 13" (14", 14", 16"), ending by working a wrong side row. At end of last row, do not ch 3.

Armhole Shaping

Row 1: Sl st in first 7 (8, 9, 10) sts, ch 3 (counts as dc), dc in next st and in each st across to last st, 2 dc in last st: 17 (19, 21, 23) dc; ch 3, turn.

Row 2: Dc in next st and in each st across; ch 3, turn.

Row 3: Dc in next st and in each st across to last st, 2 dc in last st: 18 (20, 22, 24) dc; ch 3, turn.

Rep Row 2 until armhole measures about 9" (10", 11", 11"), ending by working a wrong side row. At end of last row, do not ch 3.

Collar Extension

Row 1: Sl st in first 10 (11, 12, 13) sts, ch 3 (counts as dc), dc in next st and in each st across: 9 (10, 11, 12) dc; ch 3, turn.

Rows 2 through 5 (5, 6, 6): Rep Row 2 of armhole shaping 4 (4, 5, 5) times more. At end of last row, do not ch 3. Finish off; weave in ends.

Right Front

Work same as left front to armhole shaping. At end of last row, ch 3, turn.

Armhole Shaping

Row 1: Dc in first st, dc in next st and in each st across to last 6 (7, 8, 9) sts: 17 (19, 21, 23) dc; ch 3, turn, leaving last 6 (7, 8, 9) sts unworked.

Row 2: Dc in next st and in each st across; ch 3, turn.

Row 3: Dc in first st, dc in next st and in each st across: 18 (20, 22, 24) dc; ch 3, turn.

Rep Row 2 until armhole measures about 9" (10", 11", 11"), ending by working a wrong side row.

Collar Extension

Row 1: Dc in next 8 (9, 10, 11) sts: 9 (10, 11, 12) dc; ch 3, turn, leaving last 9 (10, 11, 12) sts unworked.

Rows 2 through 5 (5, 6, 6): Rep Row 2 of armhole shaping 4 (4, 5, 5) times more. At end of last row, do not ch 3. Finish off; weave in ends.

Sleeves (make 2)

Ch 22 (24, 26, 28).

Row 1 (right side): Dc in 4th ch from hook and in each ch across: 20 (22, 24, 26) dc; ch 3, turn.

Row 2: Dc in first st, dc in next st and in each st across to last st, 2 dc in last st: 22 (24, 26, 28) dc; ch 3, turn.

Rows 3 through 5 (5, 7, 7): Rep Row 2 three (three, five, five) times more. At end of last row: 28 (30, 36, 38) dc.

Row 6 (6, 8, 8): Dc in next st and in each st across; ch 3, turn.

Rows 7 (7, 9, 9) through 22 (24, 24, 22): Rep Rows 2 and 6 (6, 8, 8) eight (nine, eight, seven) times more. At end of last row: 44 (48, 52, 52) dc.

Rep Row 6 (6, 8, 8) until sleeve measures about 21" (22", 22", 23"), or to desired length. At end of last row, do not ch 3. Finish off; weave in ends.

Finishing

Sew shoulder seams. Sew sleeves to front and back having center of sleeves at shoulder seams. Sew sleeve and side seams. Sew last row of collar extensions together, then sew back neck to inside edges of collar extensions. Turn collar down.

#64 BEARY CUTE JACKET

Designed by Michele Thompson for Coats & Clark

MATERIALS

Bulky weight yarn
  9 (11, 13, 15, 17) oz blue

Note: *Photographed model made with Red Heart® Baby Clouds™ # 9008 Cotton Candy*

One 1 ¹/8" diameter button

Separating zipper, 10" (12", 12", 14", 14") long

Sewing needle and sewing thread

Size P (15 mm) crochet hook (or size required for gauge)

Size K (6.5 mm) crochet hook

GAUGE

10 dc = 6" with larger hook

5 dc rows = 6"

Note: *Instructions are written for size 6 months; changes for 1, 2, 3 and 4 years are in parentheses.*

SIZES	6 months	1 year	2 years	3 years	4 years
Body Chest Measurement	18"	20"	22"	24"	26"
Finished Chest Measurement	22"	24 ¹/2"	27"	29 ¹/2"	31 ³/4"

STITCH GUIDE

Front Post double crochet (FPdc): YO, insert hook from front to back to front around post of specified st and draw up a lp; (YO and draw through 2 lps on hook) twice: FPdc made.

Back Post double crochet (BPdc): YO, insert hook from back to front to back around post of specified st and draw up a lp; (YO and draw through 2 lps on hook) twice: BPdc made.

#65 RAINBOW COVER-UP

Designed by Tammy C. Hildebrand

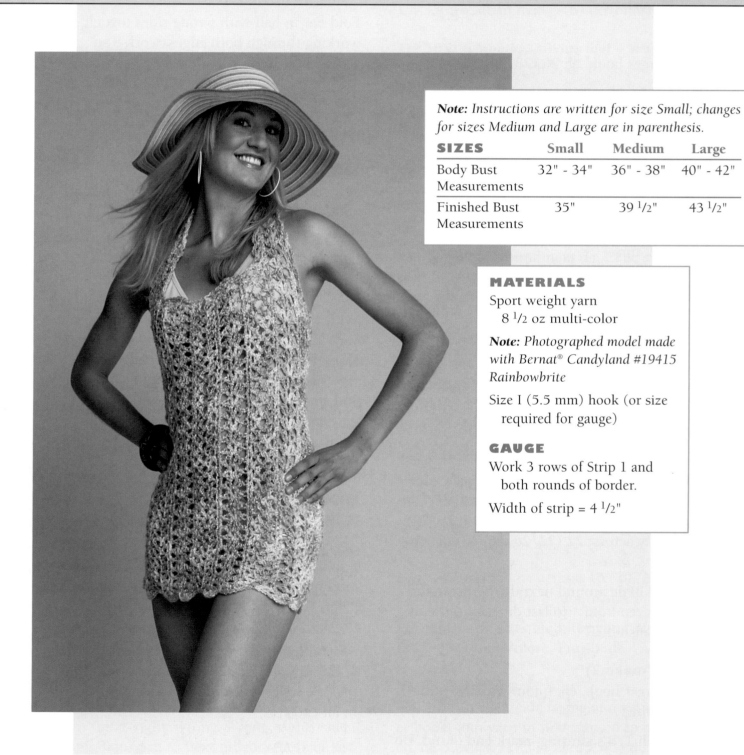

Note: *Instructions are written for size Small; changes for sizes Medium and Large are in parenthesis.*

SIZES	Small	Medium	Large
Body Bust Measurements	32" - 34"	36" - 38"	40" - 42"
Finished Bust Measurements	35"	39 $^1/_2$"	43 $^1/_2$"

MATERIALS

Sport weight yarn
  8 $^1/_2$ oz multi-color

Note: *Photographed model made with Bernat® Candyland #19415 Rainbowbrite*

Size I (5.5 mm) hook (or size
  required for gauge)

GAUGE

Work 3 rows of Strip 1 and
  both rounds of border.

Width of strip = 4 $^1/_2$"

INSTRUCTIONS

Garment consists of 8 (9, 10) strips that are joined to the previous strip as each strip is made. Weave in ends as each strip is completed.

Strip 1

Ch 9.

Row 1: Shell in 6th ch from hook (first 3 chs counts as 1 dc), skip next 2 chs, dc in last ch; ch 3, turn: 2 dc, 1 shell.

Row 2: Shell in center ch-1 sp, dc in 3rd ch; ch 3, turn.

Rep Row 2 thirty-four more times. After last row, ch 1; do not turn.

Border

Rnd 1: Working in row ends, (2 sc in each row) 36 times, ch 2; working in bottom lps of starting ch, sc in next 2 chs, sl st in next ch (under shell), sc in next 2 chs, ch 2; (2 sc in each row) 36 times, ch 2; sc in next 2 dc, sl st in center ch-1 sp, sc in next 2 dc, ch 2; join with sl st in beg sc: 152 sc.

Rnd 2: Sl st in next st, ch 6; dc in skipped beg sc; (skip next sc, dc in next sc, ch 3; dc in skipped sc) 35 times; 5 dc in next ch-2 sp, sc in same sp as sl st, 5 dc in next ch-2 sp; (skip next sc, dc in next sc, ch 3; dc in skipped sc) 36 times; (3 dc, ch 2, 3 dc) in ch-2 sp, skip next 2 sts, dc in sl st, (3 dc, ch 2, 3 dc) next ch-2 sp, join with sl st in 3rd ch of beg ch 6: 168 sts. Finish off.

Strips 2 and 3

Rep Rows 1 through 28 of Strip 1. At the end of Row 28, ch 1; do not turn.

Border

Rnd 1: Work in same manner as Rnd 1 of Strip 1 Border.

Rnd 2: Sl st in next st, ch 6; dc in skipped beg sc; (skip next sc, dc in next sc, ch3; dc in skipped sc) 27 times; 5 dc in next ch-2 sp, sc in same sp as sl st, 5 dc in next ch-2 sp; (skip next sc, dc in next sc; remove lp from hook, insert hook from the front in middle ch of corresponding ch-3 in previous strip, pull dropped lp through, ch 1) 28 times; (dc, ch 1; remove lp from hook, insert hook from the front in middle ch of corresponding ch-3 in previous strip, pull dropped lp through, ch 1; dc) in ch-2 sp, sk next 2 sts, (2 dc, ch 1, 2 dc) in sl st, sk next 2 sts, (dc, ch 3, dc) in next ch-2 sp, join with sl st in 3rd ch of beg ch-6: 131 sts. Finish off.

Strip 4

Rep Rows 1 through 34 of Strip 1.

Border

Rnd 1: Work in same manner as Rnd 1 of Strip 1 Border.

Rnd 2: Ch 6, dc in skipped beg sc; (skip next sc, dc in next sc, ch 3; dc in skipped sc) 35 times; 5 dc in next ch-2 sp, sc in same sp as sl st, 5 dc in next ch-2 sp; (skip next sc, dc in next sc; remove lp from hook, insert hook from the front in middle ch of corresponding ch-3 in previous strip, pull dropped lp through, ch 1) 29 times; (skip next sc, dc in next sc, ch 3; dc in skipped sc) 7 times; (3 dc, ch 2, 3 dc) in ch-2 sp, sk next 2 sts, dc in sl st, (3 dc, ch 2, 3 dc) next ch-2 sp, join with sl st in 3rd ch of beg ch 6: 168 sts. Finish off.

Strips 5 through 7
(5 through 8, 5 through 9)
Rep Rows 1 through 28 of Strip 2.

Border
Rnd 1: Work in same manner as Rnd 1 of Strip 1 Border.

Rnd 2: Ch 6, dc in skipped beg sc; (skip next sc, dc in next sc, ch 3; dc in skipped sc) 27 times; 5 dc in next ch-2 sp, sc in same sp as sl st, 5 dc in next ch-2 sp; (skip next sc, dc in next sc; remove lp from hook, insert hook from the front in middle ch of corresponding ch-3 in previous strip, pull dropped lp through, ch 1) 28 times; sc in ch-2 sp, sc in next 4 sc, sc in ch-2 sp, join with sl st in 3rd ch of beg ch 6: 129 sts. Finish off.

Strip 8 (9, 10)
Rep Rows 2 through 28 of Strip 2.

Border
Rnd 1: Work in same manner as Rnd 1 of Strip 1 Border.

Rnd 2: Sl st in next st, ch 4, drop lp and insert hook from the front in corresponding ch-3 on first strip, pick up dropped lp and draw through, ch 1, dc in skipped sc: (sk next sc, dc in next sc; remove lp from hook, insert hook from the front in middle ch of corresponding ch-3 in first strip, pull dropped lp through, ch 1) 27 times; 5 dc in next ch-2 sp, sc in same sp as sl st, 5 dc in next ch-2 sp; (sk next sc, dc in next sc; remove lp from hook, insert hook from the front in middle ch of corresponding ch-3 in previous strip;) 28 times, sc in next ch-2 sp, sc in next 4 sts, sc in next ch-2 sp, join with sl st in 3rd ch of beg ch-4. Finish off.

Back Shaping
Working in sts across Strips 5 through 8 (9, 10), join with sc in first sc of Strip 5, [(sc2tog) twice, sc in next st, (dc, ch 1, dc) in center of strip joining, sc in next st] 3 (4, 5) times, (sc2tog) twice, sc in last st. Finish off.

Matching stitches of Strips 1 and 4, with tapestry needle, sew seam.

#66 SWEET SACHET

Designed by Janie Herrin

SIZE

4" diameter

MATERIALS

Size 10 crochet thread white

Note: Photographed model made with Royale Classic Crochet Thread #201 White

18" satin ribbon, 3/8" wide

Small amount fiber fill

Scented oil

Size 7 (1.65 mm) steel crochet hook (or size required for gauge)

GAUGE

16 dc = 2"

STITCH GUIDE

Shell: (2 dc, ch 2, 2 dc) in sp indicated: shell made.

INSTRUCTIONS

Top

Ch 5, join with sl st to form a ring.

Rnd 1: Ch 3 (counts as a dc), 15 dc in ring, join with sl st in 3rd ch of beg ch-3: 16 dc.

Rnd 2: Ch 6 (counts as first dc plus ch-3 sp); * dc in next dc, ch 3; rep from * around, join in 3rd ch of beg ch-6: 16 ch-3 sps.

Rnd 3: Ch 1, sc in same st; *ch 2, sc in next ch-3 sp, ch 2, sc in next dc; rep from * around, ending with ch 1, sc in beg sc to form last ch-2 sp: 32 ch-2 sps.

Rnds 4 through 7: Ch 1, sc in same sp; *ch 2, sc in next ch-2 sp; rep from * around, ending last rep with ch 1, sc in beg sc.

Rnd 8: Ch 7; *tr in next ch-2 sp, ch 3; rep from * around, join with sl st in 4th ch of beg ch-7.

Rnd 9: Sl st in next sp, ch 3, in same sp work (dc, ch 2, 2 dc); *ch 2, sc in next sp, ch 2, shell in next sp; rep from * around, ending last rep with ch 2, join in 3rd ch of beg ch-3: 16 shells. Finish off; weave in ends.

Bottom

Work same as top.

Finishing

Apply scent to fiber fill, set aside.

Hold Top and Bottom with wrong sides tog; weave ribbon through Rnd 8 on both pieces; insert scented fiber fill before closing. Tie ribbon in a bow.

PICK A PRETTY PAIR

Designed by Vashti Braha

Note: *Instructions are written for size Small; changes for sizes Medium and Large are in parentheses.*

SKIRT SIZES	Small	Medium	Large
Body hip Measurements	32" - 34"	36" - 38"	40" - 42"
Finished hip Measurements	34 1/4"	37 3/4"	41 3/4"

Length: About 22" laid flat (stretches to about 25" while worn)

STOLE SIZE

18" wide x 70" long (stretches to 84" while worn)

MATERIALS

Worsted weight yarn
 21 (24 1/2, 28) oz gray (for skirt)
 31 1/2 oz gray (for stole)

Note: *Photographed model made with Patons Katrina #10217 Frost*

Size H (5 mm) crochet hook (or size required for gauge for skirt)

Size K (6.5 mm) crochet hook (or size required for gauge for stole)

1/8" wide braided elastic, 2 - 3 yds

Stitch markers

SKIRT GAUGE

14 linked tr = 4"

2 rows sc plus 2 rows linked tr = 2 1/8"

STOLE GAUGE

11 linked tr = 4"

3 rows sc plus 3 rows linked tr = 3 3/4"

Beginning linked treble (beg linked tr): Insert hook in one lp of 2nd ch from hook and draw up a lp, insert hook in one lp of next ch from hook and draw up a lp, insert hook in top of first st and draw up a lp, (YO and draw through 2 lps on hook) 3 times: beg linked tr made.

Linked treble (linked tr): Insert hook in first horizontal bar below top of previous linked tr and draw up a lp, insert hook in next horizontal bar below first horizontal bar of same linked tr and draw up a lp, insert hook in top of next st and draw up a lp, (YO and draw through 2 lps on hook) 3 times: linked tr made.

Slanted puff stitch (slanted puff st): (YO, insert hook in specified st and draw up a $3/4"$ lp) 3 times; (YO, insert hook in next specified st and draw up a $1/4"$ lp) 2 times; hold hook at 45 degree angle, pull up on lps so they are taut, YO and draw through all 11 lps on hook: slanted puff st made.

Half slanted puff stitch (half slanted puff st): (YO, insert hook in specified st and draw up a $3/4"$ lp) 3 times, YO and draw through all 7 lps on hook: half slanted puff st made.

Sc decrease (sc dec): (Insert hook in specified st and draw up a lp) two times, YO and draw through all 3 lps on hook: sc dec made.

SKIRT

INSTRUCTIONS

Starting at bottom, ch 121 (133, 147).

Row 1 (wrong side): Sc in 2nd ch from hook and in each ch across: 120 (132, 146) sc; ch 4, turn.

Row 2 (right side): Work beg linked tr, work linked tr in each st across: 1 beg linked tr and 119 (131, 145) linked tr; ch 1, turn.

Row 3: Sc in both lps of first st, sc in front lp of next st and in front lp of each st across to last st, sc in both lps of last st: 120 (132, 146) sc; ch 4, turn.

Row 4: Rep Row 2. At end of row, ch 2 instead of ch 1.

Row 5: Hdc in first st; *ch 1, skip next st, hdc in next st; rep from * across to last st; hdc in last st: 61 (67, 74) hdc and 59 (65, 72) chs; ch 1, turn.

Row 6: Sc in space between first 2 hdc, 2 sc in each ch-1 sp across, sc in space between last hdc and turning ch-2: 120 (132, 146) sc; ch 3, turn.

Row 7: Work slanted puff st in first 2 sts; *ch 1, work slanted puff st in same st as end of last slanted puff st and in st after next st (skip one st in center of slanted puff st); rep from * across to last 2 sts; ch 1, work slanted puff st in same st as end of last slanted puff st and in next st, dc in last st: 60 (66, 73) slanted puff sts, 59 (65, 72) chs and 1 dc; ch 3, turn.

Row 8: Work slanted puff st in top of first 2 slanted puff sts (skip ch between slanted puff sts); *ch 1, work slanted puff st in top of same st as end of last slanted puff st and in top of next slanted puff st (skip ch between slanted puff sts); rep from * across to last slanted puff st; ch 1, work half slanted puff st in top of same st as end of last slanted puff st, dc in 3rd ch of turning ch-3: 59 (65, 72) slanted puff sts, 1 half slanted puff st, 59 (65, 72) chs and 1 dc; ch 2, turn.

Row 9: Hdc in top of half slanted puff st; *ch 1, skip next st, hdc in top of next slanted puff st; rep from * across; hdc in 3rd ch of turning ch-3: 61 (67, 74) hdc and 59 (65, 72) chs; ch 4, turn.

Row 10: Work beg linked tr; *work linked tr in next hdc, work linked tr in next ch; rep from * across; work linked tr in last hdc: 1 beg linked tr and 119 (131, 145) linked tr; ch 1, turn.

Rep Rows 3 and 2 until skirt measures about 16" (for 22" long skirt laid flat), or to desired length. Place stitch markers in first, last, and middle st of last row.

Waist Shaping

Row 1: Sc in first st, sc dec in front lp of next 2 sts, sc in front lp of each st across to 2 sts before middle stitch marker; sc dec in front lp of next 2 sts; sc in front lp of next st, sc dec in front lp of next 2 sts; sc in front lp of each st across to last 3 sts; sc dec in front lp of next 2 sts, sc in last st: 116 (128, 142) sc; ch 4, turn.

Row 2: Rep Row 2: 1 beg linked tr and 115 (127, 141) linked tr. Place stitch marker in linked tr above middle stitch marker.

Rows 3 through 6: Rep Rows 1 and 2 of waist shaping two times more. At end of Row 5: 108 (120, 134) sc. At end of Row 6: 1 beg linked tr and 107 (119, 133) linked tr.

Row 7: Sc in first st, (sc dec in front lp of next 2 sts) 2 times, sc in front lp of each st across to 4 sts before middle stitch marker; (sc dec in front lp of next 2 sts) 2 times; sc in front lp of next st, (sc dec in front lp of next 2 sts) 2 times; sc in front lp of each st across to last 5 sts; (sc dec in front lp of next 2 sts) 2 times, sc in last st: 100 (112, 126) sc; ch 4, turn.

Rows 8 through 12: Rep Rows 2 and 7 of waist shaping two times more, then rep Row 2 once more. At end of Row 11: 84 (96, 110) sc. At end of Row 12: 1 beg linked tr and 83 (95, 109) linked tr. At end of Row 12, do not ch 4. Finish off; weave in ends.

Sew side seam.

Puff Border Hem

With right side facing, join with sl st in sc at side seam, ch 3, work slanted puff st in same st as joining and in next st; *ch 1, work slanted puff st in same st as end of last slanted puff st and in st after next st (skip one st in center of slanted puff st); rep from * across to last st; ch 1, work slanted puff st in same st as end of last slanted puff st and in same st as beg ch-3: 59 (65, 72) slanted puff sts and 59 (65, 72) chs; ch 1, join with sl st in 3rd ch of beg ch-3. Finish off; weave in ends.

Elasticized Waistband

Cut 2 pieces of elastic 6" longer than waist measurement.

Row 1: With right side facing, join with sl st in side seam, ch 2 (counts as hdc), hdc over first piece of elastic in next st and in each st across top of skirt: 84 (96, 110) hdc; join with sl st in 2nd ch of beg ch-2.

Row 2: Ch 2, hdc over second piece of elastic in next st and in each st across; join with sl st in 2nd ch of beg ch-2. Finish off; weave in ends.

Adjust elastic as necessary, tie knot and weave in ends.

STOLE

INSTRUCTIONS

First Half
Ch 195.

Row 1 (wrong side): Sc in 2nd ch from hook and in each ch across: 194 sc; ch 4, turn.

Row 2 (right side): Work beg linked tr, work linked tr in each st across: 1 beg linked tr and 193 linked tr; ch 1, turn.

Row 3: Sc in both lps of first st, sc in front lp of next st and in front lp of each st across to last st, sc in both lps of last st: 194 sc; ch 4, turn.

Rows 4 and 5: Rep Rows 2 and 3.

Row 6: Rep Row 2. At end of row, ch 2 instead of ch 1.

Row 7: Hdc in first st; *ch 1, skip next st, hdc in next st; rep from * across to last st; hdc in last st: 98 hdc and 96 chs; ch 1, turn.

Row 8: Sc in space between first 2 hdc, 2 sc in each ch-1 sp across, sc in space between last hdc and turning ch-2: 194 sc; ch 4, turn.

Row 9: Work slanted puff st in first 2 sts; *ch 1, work slanted puff st in same st as end of last slanted puff st and in st after next st (skip one st in center of slanted puff st); rep from * across to last 2 sts; ch 1, work slanted puff st in same st as end of last slanted puff st and in next st, dc in last st: 97 slanted puff sts, 96 chs and 1 dc; ch 4, turn.

Row 10: Work slanted puff st in top of first 2 slanted puff sts (skip ch between slanted puff sts); *ch 1, work slanted puff st in top of same st as end of last slanted puff st and in top of next slanted puff st (skip ch between slanted puff sts); rep from * across to last slanted puff st; ch 1, work half slanted puff st in top of same st as end of last slanted puff st, dc in 3rd ch of turning ch-4: 96 slanted puff sts, 1 half slanted puff st, 96 chs and 1 dc; ch 2, turn.

Row 11: Hdc in top of half slanted puff st; *ch 1, skip next st, hdc in top of next slanted puff st; rep from * across; hdc in 4th ch of turning ch-4: 98 hdc and 96 chs; ch 4, turn.

Row 12: Work beg linked tr; *work linked tr in next hdc, work linked tr in next ch; rep from * across; work linked tr in last hdc: 1 beg linked tr and 193 linked tr; ch 1, turn.

Rows 13 and 14: Rep Rows 3 and 2. At end of Row 14, ch 3 instead of ch 1.

Row 15: Work short slanted puff st (with three 3/4" lps and two 1/4" lps) in first st and in st after next st (skip one st in center of short slanted puff st); *ch 1, work short slanted puff st in same st as end of last short slanted puff st and in st after next st (skip one st in center of short slanted puff st); rep from * across to last st; ch 1, work short half slanted puff st (with three 3/4" lps) in same st as end of last short slanted puff st, dc in last st: 96 short slanted puff sts, 1 short half slanted puff st, 96 chs and 1 dc. Finish off; weave in ends.

Second Half
Row 1: With right side facing, join with sl st around first sc on Row 1 of first half, ch 4, work beg linked tr, work linked tr in each st across: 1 beg linked tr and 193 linked tr; ch 1, turn.

Rows 2 through 12: Rep Rows 5 through 15 on first half.

#69 SHEEP MITTENS

Designed by Kathleen Stuart

SIZE
Child size (up to 2 1/2" wide at palm)

MATERIALS
Worsted weight yarn
  3 oz off-white
  3 oz black
  1 yd blue
  1 yd pink

Note: *Photographed model made with Lion Brand® Wool-Ease® #99 Fisherman and #153 Black*

Size G (4 mm) crochet hook (or size required for gauge)

Tapestry needle

Stitch marker

INSTRUCTIONS

Note: *Do not join rnds unless otherwise noted; mark first stitch in each rnd with a stitch marker.*

Mitten (make 2)
With black, ch 24, sl st in first ch to form a ring.

Rnd 1: Ch 3 (counts as dc), dc in next ch and in each ch around: 24 dc; join with sl st in 3rd ch of beg ch-3.

Rnds 2 through 5: Ch 2 (counts as dc), FPdc in next st; *BPdc in next st, FPdc in next st; rep from * around: 12 FPdc, 11 BPdc and 1 dc; join with sl st in 2nd ch of beg ch-2. At end of Rnd 5, change to off-white in last FPdc.

Rnd 6: Ch 1, sc in same ch as joining, sc in next 2 sts, 2 sc in next st; *sc in next 3 sts, 2 sc in next st; rep from * 3 times more; sc in last 4 sts: 29 sc.

Rnd 7: *Sc in next st, tr in next st; rep from * around to last st, ending with sc in last st: 15 sc and 14 tr.

Rnd 8: *Tr in next st, sc in next st; rep from * around to last st, ending with tr in last st: 14 sc and 15 tr.

Rnds 9 through 11: Rep Rnds 7 and 8 once, then rep Rnd 7.

Rnd 12: Ch 6, skip first 10 sts; *tr in next st, sc in next st; rep from * around to last st, ending with tr in last st: 10 tr, 9 sc and 6 chs.

Rnd 13: Sc in first ch, tr in next ch; *sc in next ch, tr in next ch; rep from * once; **sc in next st, tr in next st; rep from ** around to last st, ending with sc in last st: 13 sc and 12 tr.

Rnds 14 through 21: Rep Rnds 8 and 7 four times more.

Rnd 22: *Tr in next st, sc in next st, sc dec in next 2 sts; rep from * around to last st, ending with tr in last st: 7 tr and 12 sc.

Rnd 23: *Sc in next st, sc dec in next 2 sts; rep from * around to last st, ending with sc in last st: 13 sc.

Rnd 24: *Sc dec in next 2 sts; rep from * around to last st, ending with sc in last st: 7 sc. Finish off. Using tapestry needle, draw yarn through sts to close up opening.

Thumb

Rnd 1: Join black with sc in first skipped st on Rnd 12, sc in next 9 skipped sts, sc in free lp of each of 6 chs added on Rnd 12: 16 sc.

Rnd 2: Sc in each st around.

Rnd 3: *Sc in next 6 sts, sc dec in next 2 sts; rep from * once: 14 sc.

Rnds 4 through 10: Sc in each st around.

Rnd 11: *Sc dec in next 2 sts; rep from * around: 7 sc. Finish off. Using tapestry needle, draw yarn through sts to close up opening.

Face (make 2)

With black, ch 2.

Rnd 1: 6 sc in 2nd ch from hook: 6 sc.

Rnd 2: *Sc in next st, 2 sc in next st; rep from * around: 9 sc.

Rnd 3: *Sc in next 2 sts, 2 sc in next st; rep from * around: 12 sc.

Rnd 4: *Sc in next st, 2 sc in next st; rep from * around: 18 sc.

Rnd 5: *Sc in next 2 sts, 2 sc in next st; rep from * around: 24 sc.

Rnd 6 (ear rnd): Sl st in next st, ch 6, sc in 2nd ch from hook and in next 4 chs, skip next st on Rnd 5, sl st in next 5 sts, ch 6, sc in 2nd ch from hook and in next 4 chs, skip next st on Rnd 5, sl st in next st. Finish off, leaving 10" length for sewing.

Sew face on top side of each mitten as shown in photograph, making sure to sew face on opposite side of each mitten for pair. Embroider eyes with blue yarn and nose with pink yarn using small straight stitches as shown in photograph.

#70 RIBBON FRINGE SHAWL

Designed by Janie Herrin

SIZE
54" wide x 35" long
   before fringe

MATERIALS
Worsted weight mohair
   sparkle yarn
   7 1/2 oz violet

Bulky weight ribbon yarn
   220 yds multicolored

Note: *Photographed model
made with Anna Gratton's
Filaro Sparkle Mohair Violet
and Lion Brand® Incredible
#201 Rainbow*

Size N (10 mm) crochet hook
   (or size required for gauge)

GAUGE
10 dc = 4"

INSTRUCTIONS

Beginning at center of neck edge, ch 4, join with a sl st to form a ring.

Row 1: Ch 4 (equals 1 dc and 1 ch-1 sp); in ring work (V-st, ch 3, V-st, ch 1, dc): 6 dc; ch 3, turn.

Row 2: Dc in first dc (increase made); (dc in next ch-1 sp and in next dc) twice, shell in ch-3 sp; (dc in next dc, dc in next ch-1 sp) twice, 2 dc in 3rd ch of ch-4 (increase made): 16 dc; ch 3, turn.

Row 3: Dc in first dc (increase made) and in each dc across to ch-3 sp; shell in ch-3 sp, dc in each rem dc, 2 dc in 3rd ch of turning ch (increase made); ch 4 (counts as a dc and ch-1 sp), turn.

Row 4: Dc in first dc; *ch 1, skip next dc, dc in next dc; rep from * to ch-3 sp, ch 1, work V-st Shell in ch-3 sp, ch 1; **dc in next dc, ch 1, skip next dc; rep from ** to last dc, ch 1, V-st in 3rd ch of turning ch; ch 4, turn.

Row 5: Dc in first dc, (ch 1, dc in next dc) across to ch-3 sp, ch 1, V-st Shell in ch-3 sp; (ch 1, dc in next dc) across to last dc, ch 1, V-st in 3rd ch of turning ch; ch 3, turn.

Row 6: Dc in first dc; *dc in ch-1 sp and in next dc*; rep from * to * to ch-3 sp, in sp work shell; rep from * to * to last st, 2 dc in 3rd ch of turning ch; ch 3, turn.

Rows 7 through 22: Rep Rows 3 through 6 consecutively, ending by working a Row 6.

At end of last row, do not finish off, do not turn.

Edging

Ch 1, work corner of (sc, ch 3, sc) in same st as last dc made; working across long shoulder edge, 2 sc in end st of each row, work corner as before in top of last dc; working across last 2 sides, sc in each dc and in each ch-1 sp, working corner in ch-3 sp of point, end with sl st in beg sc. Finish off; weave in ends.

Ribbon Fringe

Cut ribbon yarn into one-yard lengths. Following fringe instructions on page 255, knot one strand in each sc along each side edge; trim if desired..

SARONG

SIZE
About 40" wide x 28" long

MATERIALS
Sport weight yarn
  14 oz blue
  1 ³/₄ oz white
  1 ³/₄ oz red

Note: Photographed model made with Patons® Grace #60733 Peacock, #60005 Snow and #60438 Fuchsia

Size 7 (4.5 mm) crochet hook
  (or size required for gauge)

Stitch Markers

GAUGE
17 dc = 4"

8 dc rows = 4"

INSTRUCTIONS

Starting at lower edge with blue, ch 150.

Row 1 (right side): Work dc cl inserting hook first in 4th ch from hook (3 skipped chs count as dc), ch 1; *work dc cl inserting hook first in same ch as end of previous dc cl, ch 1; rep from * across; dc in same ch as last dc cl: 73 dc cl, 73 ch-1 sps and 2 dc; ch 3 (counts as dc on next row now and throughout), turn.

Dc cluster (dc cl): *YO, insert hook in specified ch or st, YO and draw up a lp, YO and draw through 2 lps on hook*, skip next ch or st; rep from * to * in next ch or st, YO and draw through all 3 lps on hook: dc cl made.

Reverse sc (rev sc): Ch 1; *Insert hook in st to right of previous st, YO and draw up a lp. YO and draw through both lps on hook; rep from *: rev sc made.

Work Around Post: To work around the post (vertical bar) of a st, insert hook from front to back to front around specified st, complete st in usual manner.

Picot: Ch 3, sl st in 3rd ch from hook: picot made.

Long sc: Insert hook in top of next st 3 rnds below, YO and draw up a lp to height of current row, YO and draw through both lps on hook: long sc made.

To change color: Work st until 2 lps rem on hook, drop old color, pick up new color and draw through both lps on hook, cut dropped color.

Hdc decrease (hdc dec): (YO, insert hook in next st, YO and draw up a lp) twice, YO and draw through all 5 lps on hook: hdc dec made.

Row 2: Work dc cl inserting hook first in next ch, ch 1; *work dc cl inserting hook first in same ch as end of previous dc cl, ch 1; rep from * across; dc in same ch as end of last dc cl; ch 3, turn.

Row 3: 2 dc in first st, work dc cl inserting hook first in next ch, ch 1; *work dc cl inserting hook first in same ch as end of previous dc cl, ch 1; rep from * across; 3 dc in same ch as end of last dc cl: 73 dc cl, 73 ch-1 sps and 6 dc; ch 3, turn.

Row 4: Work dc cl inserting hook first in middle dc of 3 dc, ch 1; *work dc cl inserting hook first in same st as end of previous dc cl, ch 1; rep from * across; dc in same ch as end of last dc cl: 75 dc cl, 75 ch-1 sps and 2 dc; ch 3, turn.

Rows 5 through 34: Rep Rows 3 and 4 fifteen times more. At end of Row 34: 105 dc cl, 105 ch-1 sps and 2 dc.

Rows 35 through 52: Rep Row 2 eighteen times more. At end of Row 52, ch 1 instead of ch 3.

Row 53 (top edge): Sc in each st across: 212 sc. Finish off; weave in ends.

Edging

Place markers on both sides of Row 33, 21 rows down from top edge. With right side facing, join fuchsia with sl st around dc post (vertical bar) at marker on left side.

Row 1: Ch 1, sc around same dc post as joining, work 2 sc in each ch-3 sp and around each dc post along left side to corner st (first ch of foundation ch), 3 sc in free lp of corner st, sc in free lp of next 146 foundation chs to next corner st (148th ch of foundation ch), 3 sc in free lp of corner st, work 2 sc in each ch-3 sp and around each dc post, ending with 2 sc in marked ch-3 sp on right side: 283 sc; ch 4 (counts as dc and ch-1 sp on next row), turn.

Row 2: Skip first 2 sc, dc in next sc; *ch 1, skip next sc, dc in next sc*; rep from * to * 31 times more; **ch 1, skip next sc, (dc, ch 1, dc) in next sc (corner ch-1 sp made)**; rep from * to * 73 times more; rep from ** to ** once; rep from * to * 33 times more: 144 dc and 143 ch-1 sps; ch 2 (counts as hdc on next row), turn.

Row 3: Skip first dc; *hdc in next ch-1 sp, hdc in next dc; rep from * around, working 3 hdc in corner ch-1 sps: 291 hdc. Finish off.

Row 4: With wrong side facing, join white with sl st in beg ch-3 sp on right side of Row 33, ch 3, sl st around dc post at edge of Row 2 of Edging, ch 3, sc in top of last hdc on Row 3 of Edging; *(sc, ch 5, sc) in next hdc, sc in each of next 7 hdc; rep from * to last 2 hdc; (sc, ch 5, sc) in next hdc, sc in last hdc, ch 3, sl st around dc post at edge of Row 2 of Edging, ch 3, sl st around dc post on left side of Row 33: 328 sc, 37 ch-5 sps, 4 ch-3 sps and 4 sl st. Finish off.

Row 5: With right side facing, join white with sc in last sc on Row 4 of Edging, skip sc at base of next ch-5; *(hdc, 11 dc, hdc) in next ch-5 sp, skip sc at base of same ch-5 and next sc, sc in each of next 5 sc, skip next sc and sc at base of next ch-5; rep from * to last ch-5 sp; (hdc, 11 dc, hdc) in last ch-5 sp, skip sc at base of same ch-5, sc in last sc: 182 sc, 74 hdc and 407 dc. Finish off.

Row 6: With right side facing, join blue with sl st in edge of last sc on Row 53, ch 1, sc in same st; 2 sc in each ch-3 sp and around each dc post on left side down to and including Row 34; ch 1, sc in last ch-3 sp on Row 4 of Edging, ch 3, sc in next ch-3 sp, ch 4, sc in first sc on Row 5 of Edging; *skip next hdc and next 3 dc, (sc in next dc, picot, ch 1, skip next dc) twice; sc in next dc, picot, ch 4, skip next 3 dc and next hdc, sc in next sc**; ch 4, skip next 3 sc, sc in next sc, ch 4; rep from * around, ending at **, ch 4, sc in 2nd ch-3 sp on Row 4 of Edging, ch 3, sc in next ch-3 sp, ch 1, 2 sc around dc post on right side of Row 34, 2 sc in each ch-3 sp and around each dc post on right side up to and including Row 52, sc in edge of first sc on Row 53. Finish off; weave in ends.

HALTER TOP

SIZE
One adjustable size

MATERIALS
Sport weight yarn
   5 1/4 oz green
   1 3/4 oz white
   1 3/4 oz fuchsia

Note: Photographed model made with Patons® Grace #60712 Lime, #60005 Snow and #60438 Fuchsia

Size E (3.5 mm) crochet hook

Size C (2.75 mm) crochet hooks (or size required for gauge)

GAUGE
22 hdc = 4" with C hook

15 hdc rows = 4"

INSTRUCTIONS

With C hook and green, ch 111.

Row 1 (right side): Hdc in 3rd ch from hook (2 skipped chs count as hdc), hdc in each rem ch across: 110 hdc; ch 2 (counts as hdc on next row now and throughout), turn.

Row 2: Skip first hdc, hdc in each rem hdc across: 110 hdc; ch 3 (counts as dc on next row now and throughout), turn.

Row 3: Work dc cl inserting hook first in next hdc, ch 1; *work dc cl inserting hook first in same hdc as end of previous dc cl, ch 1; rep from * across; dc in same ch as end of last dc cl: 54 dc cl, 54 ch-1 sps and 2 dc; ch 3, turn.

Row 4: Work dc cl inserting hook first in next ch, ch 1; *work dc cl inserting hook first in same ch as end of previous dc cl, ch 1; rep from * across; dc in same ch as end of last dc cl: 54 dc cl, 54 ch-1 sps and 2 dc; ch 3, turn.

Rows 5 and 6: Rep Row 4 two times more. At end of Row 6, ch 2 instead of ch 3.

Row 7: Skip first st, hdc in each st or ch-1 sp across, hdc in 3rd ch of turning ch-3: 110 hdc; ch 2, turn.

Row 8: Skip first hdc, hdc in each hdc across: 110 hdc; ch 3, turn.

Rows 9 through 12: Rep Rows 3 through 6.

Row 13: Rep Row 7.

Rows 14 through 24: Rep Row 8 eleven times more. At end of Row 24, do not ch 3.

Front Shaping

Row 25 (right side): Sl st in each of first 19 hdc, ch 2 (counts as hdc), hdc in each of next 73 hdc: 74 hdc; ch 2, turn, leaving rem 18 hdc unworked.

Row 26: Hdc dec in next 2 sts, hdc in each hdc to last 2 sts, hdc dec in last 2 sts: 72 sts; ch 2, turn.

Rows 27 through 43: Rep Row 26 seventeen times more: 2 sts fewer on each row than previous row. At end of Row 43: 38 sts.

Left Front Shaping

Row 44: Hdc dec in next 2 sts, hdc in each of next 8 hdc, hdc dec in next 2 sts: 11 sts; ch 2, turn, leaving rem 26 sts unworked.

Rows 45 through 47: Hdc dec in first 2 sts, hdc in each hdc to last 2 sts, hdc dec in last 2 sts; ch 2, turn. At end of Row 47: 5 sts.

Row 48: (Hdc dec in next 2 sts) twice: 3 sts; ch 2, turn.

Row 49: Hdc dec in next 2 sts: 2 sts. Finish off; weave in ends.

Right Front Shaping

Row 44: With wrong side facing, skip next 13 sts on Row 43, join green with sl st in next st, ch 2 (counts as hdc), hdc dec in next 2 sts, hdc in each of next 8 hdc, hdc dec in last 2 sts: 11 sts; ch 2, turn.

Rows 45 through 49: Rep Rows 45 through 49 on Left Front Shaping.

Finishing

With right side facing and C hook, join green with sl st around ch-2 on Row 25 of Front Shaping after 19 sl sts, ch 1, sc in same sp, work 29 more sc along left side to neck edge, ch 70 for left neck tie, sl st in 2nd ch from hook and in each ch across; work 1 row of sc evenly around neck edge, ch 70 for right neck tie, sl st in 2nd ch from hook and in each ch across, work 30 sc down right side to last hdc on Row 25. Finish off; weave in ends.

With right side facing, join green with sl st in top corner of Right Back opening, work 40 sc evenly down side edge of Back opening. Rep for left side joining green with sl st in bottom corner of Left Back opening.

Bottom Edging

Row 1: Hold piece with right side facing and beg ch at top; working in unused lps of beg ch with C hook, join fuchsia with sl st in first lp, ch 1, sc in each rem lp across to last lp, 2 sc in last lp: 111 sc; ch 4 (counts as dc and ch-1 sp on next row), turn.

Row 2: Skip first 2 sc, dc in next sc; *ch 1, skip next sc, dc in next sc; rep from * across: 56 dc and 55 ch-1 sps; ch 2 (counts as hdc on next row), turn.

Row 3: *Hdc in next ch-1 sp, hdc in next dc; rep from * across, changing to white in last st: 111 hdc; ch 1, turn.

Row 4: Sc in each of first 7 hdc, *(sc, ch 5, sc) in next hdc, sc in each of next 7 hdc; rep from * to last 8 hdc; (sc, ch 5, sc) in next hdc, sc in each of last 7 hdc: 124 sc and 13 ch-5 sps; ch 1, turn.

Row 5: Sc in first 6 sc, skip next sc and sc at base of next ch-5; *(hdc, 11 dc, hdc) in next ch-5 sp, skip sc at base of same ch-5 and next sc, sc in each of next 5 sc, skip next sc and sc at base of next ch-5; rep from * to last ch-5 sp; (hdc, 11 dc, hdc) in last ch-5 sp, skip sc at base of same ch-5 and next sc, sc in last 6 sc, changing to blue in last sc; ch 1, turn.

Row 6: Sc in first sc, ch 5, skip next 4 sc, sc in next sc; *skip next hdc and next 3 dc; (sc in next dc, picot, ch 1, skip next dc) twice; sc in next dc, picot, ch 4, skip next 3 dc and next hdc, sc in next sc**, ch 4, skip next 3 sc, sc in next sc, ch 4; rep from * across, ending at **; ch 5, skip next 4 sc, sc in last sc. Finish off; weave in ends.

Cord

With E hook and 2 strands of green, ch 270. Finish off; weave in ends. Thread cord through Left and Right Back edges as shown in photograph.

TOTE BAG

SIZE
13" wide x 15" long

MATERIALS
Sport weight yarn
  1 ³/₄ oz blue
  1 ³/₄ oz green
  3 ¹/₂ oz white
  1 ³/₄ oz red

Note: Photographed model made with Patons® Grace #60733 Peacock, #60712 Lime, #60005 Snow and #60438 Fuchsia

Size 7 (4.5 mm) crochet hook

Sizes C (2.75 mm) crochet hook (or size required for gauge)

GAUGE
22 dc = 4" with C hook

11 dc rows = 4" with C hook

INSTRUCTIONS

Front

Center Strip
With C hook and green, ch 30.

Row 1 (right side): Inserting hook first in 4th ch from hook (3 skipped chs count as dc), work dc cl, ch 1; *work dc cl inserting hook first in same ch as end of previous dc cl, ch 1; rep from * across; dc in same ch as last dc cl: 13 dc cl, 13 ch-1 sps and 2 dc; ch 3 (counts as dc on next row now and throughout), turn.

Row 2: Work dc cl, inserting hook first in next ch, ch 1; *work dc cl, inserting hook first in same ch as end of previous dc cl, ch 1; rep from * across; dc in same ch as end of last dc cl; ch 3, turn.

Row 3: Rep Row 2, changing to white in last st.

Rows 4 through 6: Rep Row 2 three times more, changing to blue in last st on Row 6.

Rows 7 through 9: Rep Row 2 three times more, changing to white in last st on Row 9.

Rows 10 through 23: Rep Row 2 fourteen times more, changing to blue in last st on Row 23.

Rows 24 through 26: Rep Row 2 three times more, changing to white in last st on Row 26.

Rows 27 through 29: Rep Row 2 three times more, changing to green in last st on Row 29.

Rows 30 through 32: Rep Row 2 three times more. At end of Row 32, finish off; weave in ends.

Top Strip

Row 1: With right side facing and C hook, join blue with sl st in ch-3 sp at beg of Row 1, ch 1, 2 sc in same sp as joining; *2 sc around next dc post, 2 sc in next ch-3 sp; rep from * across to last dc post; 2 sc around last dc post: 64 sc; ch 3, turn.

Row 2: Skip first sc, work dc cl, inserting hook first in next sc, ch 1; *work dc cl inserting hook first in same sc as end of previous dc cl, ch 1; rep from * across; dc in same sc as end of last dc cl: 31 dc cl, 31 ch-1 sps and 2 dc; ch 3, turn.

Row 3: Work dc cl, inserting hook first in next ch, ch 1; *work dc cl, inserting hook first in same ch as end of previous dc cl, ch 1; rep from * across; dc in same ch as end of last dc cl; ch 3, turn.

Row 4: Rep Row 3 once more, changing to white in last st.

Rows 5 and 6: Rep Row 3 two times more, changing to green in last st on Row 6.

Rows 7 through 9: Rep Row 2 three times more. At end of Row 9, finish off; weave in ends.

Bottom Strip

Row 1: With right side facing and C hook, join blue with sl st in ch-3 sp at beg of Row 32, ch 1, 2 sc in same sp, *2 sc around next dc post, 2 sc in next ch-3 sp; rep from * across to last dc post; 2 sc around last dc post: 64 sc; ch 3 (counts as dc on next row), turn.

Rows 2 through 9: Rep Rows 2 through 9 of Top Strip.

Back

Work same as Front.

Join Front and Back

With wrong sides of Front and Back together, working through both thicknesses with C hook, join green with sl st in top left edge, ch 1, sc in same sp as joining, work 1 row sc evenly down left side to bottom, 3 sc in corner st (place marker in center sc of 3 sc), work 62 sc along bottom edge, 3 sc in corner st (place marker in center sc of 3 sc), work 1 row sc evenly up right side. Finish off; weave in ends.

Top Edging

Row 1: With right side facing and C hook, join green with sl st in first st on Row 9 of Top Strip of Back, work 1 row sc evenly around top edge; join with sl st in first sc.

Row 2: Ch 1, work 1 rev sc in each sc around; join with sl st in first sc. Finish off; weave in ends.

Bottom Edging

Row 1: With C hook, join red with sl st in first marked sc on bottom edge, ch 2 (counts as hdc), hdc in same sc as joining, hdc in each sc along lower edge of bag to next marker, hdc in marked sc: 67 hdc; ch 4 (counts as hdc and ch-1 sp on next row), turn.

Row 2: Skip first hdc and next hdc, dc in next hdc, *ch 1, skip next hdc, dc in next hdc; rep from * across: 34 dc and 33 ch-1 sps; ch 2 (counts as hdc on next row), turn.

Row 3: Skip first dc; *hdc in next ch-1 sp, hdc in next dc; rep from * across, changing to white in last st: 67 hdc; ch 1, turn.

Row 4: Sc in first hdc; *(sc, ch 5, sc) in next hdc, sc in each of next 7 hdc; rep from * to last 2 hdc; (sc, ch 5, sc) in next hdc, sc in last hdc: 76 sc and 9 ch-5 sps; ch 1, turn.

Row 5: Sc in first sc, skip sc at base of ch-5; *(hdc, 11 dc, hdc) in next ch-5 sp, skip sc at base of same ch-5 and next sc, sc in each of next 5 sc, skip next sc and sc at base of next ch-5; rep from * to last ch-5 sp; (hdc, 11 dc, hdc) in last ch-5 sp, skip sc at base of same ch-5, sc in last sc, changing to green: 42 sc, 18 hdc and 99 dc; ch 4, turn.

Row 6: Skip first sc; *skip next hdc and next 3 dc; (sc in next dc, picot, ch 1, skip next dc) twice; sc in next dc, picot, ch 4, skip next 3 dc and next hdc, sc in next sc**; ch 4, skip next 3 sc, sc in next sc, ch 4; rep from * across, ending at **. Finish off; weave in ends.

Medallion

With C hook and red, ch 5; join with sl st in first ch to form a ring.

Rnd 1: Ch 1, 16 sc in ring: 16 sc; join with sl st in first sc.

Rnd 2: Ch 1, sc in same sc as joining, sc in next sc; *(sc, ch 9, sc) in next sc**, sc in each of next 3 sc; rep from * twice more, then rep from * to ** once; sc in next sc: 20 sc and 4 ch-9 sps; join with sl st in first sc.

Rnd 3: Ch 1, sc in same sc as joining; *skip next sc and sc at base of next ch-9, (2 hdc, 17 dc, 2 hdc) in next ch-9 sp, skip sc at base of same ch-9 and next sc**, sc in next sc; rep from * twice more, then rep from * to ** once; join with sl st in first sc.

Rnd 4: Ch 1, work long sc; *ch 5, skip next 2 hdc and next 3 dc, sc in next dc, picot, (ch 5, skip next 4 dc, sc in next dc, picot) twice, ch 5, skip next 3 dc and next 2 hdc**, work long sc; rep from * twice more, then rep from * to ** once; join with sl st in first long sc. Finish off. Sew to center Front of Bag as shown in photograph.

Handles (make 2)

With size 7 hook and 3 strands of blue, ch 65.

Row 1: Dc in 4th ch from hook, dc in each ch across: 63 dc; ch 3, turn.

Row 2: Dc in next dc and in each dc across; ch 1, turn.

Fold Strap in half lengthwise. Working through both layers, sc in first dc and in free lp of 63rd foundation ch; *sc in next dc and in free lp of next foundation ch; rep from * across: 63 sc. Finish off. Sew handles to top of bag as shown in photograph.

#74 A LA FOO-FOO POTHOLDER

DESIGNED BY JANIE HERRIN

SIZE
7 ½" x 7 ½"

MATERIALS
Worsted weight cotton yarn
  2 oz white
  2 oz coral

Small safety pin

Size H (5 mm) crochet hook
  (or size required for gauge)

GAUGE
First four rnds = 3"

STITCH GUIDE

Sc around post: Insert hook from front to back to front around post (vertical bar) of specified st and draw up a lp; YO and draw through both lps on hook:sc around post made.

Reverse sc: Ch 1; working from left to right, sc in each sc around.

INSTRUCTIONS

Front

With white, ch 4, join with sl st to form a ring.

Rnd 1 (right side): Ch 1, 8 sc in ring, join in beg sc.

Rnd 2: Ch 1, sc in same st, ch 3; (sc in next sc, ch 3) around: 8 ch-3 lps; join.

Rnd 3: Sl st in ch-3 sp, ch 1, in same sp and in each sp around work (sc, hdc, dc, hdc, sc); join beg sc: 8 petals made.

Rnd 4: Ch 2, turn; working on wrong side, sc around post of sc on Rnd 2, ch 4; *sc around post of next sc on Rnd 2, ch 4; rep from * around, join in beg sc: 8 ch-4 lps.

Rnd 5: Ch 1, turn; working on right side, in next lp and in each lp around work (sc, hdc, 2 dc, hdc, sc), end with sl st in beg sc, ch 1, pull up a long lp (to be picked up later), drop but do not cut yarn; place a safety pin in lp and remove hook.

Rnd 6: With right side facing, join coral with sc around post of any sc on Rnd 2, ch 3; *(sc around post of next sc, ch 3; rep from * around, join in beg sc: 8 ch-3 lps around center of flower.

Rnd 7: Ch 3; *sc in first sc of next petal on Rnd 3, ch 2, (sc in next st, ch 2) 3 times; sc in last sc of same petal, dc in sc below on Rnd 6; rep from * around, end with last sc, join in top of beg ch-3.

Rnd 8: Ch 2, working around petals on Rnd 5, (sc, ch 2) in each st around, join in beg sc. Finish off.

Rnd 9: Insert hook in dropped lp on Rnd 5 (remove safety pin), pick up white and sc in ch-2 sp between 2 petals on Rnd 8, ch 4, skip 2 lps, sc in next lp (you should be in center lp of petal); (ch 4, skip 2 lps, sc in next lp) around, ch 4, join in beg sc: 16 ch-4 lps.

Rnd 10: Sl st in next ch-4 sp, ch 3 (equals first dc), 4 dc in same lp; (5 dc in next lp) around, join in beg dc: 80 dc. Finish off.

Back

Ch 5, join with sl st to form a ring.

Rnd 1: Ch 1, 10 sc in ring, join in beg sc.

Rnd 2: Ch 2 (Note: do not count beg ch-2 as a st), 2 hdc in same st, 2 hdc in each sc around, join: 20 hdc.

Rnd 3: Ch 2, 2 hdc in same st; *hdc in next st, 2 hdc in next st; rep from * around, hdc in last st, join: 30 hdc.

Rnd 4: Ch 2, 2 hdc in same st; *hdc in next 2 sts, 2 hdc in next st; rep from * around, hdc in last 2 sts, join: 40 hdc.

Rnd 5: Ch 2, 2 hdc in same st; * hdc in next 3 sts, 2 hdc in next st; rep from * around, hdc in last 3 sts, join: 50 hdc.

Rnd 6: Ch 2, 2 hdc in same st; * hdc in next 4 sts, 2 hdc in next st; rep from * around, hdc in last 4 sts, join: 60 hdc.

Rnd 7: Ch 2, 2 hdc in same st; *hdc in next 5 sts, 2 hdc in next st; rep from * around, hdc in last 5 sts, join: 70 hdc.

Rnd 8: Ch 2, 2 hdc in same st; *hdc in next 6 sts, 2 hdc in next st; rep from * around, hdc in last 6 sts, join: 80 hdc. Do not finish off.

Assembly

Hold front and back with wrong sides tog. Carefully matching sts, work through both pieces, sc front and back tog. At end of rnd, join in beg sc, ch 12 for hanger, sl st in base of ch. Finish off.

With front facing, join coral with sc in any st, and work 1 rnd reverse sc around, join. Finish off.

#75 MERRY-GO-ROUND BLANKET

Designed by Mary Jane Protus for Coats & Clark

Note: *Pattern for teddy bear appears on pages 214-215.*

SIZE
56" across from point to point

MATERIAL
Bulky weight yarn
  23 oz blue (A)
  6 oz white (B)

Note: *Photographed model made with Red Heart® Baby Clouds #9008 Cotton Candy (A) and #9311 Cloud (B)*

Size N (10 mm) crochet hook
  (or size required for gauge)

GAUGE
Rnds 1 and 2 = 6" across
  (not including ch-3 lps)

INSTRUCTIONS

With A, ch 6; join with sl st to form a ring.

Rnd 1: Ch 3 (counts as first dc), 15 dc in ring; join with sl st to top of ch-3; 16 sts.

Rnd 2: Ch 3, dc in next dc, ch 3; (dc in next 2 dc, ch 3) 7 times; join in top of beg ch-3. Finish off.

Rnd 3: Join Color B in any ch-3 sp; ch 6 (counts as a dc and a ch-3 sp), 3 dc in same sp; [(3 dc, ch 3, 3 dc) all in next ch-3 sp] 7 times, 2 dc in first sp; join in 3rd ch of ch-6. Finish off.

Rnd 4: Join Color A in ch-3 sp just after joining; ch 6, 2 dc in same sp; *dc in next 2 dc, skip next 2 dc **, dc in next 2 dc: (2 dc, ch 3, 2 dc) in ch-3 sp: corner made; rep from * to last 2 sts, end at **; dc in next dc, dc in same ch as joining of previous rnd, dc in first sp; join in 3rd ch of ch-6.

Rnd 5: Sl st in next ch of ch-6, sl st in sp, ch 6, 2 dc in same sp; * dc in next 3 dc, skip next 2 dc **, dc in next 3 dc, work corner; rep from * to last 3 sts, end at **; dc in next 2 dc, dc in same ch as joining of previous rnd, dc in first sp; join in 3rd ch of ch-6.

Rnd 6: Sl st in next ch of ch-6, sl st in sp, ch 6, 2 dc in same sp; * dc in next 4 dc, skip next 2 dc **, dc in next 4 dc, work corner; rep from * to last 4 sts, end at **; dc in next 3 dc, dc in same ch as joining of previous rnd, dc in first sp; join in 3rd ch of ch-6. Finish off.

Rnd 7: Join Color B in ch-3 sp after joining; ch 6, 2 dc in same sp; *dc in next 5 dc, skip next 2 dc **, dc in next 5 dc, work corner; rep from * to last 5 sts, end at **; dc in next 4 dc, dc in same ch as joining of previous rnd, dc in first sp; join in 3rd ch of ch-6. Finish off.

Rnd 8: Work same as Rnd 4 EXCEPT work 6 dc on each side of corner.

Rnd 9: Work same as Rnd 5 EXCEPT work 7 dc on each side of corner.

Rnd 10: Work same as Rnd 6 EXCEPT work 8 dc on each side of corner.

Rnd 11: Work same as Rnd 7 EXCEPT work 9 dc on each side of corner.

Rnd 12: Work same as Rnd 4 EXCEPT work 10 dc on each side of corner.

Rnd 13: Work same as Rnd 5 EXCEPT work 11 dc on each side of corner.

Rnd 14: Work same as Rnd 6 EXCEPT work 12 dc on each side of corner.

Rnd 15: Work same as Rnd 7 EXCEPT work 13 dc on each side of corner.

Rnd 16: Work same as Rnd 4 EXCEPT work 14 dc on each side of corner.

Rnd 17: Work same as Rnd 5 EXCEPT work 15 dc on each side of corner.

Rnd 18: Work same as Rnd 6 EXCEPT work 16 dc on each side of corner.

Weave in all ends.

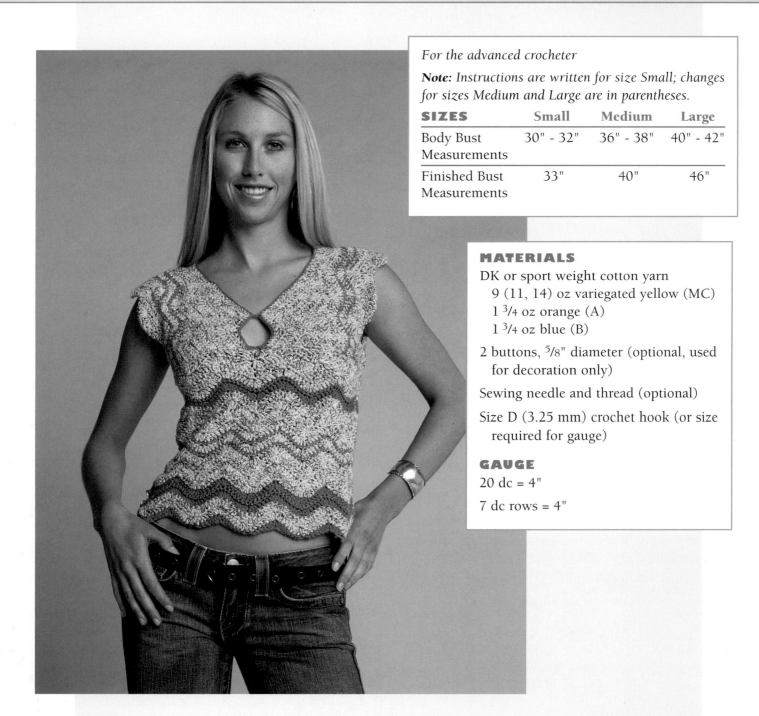

For the advanced crocheter

Note: *Instructions are written for size Small; changes for sizes Medium and Large are in parentheses.*

SIZES	Small	Medium	Large
Body Bust Measurements	30" - 32"	36" - 38"	40" - 42"
Finished Bust Measurements	33"	40"	46"

MATERIALS

DK or sport weight cotton yarn
   9 (11, 14) oz variegated yellow (MC)
   1 ³/₄ oz orange (A)
   1 ³/₄ oz blue (B)

2 buttons, ⁵/₈" diameter (optional, used for decoration only)

Sewing needle and thread (optional)

Size D (3.25 mm) crochet hook (or size required for gauge)

GAUGE

20 dc = 4"

7 dc rows = 4"

INSTRUCTIONS

Front

Lower Bodice

Starting at hemline with A, ch 73 (87, 101).

Row 1 (wrong side): 2 dc in 4th ch from hook; *dc in next 3 chs, (3 dc tog) 2 times, dc in next 3 chs, (3 dc in next ch) 2 times; rep from * across, ending with 3 dc in last ch; change to MC, ch 3 (counts as a dc on the following row throughout pattern), turn: 70 (84, 98) dc for a total of 5 (6, 7) "waves" or chevrons.

Rows 2 through 3 (5, 5): With MC, 2 dc in first dc; *dc in next 3 dc, (3 dc tog) 2 times, dc in next 3 dc, (3 dc in next dc) 2 times; rep from * across, ending with 3 dc in turning ch; ch 3, turn. At end of Row 3 (5, 5), change to A in last st, ch 3, turn.

Row 4 (6, 6): With A, dc in first dc, dc in next 3 dc, (3 dc tog) 2 times; *dc in next 3 dc, (3 dc in next dc) 2 times, dc in next 3 dc, (3 dc tog) 2 times; rep from * to last 4 sts, dc in next 3 dc, 2 dc in turning ch; change to B; ch 1, turn: 68 (82, 96) dc.

Row 5 (7, 7): With B, sc in each dc across; change to A in last st, ch 3, turn.

Row 6 (8, 8): With A, 2 dc in first sc, dc in next 2 sc, (3 dc tog) 2 times; *dc in next 3 sc, (3 dc in next sc) 2 times, dc in next 3 sc, (3 dc tog) 2 times; rep from * to last 3 sts, dc in next 2 sc, 3 dc in last sc; change to MC; ch 3, turn.

Row 7 (9, 9): With MC, 2 dc in first dc, 2 dc tog, (3 dc tog) 2 times; *dc in next 3 dc, (3 dc in next dc) 2 times, dc in next 3 dc, (3 dc tog) 2 times; rep from * to last 3 sts, 2 dc tog, 3 dc in turning ch; ch 3, turn: 66 (80, 94) dc.

Row 8 (10, 10): 2 dc in first dc, dc in next dc, (3 dc tog) 2 times; *dc in next 3 dc, (3 dc in next dc) 2 times, dc in next 3 dc, (3 dc tog) 2 times; rep from * to last 2 sts, dc in next dc, 3 dc in turning ch: ch 3, turn.

Row 9 (11, 11): Dc in first dc, dc in next dc, (3 dc tog) 2 times; *dc in next 3 dc, (3 dc in next dc) 2 times, dc in next 3 dc, (3 dc tog) 2 times; rep from * to last 2 sts, dc in next dc, 2 dc in turning ch; ch 3, turn: 64 (78, 92) dc.

Row 10 (12, 12): 2 dc in first dc, (3 dc tog) 2 times; *dc in next 3 dc, (3 dc in next dc) 2 times, dc in next 3 dc, (3 dc tog) 2 times; rep from * to last st (turning ch), 3 dc in turning ch, change to A in last st; ch 1, turn.

Row 11 (13, 13): With A, sc in each dc across; change to MC; ch 3, turn.

Row 12 (14, 14): With MC, dc in first sc, (3 dc tog) 2 times; *dc in next 3 sc, (3 dc in next sc) 2 times, dc in next 3 sc, (3 dc tog) 2 times; rep from * to last sc, 2 dc in last sc; for Small and Medium only, change to A in last st; ch 1 (1, 3), turn: 62 (76, 90) dc.

For Size Large Only

Row 15: With MC, dc in first dc, 2 dc tog, 3 dc tog; *dc in next 3 dc, (3 dc in next dc) 2 times, dc in next 3 dc, (3 dc tog) 2 times; rep from * to last 14 sts, dc in next 3 dc, (3 dc in next dc) 2 times, dc in next 3 dc, 3 dc tog, 2 dc tog, 2 dc in turning ch; ch 3, turn.

Row 16: Rep Row 15; at end of row, do not ch 3; change to A; ch 1, turn.

For All Sizes

Row 13 (15, 17): With A, sc in each dc across; change to MC; ch 3, turn.

Row 14 (16, 18): With MC, 2 dc in first dc, 2 dc tog, 3 dc tog; *dc in next 3 dc, (3 dc in next dc) 2 times, dc in next 3 dc, (3 dc tog) 2 times; rep from * to last 14 sts, dc in next 3 dc, (3 dc in next dc) 2 times, dc in next 3 dc, 3 dc tog, 2 dc tog, 3 dc in turning ch; ch 3, turn: 64 (78, 92) dc.

Row 15 (17, 19): 2 dc in first dc, dc in next dc, 2 dc tog, 3 dc tog; *dc in next 3 dc, (3 dc in next dc) 2 times, dc in next 3 dc, (3 dc tog) 2 times; rep from * across ending last rep with 3 dc tog, 2 dc tog, then dc in next dc, 3 dc in turning ch; ch 3, turn: 66 (80, 94) dc.

Row 16 (18, 20): 2 dc in first dc, dc in next dc, (3 dc tog) 2 times; *dc in next 3 dc, (3 dc in next dc) 2 times, dc in next 3 dc, (3 dc tog) 2 times; rep from * to last 2 sts, dc in next dc, 3 dc in turning ch; ch 3, turn.

Row 17 (19, 21): 2 dc in first dc, 2 dc in next dc, (3 dc tog) 2 times; *dc in next 3 dc, (3 dc in next dc) 2 times, dc in next 3 dc, (3 dc tog) 2 times; rep from * to last 2 sts, 2 dc in next dc, 3 dc in turning ch; change to A; ch 3, turn: 68 (82, 96) dc.

Row 18 (20, 22): With A, 2 dc in first dc, dc in next 2 dc, (3 dc tog) 2 times; *dc in next 3 dc, (3 dc in next dc) 2 times, dc in next 3 dc, (3 dc tog) 2 times; rep from * to last 3 sts, dc in next 2 dc, 3 dc in turning ch; change to B; ch 1, turn.

Row 19 (21, 23): With B, sc in each dc across; change to MC; ch 3, turn.

Row 20 (22, 24): With MC, rep Row 18 (20, 22). At end of row, do not change color; ch 3, turn.

Row 21 (23, 25): 2 dc in first dc, 2 dc in next dc, dc in next dc, (3 dc tog) 2 times; *dc in next 3 dc, (3 dc in next dc) 2 times, dc in next 3 dc, (3 dc tog) 2 times; rep from * to last 3 sts, dc in next dc, 2 dc in next dc, 3 dc in turning ch, ch 3, turn: (70 (84, 98) dc.

Rows 22 (24, 26) through 23 (27, 29): Rep Row 2; at end of last row ch 1 instead of ch 3; do not change color.

Row 24 (28, 30): Sl st in first dc, sl st in next dc; * sc in next 2 dc, hdc in next dc, dc in next dc, tr in next 2 dc, dc in next dc, hdc in next dc, sc in next 2 dc, sl st in next 4 dc; rep from * across, ending last rep with sl st in last 2 dc. Finish off; weave in all ends.

Back

Lower Bodice
Work same as Front Lower Bodice.

Right Yoke
Note: *The yoke is worked sideways in 2 pieces; the chevrons now run vertically up and down the yoke rather than horizontally.*

Starting at back underarm, with MC, ch 87 (87, 101).

Row 1 (wrong side): 2 dc in 4th ch from hook; *dc in next 3 ch, (3 dc tog) 2 times, dc in next 3 ch, (3 dc in next ch) 2 times; rep from * across, ending with 3 dc in last ch; ch 3, turn: 84 (84, 98) dc for a total of 6 (6, 7) chevrons.

Rows 2 through (4, 6, 6): 2 dc in first dc; *dc in next 3 dc, (3 dc tog) 2 times, dc in next 3 dc, (3 dc in next dc) 2 times; rep from * across, ending with 3 dc in turning ch; ch 3, turn. At end of Row 4 (6, 6), do not ch 3; change to A; ch 1, turn.

Row 5 (7, 7): With A, sc in each dc across; change to MC, ch 3, turn.

Row 6 (8, 8): With MC, 2 dc in first sc; *dc in next 3 sc, (3 dc tog) 2 times, dc in next 3 sc, (3 dc in next sc) 2 times; rep from * across, ending with 3 dc in last sc; change to B, ch 1, turn.

Row 7 (9, 9): With B, sc in each dc across; change to MC; ch 3, turn.

For Size Large Only

Rows 10 and 11: Rep Rows 8 and 9, with same color changes.

For All Sizes

Row 8 (10, 12): With MC, 2 dc in first sc; *dc in next 3 sc, (3 dc tog) 2 times, dc in next 3 sc, (3 dc in next sc) 2 times; rep from * across, ending with 3 dc in last sc; ch 3, turn.

Rows 9 (11, 13) through 11 (15, 17): 2 dc in first dc; *dc in next 3 dc, (3 dc tog) 2 times, dc in next 3 dc, (3 dc in next dc) 2 times; rep from * across, ending with 3 dc in turning ch; ch 3, turn.

Shape Front Neckline

Row 12 (16, 18) (right side): 2 dc in first dc, dc in next 3 dc, (3 dc tog) 2 times, dc in next 3 dc, (3 dc in next dc) 2 times, dc in next 3 dc, (3 dc tog) 2 times, dc in next 4 dc; ch 3, turn: 26 dc.

Row 13 (17, 19): Dc in next dc, (3 dc tog) 2 times, dc in next 3 dc, (3 dc in next dc) 2 times, dc in next 3 dc, (3 dc tog) 2 times, dc in next 3 dc, 3 dc in turning ch; ch 3, turn: 24 dc.

Row 14 (18, 20): 2 dc in first dc, dc in next 3 dc, (3 dc tog) 2 times, dc in next 3 dc, (3 dc in next dc) 2 times, dc in next 2 dc, (3 dc tog) 2 times, dc in turning ch: ch 3, turn: 22 dc.

Row 15 (19, 21): Beg with next dc, 3 dc tog; dc in next 3 dc, (3 dc in next dc) 2 times, dc in next 3 dc, (3 dc tog) 2 times, dc in next 3 dc, 3 dc in turning ch; finish off.

Shape Back Neckline

Row 12 (16, 18) (right side): With right side facing and skipping 28 (28, 42) dc of previous row, join MC in next dc; ch 3, 2 dc in same dc; dc in next 3 dc, (3 dc tog) 2 times, dc in next 3 dc, (3 dc in next dc) 2 times, dc in next 3 dc, (3 dc tog) 2 times, dc in next 3 dc, 3 dc in turning ch; ch 3, turn: 28 dc.

Rows 13 (17, 19) through 15 (19, 21): 2 dc in first dc, *dc in next 3 dc, (3 dc tog) 2 times, dc in next 3 dc, (3 dc in next dc) 2 times; rep from * across, ending with 3 dc in turning ch; ch 3, turn. At end of last row, do not ch 3. Finish off; weave in all ends.

Left Yoke

Starting at front underarm, with MC, ch 87 (87, 101).

Rows 1 through 11 (15, 17): Work same as Right Yoke.

Shape Back Neckline

Row 12 (16, 18) (right side): 2 dc in first dc; dc in next 3 dc, (3 dc tog) 2 times, dc in next 3 dc, (3 dc in next dc) 2 times, dc in next 3 dc, (3 dc tog) 2 times, dc in next 3 dc, 3 dc in turning ch; ch 3, turn: 28 dc.

Rows 13 (17, 19) through 15 (19, 21): 2 dc in first dc; *dc in next 3 dc, (3 dc tog) 2 times, dc in next 3 dc, (3 dc in next dc) 2 times; rep from * across, ending with 3 dc in turning ch; ch 3, turn. At end of last row, do not ch 3; finish off.

Shape Front Neckline

Row 12 (16, 18) (right side): With right side facing and skipping 28 (28, 42) dc of previous row, join MC in next dc; ch 3 (counts as dc), dc in next 3 dc, (3 dc tog) 2 times, dc in next 3 dc, (3 dc in next dc) 2 times, dc in next 3 dc, (3 dc tog 2 times), dc in next 3 dc, 3 dc in turning ch; ch, turn: 26 dc.

Row 13 (17, 19): 2 dc in first dc, dc in next 3 dc, (3 dc tog) 2 times, dc in next 3 dc, (3 dc in next dc) 2 times, dc in next 3 dc, (3 dc tog) 2 times, dc in next dc, dc in turning ch; ch 3, turn: 24 dc.

Row 14 (18, 20): Beg with next dc, (3 dc tog) 2 times; dc in next 2 dc, (3 dc in next dc) 2 times, dc in next 3 dc, (3 dc tog) 2 times, dc in next 3 dc, 3 dc in turning ch; ch 3, turn: 22 dc.

Row 15 (19, 21): 2 dc in first dc, dc in next 3 dc, (3 dc tog) 2 times, dc in next 3 dc, (3 dc in next dc) 2 times, dc in next 3 dc, 3 dc tog, dc in turning ch. Finish off; weave in all ends.

Assembling and Finishing

Sew Front Bodice to Back Bodice along sides, carefully matching rows.

Fold Right Yoke in half so that narrow ends meet for the bottom edge, with fold forming shoulder. Create right armhole by sewing right side seam from bottom edge towards shoulder for 7 stitches; you will be joining the first 7 stitches and last 7 stitches of Row 1 of the Right Yoke. Fold and stitch Left Yoke in same manner to form left armhole and left side seam.

Sew both Right Yoke and Left Yoke pieces to Lower Bodice, making sure the yoke pieces meet in center front and center back of the garment.

Neckline border

With right side facing, join A with sl st in any st of back neckline. Sc evenly around neckline, adjusting sts as needed to keep neckline smooth. To create keyhole effect in front and back necklines, work sc around keyhole opening, then join right side of neckline to left side with a loose sl st. When border is complete, finish off and weave in ends.

Buttons
(optional, used for decoration only)
With sewing needle and thread, sew buttons to lower right seam of bodice, spacing them 1" apart.

#77 PINNING UP ROSES

Designed by Janie Herrin

SIZE
5" diameter

MATERIALS
Sport weight yarn
  30 yds

Note: *Photographed model made with Red Heart® Sport #922 Hot Pink*

Pinback jewelry finding or large safety pin

Size F (3.75 mm) crochet hook (or size required for gauge)

GAUGE
8 dc = 2"

STITCH GUIDE
Sc around post of sc: Insert hook from front to back to front around post (vertical bar) of specified st, YO and draw up a lp; YO and draw through both lps on hook

INSTRUCTIONS

Ch 7, join with sl st to form a ring.

Rnd 1: Ch 1, in ring work *[sc, ch 1, (dc, ch 1) 5 times, sc]: petal made; ch 2; rep from * 3 times more, ch 2, join with sl st in beg sc: 4 petals made.

Rnd 2: Working behind petals, (ch 2, sc in next ch-2 sp) 4 times, do not join: 4 ch-2 lps.

Rnd 3: Sl st in same ch-2 sp, ch 1, in same sp work (sc, ch 3, sc); * ch 3, in next ch-2 sp work (sc, ch 3, sc); rep from * twice more, ch 3, join with sl st in beg sc: 8 ch-3 lps.

Rnd 4: In next ch-3 lp, work (sc, ch 1, 5 dc, ch 1, sc): petal made; (in next ch-3 lp work petal) 7 times: 8 petals made; do not join.

Rnd 5: Working behind petals, sc around post of next sc on Rnd 3, (ch 4, sc around post of next sc on Rnd 3) 7 times, ch 4, join with sl st in beg sc: 8 ch-4 lps.

Rnd 6: *In next ch-4 lp work (sc, ch 1, 7 dc, ch 1, sc): petal made; rep from * 7 times more, do not join: 8 petals.

Rnd 7: Working behind petals, sc around post of next sc on Rnd 5, (ch 5, sc around post of next sc on Rnd 5) 7 times, ch 5, join with sl st in beg sc.

Rnd 8: *In next ch-5 lp work (sc, ch 1, 9 dc, ch1, sc): petal made; rep from * 7 times more, join with sl st in beg sc. Finish off; weave in ends.

Sew pin back finding on back of flower at top of one petal, or use a safety pin.

#78 BY THE SEA

Designed by Patons Design Staff

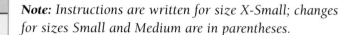

Note: *Instructions are written for size X-Small; changes for sizes Small and Medium are in parentheses.*

SIZES	X-Small	Small	Medium
Body Bust Measurements	32"	34"	36"
Finished Bust Measurement	33"	35"	37"

MATERIALS:

Sport weight yarn
  8 (8 $^3/_4$, 10) oz white
  $^1/_2$ oz blue

Note: *Photographed model made with Patons® Grace #60005 Snow and #60104 Azure*

Size C (2.75 mm) crochet
  hook (or size required for
  gauge)

GAUGE

22 dc = 4"

11 dc rows = 4"

INSTRUCTIONS

Front

With blue, ch 94 (100, 104).

Row 1 (right side): Dc in 4th ch from hook (3 skipped chs count as dc), *ch 1, skip next ch, dc in next ch; rep from * across, changing to white in last dc: 47 (50, 52) dc and 45 (48, 50) ch-1 sps; ch 3 (counts as dc on next row now and throughout), turn.

Row 2: *Dc in next ch-1 sp, dc in next dc; rep from * across, ending with dc in 3rd ch of turning ch-3: 92 (98, 102) dc; ch 3, turn.

Row 3: Dc in next dc and in each dc across, ending with dc in 3rd ch of turning ch-3: 92 (98, 102) dc; ch 3, turn.

Rep Row 3 until piece measures about 9 3/4" (10 1/2", 11") ending by working a wrong-side row. At end of last row, ch 1, turn instead of ch 3, turn.

Armhole Shaping

For Size X-Small Only

Row 1 (wrong side): Sc in first 2 dc, ch 1, dc in next dc and in each dc to last 2 dc (turning ch-3 on last row counts as last dc), sc in next dc, leaving last dc unworked: 88 dc; ch 1, turn.

Row 2: Skip first sc, sc in first 2 dc, ch 1, dc in next dc and in each dc to last 2 dc, sc in next dc, leaving last dc unworked: 84 dc; ch 1, turn.

Rows 3 through 5: Rep Row 2 three times more: 72 dc at end of Row 5.

Row 6: Skip first sc, sc in first dc, ch 1, dc in next dc and in each dc to last 2 dc, sc in next dc, leaving last dc unworked: 69 dc; ch 3, turn.

For Size Small Only

Row 1 (wrong side): Sc in first 3 dc, ch 1, dc in next dc and in each dc to last 2 dc, sc in next dc, leaving last dc unworked: 93 dc; ch 1, turn.

Row 2: Skip next sc, sc in first 3 dc, ch 1, dc in next dc and in each dc to last 2 dc, sc in next dc, leaving last dc unworked: 88 dc; ch 1, turn.

Row 3: Rep Row 2 once: 83 dc.

Row 4: Skip next sc, sc in first 2 dc, ch 1, dc in next dc and in each dc to last 2 dc, sc in next dc, leaving last dc unworked: 79 dc; ch 1, turn.

Row 5 and 6: Rep Row 4 two times more. At end of Row 6: 71 dc; ch 3 (counts as dc on next row), turn instead of ch 1, turn.

For Size Medium Only

Row 1 (wrong side): Sc in first 3 dc, ch 1, dc in next dc and in each dc to last 2 dc, sc in next dc, leaving last dc unworked: 97 dc; ch 1, turn.

Row 2: Skip next sc, sc in first 3 dc, ch 1, dc in next dc and in each dc to last 2 dc, sc in next dc, leaving last dc unworked: 92 dc; ch 1, turn.

Rows 3 through 5: Rep Row 2 three times more: 77 dc at end of Row 5.

Row 6: Skip next sc, sc in first 2 dc, ch 1, dc in next dc and in each dc to last 2 dc, sc in next dc, leaving last dc unworked: 73 dc; ch 3, turn.

For All Sizes

Row 7: Skip first sc, dc dec in next 2 dc, dc in each dc to last 3 dc, dc dec in next 2 dc, dc in last dc: 67 (69, 71) dc: ch 3, turn.

Row 8: Skip first dc, dc dec in next 2 dc, dc in each dc to last 3 dc, dc dec in next 2 dc, dc in last dc: 65 (67, 69) dc: ch 3, turn.

For Sizes X-Small and Small Only

Rows 9 and 10: Rep Row 8 two times more, changing to blue in last dc on Row 10. At end of Row 10: 61 (63) dc; ch 4 (counts as dc and ch-1 sp on next row), turn instead of working ch 3, turn.

For Size Medium Only

Rows 9 and 10: Rep Row 8 two times more: 65 dc at end of Row 10.

Row 11: Dc in next dc and in each dc across; ch 3, turn.

Row 12: Dc in next dc and in each dc across, changing to blue in last dc; ch 3, turn.

For All Sizes

Row 11 (11, 13): Skip next dc, dc in next dc; *ch 1, skip next dc, dc in next dc; rep from * across ending with dc in 3rd ch of turning ch-3, changing to white in last dc: 31 (32, 33) dc and 30 (31, 32) ch-1 sps; ch 1, turn.

Row 12 (12, 14): Sc in first dc; *sc in next ch-1 sp, sc in next dc; rep from * across ending with sc in 3rd ch of turning ch-4: 61 (63, 65) sc; ch 1, turn.

Row 13 (13, 15): Sc in each sc across; ch l, turn.

Rows 14 and 15 (14 and 15, 16 and 17): Rep Row 13 (13, 15) two times more. At end of last row, do not ch 1. Finish off; weave in ends.

Lower Edging

Hold piece with right side facing and beg ch at top; join white with sl st in unused lp of first ch.

Row 1 (right side): Ch 1, work 2 sc in next ch-1 sp and in each ch-1 sp across: 90 (96, 100) sc; ch 1, turn.

Row 2: Sc in each sc across; ch 1, turn.

Row 3: Sc in each sc across. Finish off; weave in ends.

Back

Work same as Front.

Pocket (make 2)

With white, ch 25.

Row 1 (right side): Dc in 4th ch from hook and in each ch across: 23 dc; ch 3, turn.

Row 2: Dc in next dc and in each dc across; ch 3, turn.

Rows 3 through 6: Rep Row 2 four times more, changing to blue in last dc on Row 6. At end of Row 6, ch 4 (counts as dc and ch-1 sp on next row), turn instead of working ch 3, turn.

Row 7: Skip first 2 dc, dc in next dc; *ch 1, skip next dc, dc in next dc; rep from * ending with dc in 3rd ch of turning ch-3, changing to white in last dc: 12 dc and 11 ch-1 sps; ch 1, turn.

Row 8: Sc in first dc; *sc in next ch-1 sp, sc in next dc; rep from * ending with sc in 3rd ch of turning ch-4: 23 sc; ch 1, turn.

Row 9: Sc in each sc across; ch 1, turn.

Row 10: Sc in each sc across. Finish off; weave in ends.

Finishing

Position pockets on right side of Front 1" up from bottom edge and 1 1/2" in from sides and sew in position. Sew side seams.

Armhole Edging and Strap

Right Side

Row 1: With right side facing, join white with sl st in edge of last sc on Row 15 (15, 17) of Front, ch 1, sc in edge of each row and in each st around armhole edge from Front to Back, ending with last sc in edge of first sc on Row 15 (15, 17) on Back; ch 1, turn.

Row 2: Sc in each sc across, ch 48 (foundation of strap), sl st in first sc of this row (on back for right side, front on other side) to attach strap, making sure ch does not twist; ch 1, do not turn.

Rnd 3: Sc in same sc as joining sl st, working around armhole, sc in each sc of Row 2 and in each ch of strap, sl st in first sc; ch 1, do not turn.

Rnd 4: Working around armhole, sc in same sc as joining sl st, sc in each sc around, sl st in first sc. Finish off.

With right side facing, join white with sl st in edge of last sc on Row 2 of armhole edging, sc in unused lp of first ch of ch-48 of strap on Row 2 and in unused lp of each ch around, sl st in edge of first sc on Row 2 of armhole edging. Finish off; weave in ends.

Left Side

Row 1: With right side facing, join white with sl st in edge of last sc on Row 15 (15, 17) of Back, sc in edge of each row and in each st around armhole edge from Back to Front, ending with last sc in edge of first sc on Row 15 (15, 17) on Front; ch 1, turn.

Rows 2 through 4: Work Rows 2 through 4 to correspond to Right Side of Armhole Edging.

Rep from * to * once.

#79 LAZY DAISIES FOR BABY

Designed by Michele Thompson for Coats & Clark

SIZE
40" x 40"

MATERIALS
Sport weight yarn
  18 oz green (A)
  8 oz white (B)
  2 oz yellow (C)

Note: Photographed model made with Red Heart® Soft Baby #7680 Soft Mint (A), #7001 White (B) and #7321 Powder Yellow (C)

Size G (4 mm) crochet hook

Size H (5 mm) crochet hook (or size required for gauge)

GAUGE
14 sc = 4" with larger hook

18 sc rows = 4" with larger hook

One Flower Square = 3 1/2" with larger hook

STITCH GUIDE
Puff Stitch (Pst): Drop first color to wrong side; with 2nd color (YO, insert hook in specified st and draw up a lp) 4 times; drop 2nd color to wrong side, with first color YO and draw through all 9 lps on hook: Pst made.

INSTRUCTIONS

Center
Using larger hook and A, ch 113.

Row 1 (right side): Sc in second ch from hook and each rem ch; ch 1, turn: 112 sc.

Row 2: Sc in each sc; ch 1, turn.

Rows 3 through 7: Rep Row 2.

Row 8: Attach C for Psts, carrying C along top of work when not in use, working sc over C and concealing it within sc until needed. Sc in first 6 sc; *with C, Pst in next sc; with A sc in next 8 sc; rep from * to last 7 sc; Pst in next sc, sc in last 6 sc; ch 1, turn: 12 Psts. Finish off C.

Row 9: Sc in each st; ch 1, turn.

Row 10 through 17: Rep Row 2.

Row 18: Rep Row 8.

Rep Rows 9 through 18 twelve more times.

Rep Row 2 seven more times; at end of last row, do not ch 1. Finish off.

Embroidery

Using B, embroider an 8-petal Lazy Daisy around each Puff St. (See Fig below.) Weave in ends.

Square (make 40)

Using larger hook and C, ch 4; join with sl st to form a ring.

Rnd 1: Ch 1, 8 sc in ring; join with sl st to first sc. Finish off.

Rnd 2: Join B in any sc; (ch 4, hdc in 2nd ch from hook, dc in next 2 ch, sl st in next sc) 8 times, work last sl st in same sc as joining: 8 petals. Finish off.

Rnd 3: Join A in tip of any petal, ch 1, sc in same place; *ch 3, sc in tip of next petal, ch 7 **; sc in tip of next petal; rep from * around, end at **; join in first sc.

Rnd 4: Ch 1, sc in first sc; * 3 sc in ch-3 sp, sc in next sc, (3 sc, ch 3, 3 sc) in next ch-7 sp **; sc in next sc; rep from * around, end at **; join in first sc. Finish off.

Assembly

Using A, sew squares tog through front lps, forming a large open square, with 9 Squares along each side and one square in each corner as shown in photo. Place wrong side of assembled squares over right side of Center and pin in place. Using A, sew Center to back lps of inner edge of squares.

Inner Edging

With right side facing, fold on the seam just made and hold the squares toward you and the Center away from you, exposing the rem front 1ps of the squares. With smaller hook, join B in any lp. Ch 1, sc in same lp; * ch 2, skip next lp, dc in next 1p, ch 2, skip next lp **; sc in next lp; rep from * around inner edge, adjusting sts at inner corners and at end of rnd as needed, end at **; join in first sc. Finish off.

Outer Edging

With right side facing, with smaller hook join A in any sc.

Rnd 1: Ch 1, sc in each sc and ch-2 sp around; work 3 sc in each corner; join in first sc. Finish off.

Rnd 2: With right side facing and with smaller hook, join B in any sc, ch 1, sc in first sc; * ch 2, skip next sc, dc in next sc, ch 2, skip next sc **; sc in next sc; rep from * around, adjusting sts at corners and end of rnd as needed, end at **; join in first sc. Finish off.

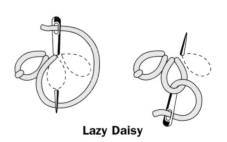

Lazy Daisy

Designed by Michele Thompson for Coats & Clark

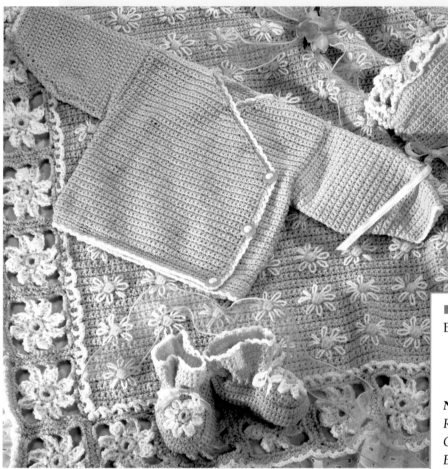

Note: *Instructions are written for size Newborn with changes for sizes 3-6 months and 9-12 months in parentheses.*

SIZES	Newborn	3-6 months	9-12 months
Body Chest Measurements	17"	18"	20"
Finished Chest Measurements	18"	20"	22"

MATERIALS

Baby fingering weight yarn
   6 oz green (A)
   1 oz white (B)
   1 oz yellow (C)

Note: *Photographed models made with Red Heart® Baby Fingering #680 Pastel Green (A), #1 White (B) and #224 Baby Yellow (C)*

3 daisy-shape buttons, 7/8" diameter

8 snap sets, 3/8" diameter

1 1/4 yds white satin ribbon, 1/8" wide

1 yd white satin ribbon, 1/4" wide

sewing thread and needle

Size E (3.5 mm) crochet hook

Size F (3.75 mm) crochet hook
   (or size required for gauge)

GAUGE

20 sc = 4" with larger hook

25 sc rows = 4" with larger hook

SWEATER

INSTRUCTIONS

Right Front

With larger hook and A, ch 39 (44, 49).

Row 1 (right side): Sc in 2nd ch from hook and in each ch; ch 1, turn: 38 (43, 48) sc.

Row 2: Sc in each sc; ch 1, turn.

Rep Row 2 until piece measures 4 1/2" (5 1/2", 6") ending by working a wrong-side row.

Right Armhole and Neck

Row 1: Draw up a lp in each of next 2 sc, YO and draw through all 3 lps on hook: sc dec made for neck edge; sc in each sc across to last sc; ch 1, turn, leaving last sc unworked for armhole edge: 36 (41, 46) sc.

Row 2: Sc in each sc across; sc dec in last 2 sc; ch1, turn.

Rep Rows 1 and 2 until 12 (14, 15) sc rem.

For the Two Larger Sizes Only

Work 1 more row even in sc. Finish off.

Left Front

Work same as Right Front until piece measures 4 1/2" (5 1/2", 6").

Shape Armhole and Neck

Row 1: Sl st in first sc for armhole edge, ch 1, sc in each sc to end; sc dec in last 2 sc for neck edge; ch 1, turn.

Row 2: Sc dec in first 2 sc, sc in each sc to end; ch 1, turn.

Row 3: Sc in each sc to end, sc dec in last 2 sc; ch 1, turn.

Rep Rows 2 and 3 until 12 (14, 15) sc rem.

For the Two Larger Sizes Only

Work 1 more row even in sc. Finish off.

Back

With larger hook and A, ch 46 (51, 56).

Row 1: Work same as Front on 45 (50, 55) sc, until piece measures 4 1/2" (5 1/2", 6"), ending by working a wrong-side row.

Shape Armholes

Sl st in first sc, ch 1, sc in each sc across, leaving last sc unworked; ch 1, turn: 43 (48, 53) sc. Work even in sc until Back is same length as Fronts to shoulder. Do not ch at end of last row. Finish off.

Sleeves (make 2)

Using larger hook and A, ch 28 (30, 32).

Row 1: Sc in 2nd ch from hook and in each rem ch; ch 1, turn: 27 (29, 31) sc.

Row 2: Sc in each sc; ch 1, turn.

Row 3: Rep Row 2.

Row 4: 2 Sc in first sc (sc inc made), sc in each sc, 2 sc in last sc; ch 1, turn.

Rows 5 through7: Rep Row 2.

Row 8: Rep Row 4.

Rep Rows 5 through 8 until there are 41 (45, 53) sc.

Work even in sc until Sleeve measure 5 (7, 8)" long. On last row do not ch 1. Finish off.

Finishing

Body Edging

Using A, sew side and shoulder seams. With right side facing and smaller hook, join A at side seam and work 2 rnds sc evenly around entire edge of garment, working 3 sc in each corner; join in first sc with sl st. Finish off. Join B in joining of previous rnd; *ch 3, skip 1 sc, sl st in next sc; rep from * around, adjusting at corners as needed; join in first ch of beg ch-3. Finish off.

Sleeve Edging

With right side facing and smaller hook, join A at lower edge and work 27 (29, 31) sc in unused lps of beg ch; ch 1, turn. Work one more row sc with A. Finish off. Turn to right side; then join B in first sc; ch 1, sl st in first sc, * ch 3, skip 1 sc, sl st in next sc; rep from * across. Finish off. Using A, sew sleeve seams and set in sleeves. Weave in all ends.

Overlap Right Front over Left Front for girls and Left Front over Right Front for boys. Sew 3 snap sets to fronts near side seam and sew 3 daisy buttons over snaps. Sew one snap set at top neck and one set at top inner corner of overlap.

BONNET

INSTRUCTIONS

Back

Square
[make 4 using smaller (larger, larger) hook]
Using C, ch 4; join with a sl st to form a ring.

Rnd 1: Ch 1, 8 sc in ring; join with a sl st to first sc. Finish off.

Rnd 2: Join B in any sc; (ch 4, hdc in 2nd ch from hook, dc in next 2 ch, sl st in next sc) 8 times, work last sl st in same sc as joining: 8 petals. Finish off.

Rnd 3: Join A in tip of any petal, ch 1, sc in same place; *ch 3, sc in tip of next petal, ch 7 **; sc in tip of next petal; rep from * around, end at **; join in first sc.

Rnd 4: Ch 1, sc in first sc; * 3 sc in ch-3 sp, sc in next sc, (3 sc, ch 3, 3 sc) in next ch-7 sp **; sc in next sc; rep from * around, end at **; join in first sc. Finish off.

Using A, sl st Squares tog through front lps to form one large square.

Brim/Casing

With right side facing and larger hook, join A in back lp of lower right-hand corner of large square and working in back lps only, work 51 (65, 71) sc evenly around 3 sides of square; ch 1, turn. Sc in each sc until Brim measures 2 1/2" (3 1/2", 4"), ending by working a right-side row. At end of last row; ch 3, turn Bonnet upside down. For ribbon casing: work dc into side of sc rows to back section, dc in back lp only of each sc across back, dc into side of sc rows to front edge. Finish off.

Edging

With right side facing and smaller hook, join B at beg of casing row and work as follows: * ch 3, skip 1 st, sl st in next st; rep from * around entire Bonnet, adjusting at corners as needed; join in first ch of beg ch-3. Finish off. Weave 1/4" ribbon through dc row of casing.

Back Edging

With right side facing and smaller hook, join B in front lp at lower corner of Back and work Edging pattern in each front lp around square Back. Finish off.

BOOTIE (make 2)

INSTRUCTIONS

Sole

Starting at heel, with larger hook and A, ch 10 (12, 14).

Row 1 (right side): Sc in second ch from hook and each rem ch: 9 (11, 13) sc; ch 1, turn.

Row 2: Sc in each sc; ch 1, turn.

Rows 3 through 18 (20, 22): Rep Row 2.

Row 19 (21, 23): Sc in first sc; draw up a lp in each of next 2 sc; YO and draw through all 3 lps on hook: decrease made; sc to last 3 sts, draw up a lp in each of next 2 sts, YO and draw through all 3 lps on hook; sc in last st: 7 (9, 11) sc; finish off. Mark this row for toe end.

Top

Ch 10 (12, 14).

Row 1: Sc in 2nd ch from hook and in each rem ch: 9 (11, 13) sc; ch 1, turn. Mark this row for instep.

Rows 2 through 8 (9, 10): Work same as Sole.

Last Row: Work Row 19 (21, 23) of Sole: 7 (9, 11) sc. Finish off. Mark this row for toe end.

Sides

Rnd 1 (right side): Working in unused lps of beg ch of sole, with larger hook, join A in center ch at heel end; ch 1, sc in joining and in each rem ch; sc in end of each row along side to row marked as toe; place a contrast piece of yarn between last and next st to indicate start of toe; sc in each sc across toe; place another marker to indicate end of toe; sc in end of each row along opposite side to beg ch, sc in rem unworked lps of ch, join with sl st in beg sc; do not turn.

Note: Move toe markers up as you work.

Rnds 2 through 6 (6, 8): Ch 1, sc in each sc around, join; do not turn.

On the next rnd, Top will be joined to sides and toe of Sole.

Rnd 7 (7, 9): Ch 1; sc in each sc to 8 (9, 10) sts before first toe marker; place one row edge of Top in front of Side and join with sc, working through both pieces, matching rows and sts, to first toe marker; sc through both pieces across toe, then sc through both pieces across rem row edges of Top and Sides; then complete rnd working sc in rem sc sts of Side; join.

Rnd 8 (8, 10): Ch 3 (counts as a dc), dc in each sc to instep (free) edge of Top; leaving joined edges of Top unworked, dc in unused lps of beg ch across instep edge and in rem unjoined sc of Side; join in 3rd ch of beg ch-3.

Rnd 9 (9, 11): Ch 1, sc in each dc around, join.

Work 5 (7, 9) more rnds in sc; at end of last rnd. Finish off; weave in all ends.

Edging

Rnd 1: With right side facing and smaller hook, join white in sc at center back joining; * ch 3, skip 1 sc, sl st in next sc; rep from * around, join in beg sc. Finish off; weave in ends.

Finishing

Following instructions for Rnds 1 and 2 of Hat Square, make 2 daisies and sew to instep of each Bootie. Cut two 20" long pieces of 1/8" ribbon and weave through dc rows at ankle. Tie ends in bow.

#83 BRONZE BEAUTY

Designed by Tammy Hildebrand

SIZE
26" wide x 25" long

MATERIALS
Worsted weight yarn
  10 ¹/₂ oz bronze

Note: *Photographed model made with Lion Brand® Glitterspun, #135 Bronze*

Size J (6 mm) crochet hook
  (or size required for gauge)

GAUGE
Rnds 1 through 4 on Large
  Motif = 5 ¹/₂" diameter

STITCH GUIDE

Ch-3 join: Ch 1, drop lp, insert hook in center ch of corresponding ch-3 on adjacent motif, pick up dropped lp and draw through ch, ch 1.

Ch-5 join: Ch 2, drop lp, insert hook in center ch of corresponding ch-5 on adjacent motif, pick up dropped lp and draw through ch, ch 2.

INSTRUCTIONS

Note: *Mark Motifs as they are worked.*

Strip 1

Large Motif 1
Ch 4; join with sl st to form a ring.

Rnd 1: Ch 3 (counts as dc), 15 dc in ring: 16 dc; join with sl st in 3rd ch of beg ch-3.

Rnd 2: Ch 1, (sc, ch 3) in same st as joining and in each st around: 16 sc and 16 ch-3 sps; join with sl st in beg sc.

Rnd 3: Sl st in next ch-3 sp, ch 3 (counts as dc), (dc, ch 3, 2 dc) in same ch-3 sp, sc in next ch-3 sp; *(2 dc, ch 3, 2 dc) in next ch-3 sp, sc in next ch-3 sp; rep from * around: 32 dc, 8 sc and 8 ch-3 sps; join with sl st in 3rd ch of beg ch-3.

Rnd 4: Sl st in next dc and in next ch-3 sp, ch 1, (sc, ch 3, sc, ch 5, sc, ch 3, sc) in same ch-3 sp, sc in next sc; *(sc, ch 3, sc, ch 5, sc, ch 3, sc) in next ch-3 sp, sc in next sc; rep from * around: 16 ch-3 sps, 8 ch-5 sps and 40 sc; join with sl st in beg sc. Finish off; weave in ends.

Strip 2

Large Motif 1

Ch 4; join with sl st to form a ring.

Rnds 1 through 3: Rep Rnds 1 through 3 on strip 1, large motif 1.

Note: Join Rnd 4 to right side of strip 1, large motif 1.

Rnd 4: Sl st in next ch-3 sp, ch 1, (sc, ch 3, sc, ch-5 join, sc, ch-3 join, sc) in same ch-3 sp, sc in next sc, (sc, ch-3 join, sc, ch-5 join, sc, ch 3, sc) in next ch-3 sp, sc in next sc; *(sc, ch 3, sc, ch 5, sc, ch 3, sc) in next ch-3 sp, sc in next sc; rep from * around: 14 ch-3 sps, 2 ch-3 joins, 6 ch-5 sps, 2 ch-5 joins and 40 sc; join with sl st in beg sc.

Strip 2

Large Motifs 2 through 6

Work same as strip 2, large motif 1, joining each large motif to bottom of previous large motif on strip 2.

Strip 3

Large Motif 1

Work same as strip 2, large motif 1, joining to right side of strip 2, large motif 2.

Strip 3

Large Motif 2

Ch 4; join with sl st to form a ring.

Rnds 1 through 3: Rep Rnds 1 through 3 on strip 1, large motif 1.

Note: Join Rnd 4 to bottom of strip 3, large motif 1 and to right side of strip 2, large motif 3.

Rnd 4: Sl st in next ch-3 sp, ch 1, (sc, ch 3, sc, ch-5 join, sc, ch-3 join, sc) in same ch-3 sp, sc in next sc, (sc, ch-3 join, sc, ch-5 join, sc, ch 3, sc) in next ch-3 sp, sc in next sc, (sc, ch 3, sc, ch-5 join, sc, ch-3 join, sc) in next ch-3 sp, sc in next sc, (sc, ch-3 join, sc, ch-5 join, sc, ch 3, sc) in next ch-3 sp, sc in next sc; *(sc, ch 3, sc, ch 5, sc, ch 3, sc) in next ch-3 sp, sc in next sc; rep from * around: 12 ch-3 sps, 4 ch-3 joins, 4 ch-5 sps, 4 ch-5 joins and 40 sc; join with sl st in beg sc.

Strip 3

Large Motifs 3 through 5

Work same as strip 3, large motif 2, joining to bottom of previous large motif on strip 3 and to right side of strip 2, large motifs 4 through 6.

Strips 4 and 5

Large Motifs 1 through 5

Work same as strip 3, large motifs 1 through 5, joining motif 1 to right side of previous strip, large motif 1 and motifs 2 through 5 to bottom of previous large motif in same strip and to right side of previous strip, large motifs 2 through 5.

Strip 6

Large Motif 1

Work same as strip 1, large motif 1.

Strip 6

Large Motifs 2 through 6

Work same as strip 3, large motif 2, joining large motif 2 to bottom of strip 6, large motif 1 and to right side of strip 5, large motif 1. Join large motif 3 to bottom of strip 6, large motif 2 and to right side of strip 5, large motif 2. Join large motifs 4 through 6 in same manner.

Strip 7

Large Motif 1

Work same as strip 2, large motif 1, joining to right side of strip 6, large motif 1.

Center Filler Motif (make 12)

Ch 4; join with sl st to form a ring.

Rnd 1: Ch 4 (counts as dc and ch-1 sp); *dc in ring, ch 1; rep from * 10 times more: 12 dc and 12 ch-1 sps; join with sl st in 3rd ch of beg ch-4.

Rnd 2: Working in open sps between 4 joined large motifs: *(sc, ch-3 join, sc) in each of next 2 ch-1 sps, (sc, ch-5 join, sc) in next ch-1 sp; rep from * around: 4 ch-5 joins, 8 ch-3 joins and 24 sc; join with sl st in beg sc.

Note: Ch-5 joins are worked in previous ch-5 joins on large motifs. Ch-3 joins are worked in unjoined ch-3 sps on large motifs.

Corner Edging Motif (make 4)

Ch 4; join with sl st to form a ring.

Rnd 1: Work same as Rnd 1 on center filler motif.

Rnd 2: Working in open sps between 3 joined large motifs on strips 2 and 6, left and right side of joined large motifs 1 and 2: *(sc, ch-5 join, sc) in next ch-1 sp, (sc, ch-3 join, sc) in each of next 2 ch-1 sps; rep from * 2 times more; (sc, ch-5 join, sc) in next ch-1 sp, (sc, ch 3, sc) in each of next 2 ch-1 sps: 4 ch-5 joins, 6 ch-3 joins, 2 ch-3 sps and 24 sc; join with sl st in beg sc. Finish off; weave in ends.

Edging Motif (make 14)

Ch 4; join with sl st to form a ring.

Rnd 1: Work same as Rnd 1 on center filler motif.

Rnd 2: Working around outer edges between 2 joined large motifs: (sc, ch-5 join, sc) in next ch-1 sp; *(sc, ch-3 join, sc) in each of next 2 ch-1 sps, (sc, ch-5 join, sc) in next ch-1 sp; rep from * once more; (sc, ch 3, sc) in each of next 2 ch-1 sps, (sc, ch 5, sc) in next ch-1 sp, (sc, ch 3, sc) in each of next 2 ch-1 sps: 3 ch-5 joins, 1 ch-5 sp, 4 ch-3 joins, 4 ch-3 sps and 24 sc; join with sl st in beg sc. Finish off; weave in ends.

FLOWERS AND BEARS IN THE DELL

Afghan designed by Mary Jane Protus for Coats & Clark

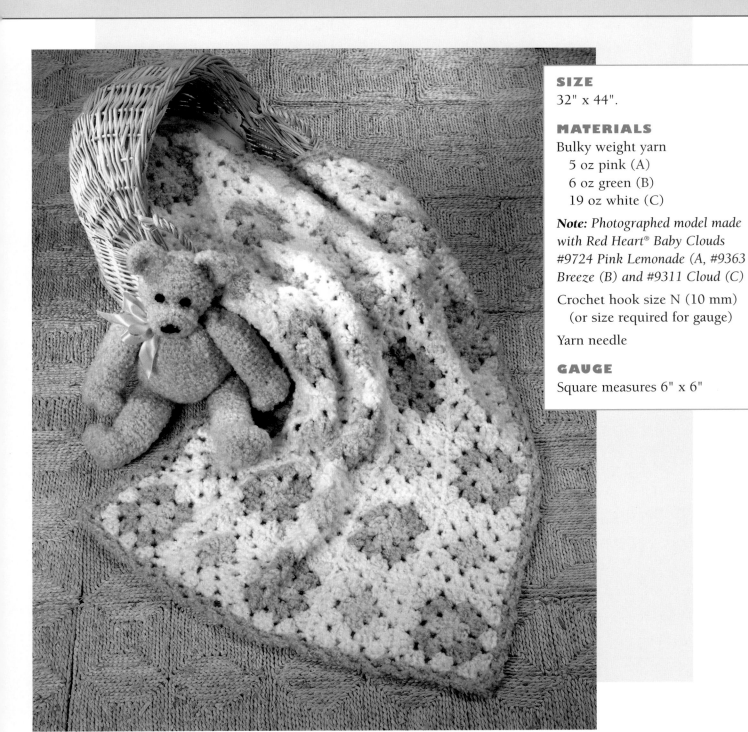

SIZE
32" x 44".

MATERIALS
Bulky weight yarn
   5 oz pink (A)
   6 oz green (B)
   19 oz white (C)

Note: *Photographed model made with Red Heart® Baby Clouds #9724 Pink Lemonade (A, #9363 Breeze (B) and #9311 Cloud (C)*

Crochet hook size N (10 mm)
   (or size required for gauge)

Yarn needle

GAUGE
Square measures 6" x 6"

INSTRUCTIONS

Square A (make 18)

With Color A, ch 4; join with a sl st to form a ring.

Rnd 1: Ch 5 (counts as a dc and a ch-2 sp), (3 dc in ring, ch 2) 3 times, 2 dc in ring; join with a sl st in 3rd ch of ch-5. Finish off.

Rnd 2: Join Color B in any ch-2 sp; ch 5, 3 dc in same sp, ch 1; [(3 dc, ch 2, 3 dc) in next ch-2 sp for corner, ch 1] 3 times, 2 dc in first sp; join in 3rd ch of beg ch-5. Finish off.

Rnd 3: Join Color C in any corner ch-2 sp; ch 5, 3 dc in same sp, ch 1, 3 dc in next ch-1 sp, ch 1; [(3 dc, ch 2, 3 dc) in corner ch-2 sp, ch 1, 3 dc in next ch-1 sp, ch 1] 3 times, 2 dc in first sp; join. Finish off; weave in all ends.

Square B (make 17)

With Color A, ch 4; join with a sl st to form a ring.

Rnd 1: Work same as Square A.

Rnd 2: Join Color C in any ch-2 sp; ch 5, 3 dc in same sp, ch 1; [(3 dc, ch 2, 3 dc) in next ch-2 sp for corner, ch 1] 3 times, 2 dc in first sp; join in 3rd ch of beg ch-5.

Rnd 3: Sl st into first sp; ch 3, (2 dc, ch 2, 3 dc) in first sp, ch 1, 3 dc in next ch-1 sp, ch 1; [(3 dc, ch 2, 3 dc) all in corner ch-2 sp, ch 1, 3 dc in next ch-1 sp, ch 1] 3 times; join.

Finish off; weave in all ends

Finishing

Join squares in 7 rows of 5 squares each; to join, hold 2 squares with right sides tog and with Color A, sew with overcast st, carefully matching sts. Sew squares alternating A and B as shown in diagram.

A	B	A	B	A
B	A	B	A	B
A	B	A	B	A
B	A	B	A	B
A	B	A	B	A
B	A	B	A	B
A	B	A	B	A

Border

With right side facing, join Color B in any outer corner ch-2 sp.

Rnd 1: Ch 1; **(sc, ch 3, sc) in corner sp, ch 3; * sc in next sp, ch 3; rep from * to next corner; rep from ** around; join with a sl st in first sc.

Rnd 2: Sl st into first sp, ch 1; **(sc, ch 3, sc) all in corner sp, ch 3; * sc in next sp, ch 3; rep from * to next corner; rep from ** around; join in first sc. Finish off; weave in ends.

TEDDY BEAR

Designed by Sue Penrod for Coats & Clark

SIZE
21" tall

MATERIALS
Bulky weight yarn
  13 oz pink (or desired color)

Worsted weight yarn
  30 yds black

Note: Photographed model made with Red Heart® Baby Clouds #9724 Pink Lemonade and Super Saver® #312 Black

Poly fiberfill for stuffing

Tapestry or yarn needle

Size I (5.5 mm) crochet hook

Size K (6.5 mm) crochet hook, or size
  required for gauge

GAUGE
7 sc = 3" with larger hook and bulky
  weight yarn

7 sc rnds = 3" with larger hook and
  bulky weight yarn

INSTRUCTIONS

Note: Use bulky weight yarn and larger hook unless otherwise specified.

Ear (make 2)
Ch 4; join with sl st to form a ring.

Rnd 1 (right side): Ch 1, 8 sc in ring; use a piece of contrasting yarn to mark end of rnd; do not join, work in continuous rnds.

Rnd 2: 2 sc in each sc: 16 sc.

Rnds 3 and 4: Sc in each sc.

Row 5: Fold ear in half with wrong sides together, ch 1, work 8 sc across working through both layers. Finish off, leaving a long yarn end for sewing.

Muzzle
Work same as ear through Rnd 2.

Rnd 3: (Sc in next sc, 2 sc in next sc) 8 times: 24 sc.

Rnds 4 and 5: Sc in each sc. Finish off, leaving a long yarn end for sewing.

Arm (make 2)
Work same as ear through Rnd 2.

Rnds 3 through 14: Sc in each sc around. Stuff lightly with poly fiberfill and roll in your hands to shape.

Rnd 15 (wrist): (Draw up a lp in next 2 sc, YO and draw yarn through all 3 loops on hook) 4 times, sc in next 8 sc: 12 sc.

Rnd 16 (paw): Sc in next 4 sc, (2 sc in next sc) 8 times: 20 sc.

Rnds 17 through 19: Sc in each sc. Stuff lightly with poly fiberfill and shape.

Rnd 20: (Sc in next 3 sc, skip next sc, sc in next sc) 4 times: 16 sc.

Rnd 21: (Sc in next sc, skip next sc): 8 sc.

Rnd 22: (Sl st in next sc, skip next sc) 4 times. Finish off.

Leg (make 2)

Work same as ear through Rnd 2.

Rnds 3 through 16: Sc in each sc. Stuff lightly with poly fiberfill and shape.

Rnd 17 (ankle): (Draw up a lp in next 2 sc, YO and draw yarn through all 3 lps on hook) 4 times, sc in next 8 sc: 12 sc.

Rnd 18: (3 sc in next sc) 4 times, sc in next 8 sc: 20 sc.

Rnds 19 through 22: Sc in each sc. Stuff lightly with poly fiberfill and shape.

Rnds 23 through 25: Work same as Arms Rnds 20 through 22. Finish off.

Head and Body

Work same as ear through Rnd 2.

Rnd 3: 2 sc in each sc: 32 sc.

Rnds 4 through 13: Sc in each sc.

Rnd 14 (neck): (Draw up a lp in next 2 sc, YO and draw yarn through all 3 lps on hook) 16 times: 16 sc.

Rnd 15 (body): 3 sc in each sc: 48 sc.

Rnds 16 through 28: Sc in each sc.

Rnd 29: (Sc in next 6 sc, skip next sc, sc in next sc) 6 times: 42 sc.

Rnd 30: (Sc in next 4 sc, skip next sc, sc in next sc) 7 times: 35 sc.

Rnd 31: (Sc in next 5 sc, skip next sc, sc in next sc) 5 times: 30 sc.

Rnd 32: (Sc in next 3 sc, skip next sc, sc in next sc) 6 times: 24 sc.

Stuff head lightly with poly fiberfill and shape before working next rnds.

Rnd 33: (Sc in next sc, skip next sc, sc in next sc) 8 times: 16 sc.

Stuff body lightly with poly fiberfill and shape. Weave yarn through the stitches of Rnd 14 (neck), gathering neck to shape. Knot yarn ends together; weave in ends.

Rnd 34: (Sc in next sc, skip next sc) 8 times: 8 sc.

Rnd 35: (Sl st in next sc, skip next sc) 4 times. Finish off; weave in all ends.

Assembly

As shown in photo, sew arms and legs onto body, leaving a 6" beginning yarn end on outer side of each limb.

Stitch through limb and into body, then back through limb several times at same point. This method allows limbs to move. Cut yarn, leaving a 6" end. Knot yarn ends tog, weave ends back into limb.

Cup ears slightly and sew them to head.

Stuff muzzle lightly with poly fiberfill and sew into place on head.

Features

Nose

With black worsted weight yarn and smaller hook, ch 3.

Rnd 1: 5 hdc in 3rd ch from hook, ch 3, sl st in same ch, Finish off, leaving a long yarn end for sewing.

Eye (make 2)

With black worsted weight yarn and smaller hook, ch 2.

Row 1: 3 sc in 2nd ch from hook. Finish off, leaving a long end for sewing.

With black worsted weight yarn, embroider mouth onto muzzle. Sew nose to muzzle above mouth; sew eyes in place, rounding them slightly.

#86 LOOPY PONCHO

Designed by Marty Miller

Note: *Instructions are written for size Small; changes for sizes Medium, Large and Extra Large are in parentheses.*

SIZES	Small	Medium	Large	X-Large
Fits Bust	32" - 34"	36" - 38"	40" - 42"	44" - 46"

MATERIALS

Sport weight yarn
   24 ¹/₂ (28, 30, 34) oz white

Note: *Photographed model made with Berroco® Chinchilla™ #5101 Vanilla*

Size K (6.5 mm) crochet hook
   (or size required for gauge)

GAUGE

10 Lp Sts = 4"

INSTRUCTIONS

Rectangles (make 2)

Starting at bottom, ch 79 (81, 84, 86).

Row 1 (right side): Sc in 2nd ch from hook and in each ch across: 78 (80, 83, 85) sc; ch 1, turn.

Row 2: LpSt in each sc; ch 1, turn.

Row 3: Sc in each LpSt; ch 1, turn.

Rep Rows 2 and 3 until piece measures 14" (15", 16", 17") from starting ch, ending by working a Row 3. Finish off.

Finishing

Join the two rectangles tog following diagrams. GB is the top of one rectangle, FD is the top of the other. Connect G to E, H to F, A to D and B to C. To join, with the right sides together, sc the two rectangles together along (GE) (HF) and then along (AD) (BC), making sure to keep the seams flat.

Neck Edging

Rnd 1: With right side facing, join yarn in the middle of one side of the neck edge. Sc in each sc around until 2 scs before the corner, work sc dbl dec; sc to next corner, work sc dbl dec as before, sc around; join with sl st in beg sc; ch 1, turn.

Rnd 2: Lp St in each sc until 2 scs before the corner; work Lp St dec; Lp St to next corner, dec as before, work Lp St around, join with sl st in beg Lp St; ch 1, turn.

Rnd 3: Rep Rnd 1. Finish off; weave in all ends.

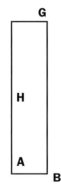

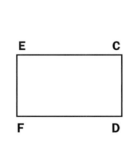

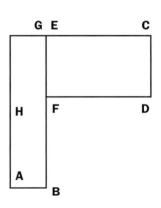

217

#87 COZY SHRUG

Designed by Kathleen Stuart

SIZE
26" wide x 60" long

MATERIALS
Bulky weight yarn
  30 oz purple

Eyelash yarn
  1 1/2 oz gray

Note: *Photographed model made with Lion Brand® Homespun® #314 Renaissance and Fun Fur #204 Lava*

Size J (6 mm) crochet hook
  (or size required for gauge)

GAUGE
11 hdc = 4"

7 hdc rows = 4"

INSTRUCTIONS

Body

With bulky yarn, ch 68.

Row 1 (right side): Hdc in 3rd ch from hook (2 skipped chs count as hdc), hdc in next ch and in each ch across: 67 hdc; ch 3 (counts as hdc and ch-1 sp on next row now and throughout), turn.

Row 2: Skip first 2 hdc, hdc in next hdc; *ch 1, skip next hdc, hdc in next hdc; rep from * across: 34 hdc and 33 ch-1 sps; ch 2 (counts as hdc on next row now and throughout), turn.

Row 3: Puff st in first ch-1 sp; *ch 1, skip next hdc, puff st in next ch-1 sp; rep from * across, ending with puff st in 3rd ch of turning ch-3, hdc in 2nd ch of turning ch-3: 33 puff sts, 32 ch-1 sps and 2 hdc; ch 3, turn.

PATTERN STITCHES

Puff st: (YO, insert hook in specified st and draw up a lp) 4 times, YO and draw through all 9 lps on hook: puff st made.

3 sc decrease (3 sc dec): (Insert hook in specified st and draw up a lp) 3 times, YO and draw through all 4 lps on hook: 3 sc dec made.

Front Post dc (FPdc): YO, insert hook from front to back to front around post of specified st and draw up a lp, (YO and draw through 2 lps on hook) twice: FPdc made.

Back Post dc (BPdc): YO, insert hook from back to front to back around post of specified st and draw up a lp, (YO and draw through 2 lps on hook) twice: BPdc made.

Row 4: Skip first puff st; *hdc in next ch-1 sp, ch 1, skip next puff st; rep from * across, ending with hdc in 2nd ch of turning ch-2: 34 hdc and 33 ch-1 sps; ch 2, turn.

Row 5: *Hdc in next ch-1 sp, hdc in next hdc; rep from * across, ending with hdc in 3rd ch of turning ch-3, hdc in 2nd ch of turning ch-3: 67 hdc; ch 3, turn.

Rep Rows 2 through 5 twenty three times mores. At end of last row, ch 1, turn.

First Cuff

Row 1: Skip first hdc, *3 sc dec in next 3 sts; rep from * across: 22 sts; ch 1, turn.

Row 2: Sc in first st and in each st across: 22 sc; join with sl st in first sc. Do not turn. Note: Cuff is worked in rnds from this point forward.

Rnd 3: Ch 3 (counts as dc), dc in next sc and in each sc around: 22 dc; join with sl st in 3rd ch of turning ch-3.

Rnds 4 through 8: Ch 2 (counts as hdc), FPdc in next st, *BPdc in next st, FPdc in next st; rep from * around: 11 FPdc, 10BPdc and 1 hdc; join with sl st in 2nd ch of beg ch-2. At end of last rnd: finish off; weave in ends.

Second Cuff

Row 1: With right side facing, join bulky yarn with sl st in free lp of first ch on Row 1 of body, ch 1; *3 sc dec in next 3 sts; rep from * across: 22 sts; ch 1, turn.

Row 2: Rep Row 2 of first cuff. Note: Cuff is worked in rnds from this point forward.

Rnds 3 through 8: Rep Rnds 3 through 8 of first cuff.

Edging

With outside facing, join bulky yarn with sc in edge of row next to cuff, sc in edge of each row across side of shrug, sc in edge of each row across other side of shrug; join with sl st in first sc. Finish off; weave in ends.

Sleeves

Starting at end of edging near cuff, whip-stitch 8" of edging on sides together. Rep on other cuff.

Fur Edging

Rnd 1: With inside facing, join eyelash yarn with sc in any sc on edging round, sc in next sc and in each sc around; join with sl st in first sc.

Rnd 2: Ch 3, dc in next sc and in each sc around, join with sl st in 3rd ch of beg ch-3. Finish off; weave in ends.

Note: *Instructions are written for size Small; changes for sizes Medium and Large are in parentheses.*

SIZES	Small	Medium	Large
Body Bust Measurements	32" - 34"	36"	38" - 40"
Finished Bust Measurements	35 1/2"	38 1/2"	41 1/2"

MATERIALS

Size 5 crochet cotton
  400 (500, 500) g cream

Note: *Photographed model made with Twilleys Lyscordet #21 Cream.*

Size C (2.75 mm) crochet hook

Size E (3.5 mm) crochet hook
  (or size required for gauge)

GAUGE

One flower square = 2 1/4" x 2 1/4"
  with larger hook.

INSTRUCTIONS

Back

First Flower Square

Rnd 1: With larger hook, ch 4, join with sl st in first ch to form a ring.

Rnd 2: Ch 1, 8 sc in ring; join with sl st in beg sc.

Rnd 3: Ch 4; *YO 3 times, insert hook in sc at base of ch-4, YO, draw up lp, [YO, draw through 2 lps] 3 times, rep from * once more; YO, draw through 3 lps on hook (first petal made); ** ch 4, trCl in next sc, ch 4, dtrCl in next sc, rep from ** twice more; ch 4, trCl in last sc, ch 4, sl st in top of first petal made: 8 petals.

Rnd 4: * Ch 3, sl st in top of same petal (picot made), 4 sc in ch-4 sp, sl st in top of next petal, rep from *; ending with sl st in top of first petal. Finish off; weave in ends.

Second Flower Square

Rnds 1 through 3: Rep Rounds 1 through 3 of First Flower Square.

Rnd 4: Work as for Round 4 of First Flower joining 5th, 6th and 7th picots to 3 corresponding picots of first flower square as follows: Instead of ch 3, work [ch 1, sl st into corresponding picot, ch 1].

Make a further 8 (8, 9) flower squares, joining them side by side into a strip of 10 (10, 11) squares.

Make another 2 strips in the same way.

The strips are now joined by working rows along their edges.

Left Side

With right side of strip facing, with larger hook, and working along one long side of first strip, join yarn to picot at right-hand corner.

Row 1: Ch 5; * sc in next picot, ch 4, sc in each of 2 joined picots, ch 4, rep from * across strip, ending with sc in last corner picot, ch 1, turn: 110 (110, 121) sts.

Row 2: Sc in first sc; * 4 sc in ch-4 sp, sc in next sc, 4 sc in ch-4 sp, sc in next 2 sc, rep from *; across, ending with 5 (5, 4) sc in ch-5 sp, sc in 5th ch of this ch-5, ch 4, turn: 111 (111, 121) sc.

Row 3: Skip first sc; * trCl in next sc, ch 1, skip 1 sc, rep from * to last 2 sc, ending with trCl in next sc, tr in last sc, ch 1, turn: 55 (55, 60) trCl.

Row 4: Sc in tr; * skip top of trCl, 2 sc in ch-1 sp; rep from * across, ending with sc under ch-4, sc in 4th ch of this ch-4; ch 4, turn. 111 (111, 121) sc.

Rows 5 through 7 (9, 9): Rep Rows 3 and 4, 1 (2, 2) more times, and Row 3 once more.

Join Second Strip of Flower Squares

Row 8 (10, 10): With wrong side of second strip facing, work jsc in [tr and first picot of long edge of second strip]; * [2 sc in next ch-sp] twice; jsc in [next ch-sp and next picot]; sc in same ch-sp, 2 sc in next ch-sp, sc in next ch-sp; jsc in [same ch-sp and next picot], jsc in [next ch-sp and next picot]; sc in same ch-sp, 2 sc in next ch-sp, sc in next ch-sp; jsc in [same ch-sp and next picot]; [2 sc in next ch-sp] twice; jsc in [next ch-sp and next picot], jsc in [same ch-sp and next picot]; rep from *; ending with jsc in [4th ch of ch-4 and last picot]. Finish off; weave in ends.

Working along opposite edge of 2nd strip, with right side of strip facing, using larger hook, join yarn to picot at right-hand corner.

Rows 9 (11, 11) through 12 (14, 14): Rep Rows 1 through 4: 111 (111, 121) sc.

For Large Size Only
Rows 15 and 16: Rep Rows 3 and 4 once more.

Shape Armhole (for all sizes)

Row 1: Ch 5, skip first sc; [trCl in next sc, ch 1, skip 1 sc] 34 (34, 37) times; trCl in next sc, skip 1 sc, tr3tog over next 3 sc; ch 1, turn, leaving 37 (37, 41) sc unworked.

Row 2: Skip top of tr3tog and top of trCl; * 2 sc in ch-1 sp, skip top of trCl, rep from * across; ending with sc under ch-5, sc in 4th ch of ch-5, ch 5, turn.

Row 3: Skip first sc; [trCl in next sc, ch 1, skip 1 sc] 32 (32, 35) times; trCl in next sc, skip 1 sc, tr3tog over next 3 sc; ch 1, turn.

Row 4: Rep Row 2.

Row 5: Skip first sc; [trCl in next sc, ch 1, skip 1 sc] 30 (30, 33) times; trCl in next sc, skip 1 sc, tr3tog over next 3 sc; ch 1, turn.

Row 6: Sc in top of tr3tog; * skip top of trCl, 2 sc in ch-1 sp, rep from *; ending with sc under ch-5, sc in 4th ch of ch-5. Finish off; weave in ends.

Right Side

With right side of work facing, begin at opposite edge of center strip and work as Left Side Rows 1 through 12 (14, 16). Finish off; weave in ends.

Shape Armhole (for all sizes)

Counting from shoulder edge, with right side of work facing, rejoin yarn in 38th (38th, 42nd) sc.

Row 1: Ch 3, tr2tog over next 2 sc; * skip 1 sc, trCl in next sc, ch 1, rep from * across; ending with tr in last sc, ch 1, turn.

Row 2: Sc in tr, sc in ch-1 sp; * skip top of trCl, 2 sc in ch-1 sp, rep from * across, ending with skip top of last trCl, sc in top of tr2tog, turn.

Row 3: Rep Row 1, ending with skip 1 sc, tr in last sc.

Rows 4 and 5: Rep Rows 2 and 3.

Row 6: Rep Row 2. Finish off; weave in ends.

Front

Work same as Back.

Sleeves (make 2)

With larger hook make a strip of 8 (8, 9) flowers in the same way as Back. Sleeves are worked sideways, in the same way as the Back.

Left Side

Working along one long side of strip, with right side of strip facing and with larger hook, join yarn to picot at right-hand corner.

Rows 1 through 4: Rep Rows 1 through 4 of Left Side of Back: 44 (44, 48) trCl.

Rows 5 through 11 (11, 13): Rep Rows 3 and 4, 3 (3, 4) more times, and Row 3 once again.

Shape Sleeve

Row 1: Ch 1, sc in tr; [skip top of trCl, 2 sc in next sp] 33 times, ch 3, turn.

Row 2: Skip 1 sc, tr3tog over next 3 sc; * skip 1 sc, trCl in next sc, ch 1, rep from * to last 2 sc; trCl in next sc, tr in last sc, ch 1, turn.

Row 3: Sc in tr, [skip top of trCl, 2 sc in next ch-sp] 24 times, ch 3, turn.

Row 4: Skip 1 sc, tr3tog over next 3 sc; * skip 1 sc, trCl in next sc, ch 1, rep from * to last 5 sc; skip 1 sc, tr3tog over next 3 sc, tr in last sc, ch 1, turn.

Row 5: Sc in tr, skip top of tr3tog, 2 sc in next sp, [skip top of trCl, 2 sc in next ch-sp] 13 times, ch 3, turn.

Row 6: Rep Row 4.

Row 7: Sc in tr, skip top of tr3tog, 2 sc in next sp, [skip top of trCl, 2 sc in next ch-sp] 3 times, ch 3, turn.

Row 8: [Skip 1 sc, tr3tog over next 3 sc] twice, tr in last sc. Finish off; weave in ends.

Right Side

Working along one long side of strip, with right side of strip facing and with larger hook, join yarn in picot at right-hand corner.

Rows 1 through 4: Rep Rows 1 through 4 of Left Side of Back: 44 (44, 48) trCl.

Rows 5 through 12 (12, 14): Rep Rows 3 and 4, 4 (4, 5) more times

Shape Sleeve

Row 1: Ch 4, skip first sc, [trCl in next sc, ch 1, skip 1 sc] 31 times, tr3tog over next 3 sc, tr in next sc; ch 1, turn.

Row 2: Skip top of tr3tog, sc in next ch-sp; * skip top of trCl, 2 sc in next ch-sp, rep from * across, ending with sc under ch-4, sc in 3rd ch of ch-4; ch 3, turn.

Row 3: Skip 1 sc; tr3tog over next 3 sc, [skip 1 sc, trCl in next sc, ch 1] 19 times; skip 1 sc, trCl in next sc, skip 1 sc; tr3tog over next 3 sc, tr in next sc; ch 1, turn.

Row 4: Skip top of tr3tog; sc in next ch-sp; * skip top of trCl, 2 sc in next ch-sp, rep from * across, ending with sc in top of tr3tog, sc in 3rd ch of ch-3, ch 3, turn.

Row 5: Skip 1 sc, tr3tog over next 3 sc, [skip 1 sc, trCl in next sc, ch 1] 9 times, skip 1 sc, trCl in next sc, skip 1 sc, tr3tog over next 3 sc, tr in next sc, ch 1, turn.

Row 6: Rep Row 4.

Row 7: Ch 3, [skip 1 sc, tr3tog over next 3 sc] twice, tr in next sc. Finish off; weave in ends.

Finishing

Shoulder seams

With right sides tog, sew row ends together at each side up to first picots of flower squares. Matching shaping rows, and centers of flower strips to shoulder seams, sew top edges of sleeves to armholes. Sew side and sleeve seams.

Cuffs

With right side of work facing, with smaller hook, join yarn to base of sleeve seam.

Rnd 1: Ch 1, [ch 4, sc in side edge of next sc row] 4 (4, 5) times, ch 4, sc2tog over side edge of next sc row and first picot, ch 4, sc in next picot, ch 4, sc2tog over next picot and following sc row, [ch 4, sc in side edge of next row] 4 (4, 5) times, ch 4, sl st in ch-1 at beg of round.

Rnd 2: Ch 1; *3 sc in next ch-sp, ch 3, sl st in last sc worked (picot made), 2 sc in same ch-sp, skip 1 sc, rep from *; ending with sl st in ch-1 at beg of round. Finish off; weave in ends.

Bottom Border

With right side of work facing, with smaller hook, join yarn to base of one side seam.

Rnd 1: Ch 1; *[ch 4, sc in side edge of next sc row] 4 (4, 5) times, [[ch 4, sc2tog over side edge of next sc row and first picot; ch 4, sc in next picot, ch 4; sc2tog over next picot and side edge of following sc row, [ch 4, sc in side edge of next row] 2 (3, 3) times] twice; ch 4, sc2tog over side edge of next sc row and following picot, ch 4; sc in next picot, ch 4; sc2tog over next picot and side edge of following sc row, [ch 4, sc in side edge of next sc row] 4 (4, 5) times with last sc in base of seam, rep from * once more; ending with sl st in ch-1 at beg of round.

Rnd 2: Rep Rnd 2 of Cuff. Finish off; weave in ends.

Neck Border

With right side of work facing, with smaller hook, join yarn in center picot at top of right hand strip of back. Work along top edge of back:

Rnd 1: *Ch 4, sc2tog over next picot and side edge of following sc row, [ch 4, sc in side edge of next sc row] 2 (3, 3) times; ch 4, sc2tog over side edge of next sc row and following picot, ch 4, * sc in next picot, rep * to * once more; sc2tog over next picot and corresponding picot of front edge; work along front edge in same way as back, ending with sc2tog over center picot of last flower strip and corresponding picot of back edge at beg of round.

Rnd 2: Rep Round 2 of Cuff, working last sc of back edge together with first sc of front edge at corner, and ending by working last sc of front edge together with sl st in first sc of round. Finish off; weave in ends.

#89 FALLING LEAVES WRAP

Designed by Zelda K

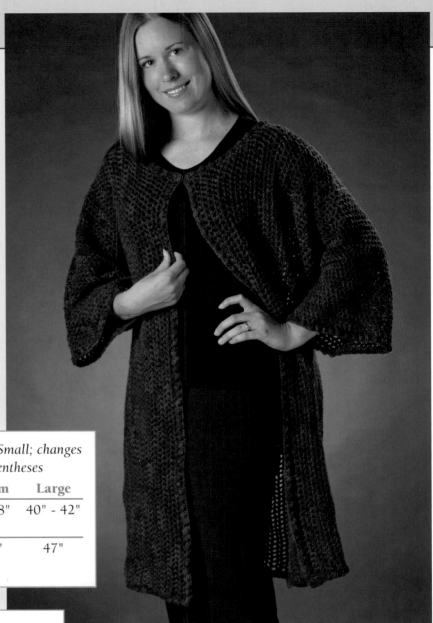

MATERIALS

Sport weight yarn
  25 (28, 30) oz multi-colored

Note: *Photographed model made with Lion Brand® Wool-Ease® Sportweight, #233 Autumn Print*

Size G (4 mm) crochet hook
  (or size required for gauge)

Matching sewing thread and
  sewing needle

1 skirt/pant hook and eye

Safety pin

GAUGE

10 dc and 10 ch-1 sps = 4 $^{1}/_{4}$"

10 dc rows = 4"

Note: *Instructions are written for size Small; changes for sizes Medium and Large are in parentheses*

SIZES	Small	Medium	Large
Body Bust Measurements	32" - 34"	36" - 38"	40" - 42"
Finished Bust Measurements	40 $^{1}/_{2}$"	43 $^{3}/_{4}$"	47"

STITCH GUIDE

Hdc/dc decrease (hdc/dc dec): (YO, insert hook in specified st or sp and draw up a lp) two times, YO and draw through 2 lps on hook, YO and draw through rem 4 lps on hook: hdc/dc dec made.

Puff st: YO, insert hook in specified st and draw up a lp, (YO, insert hook in same st and draw up a lp) 3 times, YO and draw through all 9 lps on hook: puff st made.

Reverse sc (rev sc): Working from left to right, sc in next st to the right: rev sc made.

INSTRUCTIONS

Right Sleeve

Ch 100.

Row 1 (right side): Dc in 6th ch from hook (5 skipped chs count as dc and ch-1 sp); *ch 1, skip next ch, dc in next ch; rep from * across: 49 dc and 48 ch-1 sps; ch 4 (counts as dc and ch-1 sp on next row now and throughout), turn.

Row 2: Skip first 2 dc, dc in next ch-1 sp; *ch 1, skip next dc, dc in next ch-1 sp; rep from * across to beg skipped chs; ch 1, dc in first skipped ch, ch 1, dc in next ch; ch 4, turn.

Row 3: Skip first 2 dc, dc in next ch-1 sp, *ch 1, skip next dc, dc in next ch-1 sp, rep from * across to turning ch-4; ch 1, dc in 4th ch of turning ch-4, ch 1, dc in next ch; ch 4, turn.

Row 4: Dc in first ch-1 sp; *ch 1, skip next dc, dc in next ch-1 sp; rep from * across to turning ch-4; ch 1, dc in 4th ch of turning ch-4, ch 1, dc in next ch: 50 dc and 49 ch-1 sps; ch 4, turn.

Rows 5 through 14: Rep Row 4 ten times more. At end of Row 14: 60 dc and 59 ch-1 sps.

Rows 15 and 16: Rep Row 3 two times more.

Row 17: Rep Row 4: 61 dc and 60 ch-1 sps.

Rows 18 and 19: Rep Row 3 two times more.

Rows 20 through 22: Rep Rows 17 through 19: 62 dc and 61 ch-1 sps.

Rows 23 through 28: Rep Row 4 six times more. At end of Row 28: 68 dc and 67 ch-1 sps; ch 110 (instead of ch 4), turn.

Right Body

Row 1 (right side): Dc in 6th ch from hook (5 skipped chs count as dc and ch-1 sp); *ch 1, skip next ch, dc in next ch*; rep from * to * across chs; **ch 1, skip next dc, dc in next ch-1 sp; rep from ** across to turning ch-4; ch 1, dc in 4th ch of turning ch-4. Remove lp from hook and secure with safety pin so work does not unravel. Join new skein of yarn with sl st in 3rd ch of turning ch-4 at beg of Row 28 on right sleeve, ch 108. Finish off new skein. Remove safety pin and place dropped lp onto hook, ch 1, skip 3rd ch of turning ch-4, dc in first ch of added ch-108;

rep from * to * across to last ch; dc in last ch: 176 dc and 174 ch-1 sps; ch 4, turn.

Row 2: Skip first 2 dc, dc in next ch-1 sp; *ch 1, skip next dc, dc in next ch-1 sp; rep from * across to turning ch-4; ch 1, dc in 4th ch of turning ch-4, dc in next ch; ch 4, turn.

Rows 3 through 15 (17, 19): Rep Row 2 thirteen (fifteen, seventeen) times more.

Back

Row 1 (wrong side): Skip first 2 dc, dc in next ch-1 sp; *ch 1, skip next dc, dc in next ch-1 sp; rep from * 85 times more; dc in next dc: 89 dc and 87 ch-1 sps; ch 4, turn, leaving rem sts unworked.

Rows 2 through 20: Rep Row 2 of right body 19 times more. At end of Row 20, remove lp from hook and secure with safety pin so work does not unravel.

Right Front

Row 1: With wrong side facing, skip next 2 dc on Row 15 (17, 19) of right body, join with sl st in next dc, hdc/dc dec in next 2 ch-1 sps; *ch 1, skip next dc, dc in next ch-1 sp; rep from * across to turning ch-4; ch 1, dc in 4th ch of turning ch-4, dc in next ch: 83 dc, 82 ch-1 sps and 1 hdc/dc dec; ch 4, turn.

Row 2: Skip first 2 dc, dc in next ch-1 sp; *ch 1, skip next dc, dc in next ch-1 sp; rep from * across; ch 1, dc in hdc/dc dec: 84 dc and 83 ch-1 sps; ch 1, turn.

Row 3: Hdc in first ch-1 sp, hdc/dc dec in next dc and next ch-1 sp; *ch 1, skip next dc, dc in next ch-1 sp; rep from * across to turning ch-4; ch 1, dc in 4th ch of turning ch-4, dc in next ch: 82 dc, 81 ch-1 sps, 1 hdc/dc dec and 1 hdc; ch 4, turn.

Row 4: Skip first 2 dc, dc in next ch-1 sp; *ch 1, skip next dc, dc in next ch-1 sp; rep from * across; dc in hdc/dc dec: 83 dc and 81 ch-1 sps; ch 1, turn.

Row 5: Rep Row 3: 80 dc, 79 ch-1 sps, 1 hdc/dc dec and 1 hdc.

Row 6: Rep Row 4: 81 dc and 79 ch-1 sps.

Row 7: Rep Row 3: 78 dc, 77 ch-1 sps, 1 hdc/dc dec and 1 hdc.

Row 8: Rep Row 4: 79 dc and 77 ch-1 sps. At end of row, ch 4 (instead of ch 1), turn.

Row 9: Skip first 2 dc, dc in next ch-1 sp; *ch 1, skip next dc, dc in next ch-1 sp; rep from * across to turning ch-4; ch 1, dc in 4th ch of turning ch-4, dc in next ch: 79 dc and 77 ch-1 sps; ch 4, turn.

Row 10: Rep Row 9. At end of row, do not ch 4. Finish off; weave in ends.

Left Front

Ch 159.

Row 1 (right side): Dc in 6th ch from hook (5 skipped chs count as dc and ch-1 sp); *ch 1, skip next ch, dc in next ch; rep from * across to last ch; dc in last ch: 79 dc and 77 ch-1 sps; ch 4, turn.

Rows 2 and 3: Skip first 2 dc, dc in next ch-1 sp: *ch 1, skip next dc, dc in next ch-1 sp; rep from * across to turning ch-4; ch 1, dc in 4th ch of turning ch-4, dc in next ch: 79 dc and 77 ch-1 sps; ch 4, turn.

Row 4: Dc in first dc; *ch 1, skip next dc, dc in next ch-1 sp; rep from * across to turning ch-4; ch 1, dc in 4th ch of turning ch-4, dc in next ch: 80 dc and 78 ch-1 sps; ch 4, turn.

Row 5: Skip first 2 dc, dc in next ch-1 sp; *ch 1, skip next dc, dc in next ch-1 sp; rep from * across to turning ch-4; ch 1, dc in 4th ch of turning ch-4, ch 1, dc in next ch: 80 dc and 79 ch-1 sps; ch 4, turn.

Row 6: Dc in first dc, ch 1, dc in next ch-1 sp; *ch 1, skip next dc, dc in next ch-1 sp; rep from * across to turning ch-4; ch 1, dc in 4th ch of turning ch-4, dc in next ch: 82 dc and 80 ch-1 sps; ch 4, turn.

Row 7: Rep Row 5: 82 dc and 81 ch-1 sps; ch 4, turn.

Row 8: Rep Row 6: 84 dc and 82 ch-1 sps; ch 4, turn.

Row 9: Rep Row 5: 84 dc and 83 ch-1 sps. At end of row, do not ch 4. Finish off; weave in ends.

Left Body

Row 1 (wrong side): Remove safety pin and place dropped lp from Row 20 of back onto hook, skip first 2 dc, dc in next ch-1 sp; *ch 1, skip next dc, dc in next ch-1 sp; rep from * across to turning ch-4; ch 1, skip 4th ch of turning ch-4, dc in next ch, ch 7, with wrong side of left front facing, dc in first dc at end of Row 9 on left front, ch 1, dc in first ch-1 sp; *ch 1, skip next dc, dc in next ch-1 sp; rep from * across to turning ch-4; ch 1, dc in 4th ch of turning ch-4, dc in next ch: 173 dc, 170 ch-1 sps and 7 chs; ch 4, turn.

Row 2 (right side): Skip first 2 dc, dc in next ch-1 sp; *ch 1, skip next dc, dc in next ch-1 sp*; rep from * to * across to ch-7 sp; ch 1, dc in first ch of ch-7 sp; **ch 1, skip next ch of ch-7, dc in next ch; rep from ** 2 times more; rep from * to * across to turning ch-4; ch 1, dc in 4th ch of turning ch-4, dc in next ch: 176 dc and 174 ch-1 sps; ch 4, turn.

Row 3: Skip first 2 dc, dc in next ch-1 sp; *ch 1, skip next dc, dc in next ch-1 sp; rep from * across to turning ch-4; ch 1, dc in 4th ch of turning ch-4, dc in next ch; ch 4, turn.

Rows 4 through 16 (18, 20): Rep Row 3 thirteen (fifteen, seventeen) times more. At end of last row, do not ch 4. Finish off; weave in ends.

Left Sleeve

Row 1 (wrong side): With wrong side facing, skip first 53 ch-1 sps on left body, join with sl st in next ch-1 sp, ch 4 (counts as dc and ch-1 sp), dc in next ch-1 sp; *ch 1, skip next dc, dc in next ch-1 sp; rep from * 65 times more: 68 dc and 67 ch-1 sps; ch 4, turn, leaving rem 53 ch-1 sps unworked.

Row 2: Skip first ch-1 sp, dc in next ch-1 sp; *ch 1, skip next dc, dc in next ch-1 sp; rep from * across to turning ch-4; ch 1, skip 4th ch of turning ch-4, dc in next ch: 67 dc and 66 ch-1 sps; ch 4, turn.

Rows 3 through 7: Rep Row 2 five times more. At end of Row 7: 62 dc and 61 ch-1 sps; ch 4, turn.

Row 8: Dc in first ch-1 sp; *ch 1, skip next dc, dc in next ch-1 sp; rep from * across to turning ch-4; ch 1, skip 4th ch of turning ch-4, dc in next ch; ch 4, turn.

Row 9: Rep Row 8.

Row 10: Rep Row 2: 61 dc and 60 ch-1 sps.

Rows 11 and 12: Rep Row 8 two times more.

Row 13: Rep Row 2: 60 dc and 59 ch-1 sps.

Rows 14 and 15: Rep Row 8 two times more.

Rows 16 through 26: Rep Row 2 eleven times more. At end of Row 26: 49 dc and 48 ch-1 sps.

Rows 27 and 28: Rep Row 8 two times more. At end of Row 28, do not ch 4. Finish off; weave in ends.

Assembly

Sew side and sleeve seams.

Sleeve Edging

With right side facing, join with sl st in seam on sleeve edge.

Rnd 1: Ch 1, sc in same st as joining, sc in next st and in each st around: 96 sc; join with sl st in first sc; ch 1, turn.

Rnd 2: Sc in same sc as joining, puff st in next sc; *sc in next 2 sc, puff st in next sc; rep from * around to last sc; sc in last sc: 32 puff sts and 64 sc; join with sl st in first sc; ch 1, turn.

Rnd 3: Work rev sc in each st around: 96 rev sc; join with sl st in first rev sc. Finish off; weave in ends.

Rep on second sleeve edge.

Tunic Edging

With right side facing, join with sl st in bottom edge at right side seam.

Rnd 1: Ch 1, sc in same st as joining, work 2 sc in edge of each row across bottom edge, 2 sc in bottom right front corner, sc in each dc and in each ch-1 sp across Row 10 on right front, 2 sc in top right front corner, sc evenly around neck edge in same manner, 2 sc in top left front corner, sc in free lp of each ch across Row 1 on left front, 2 sc in bottom left front corner, 2 sc in edge of each row across bottom edge to beg; join with sl st in first sc; ch 1, turn.

Note: Count sc sts on Rnd 1 and increase or decrease 1 st evenly spaced, if necessary, to have a multiple of 3 sc around entire edge.

Rnd 2: Sc in same sc as joining, puff st in next sc; *sc in next 2 sc, puff st in next sc; rep from * around to last sc; sc in last sc; join with sl st in first sc; ch 1, turn.

Rnd 3: Work rev sc in each st around; join with sl st in first rev sc. Finish off; weave in ends.

Finishing

With needle and thread, sew hook and eye to top corners of left and right front.

#90 PINEAPPLE ROSES

Designed by Janie Herrin

SIZE

50" x 66"

MATERIALS

Worsted weight yarn
  8 oz pink
  56 oz off white

Note: Photographed model made with Red Heart® Super Saver® #316 Soft White and #372 Rose Pink

Size I (5.5 mm) crochet hook
  (or size required for gauge)

GAUGE

6 dc = 2"

block = 16 " x 16"

STITCH GUIDE

Front Post single crochet (FPsc): Insert hook from front to back to front around post (vertical bar) of specified stitch, YO and draw up a lp; YO and draw through both lps on hook: FPsc made.

INSTRUCTIONS

Block One

With rose, starting at center with flower, ch 6, join with sl st to form a ring.

Rnd 1 (right side): Ch 1, in ring work (sc, ch 1, 3 dc, ch 1) 4 times, join with sl st in beg sc: 4 petals made; ch 1, turn.

Rnd 2: Working on wrong side, FPsc around next sc, (ch 3, FPsc around of next sc) 3 times; ch 3, join in beg sc; ch 1, turn: 4 ch-3 lps.

Rnd 3: Sc in same st; *ch 1, in next lp work (3 dc, ch 1, sc, ch 1, 3 dc, ch 1), sc in next sc; rep from * around, end with last ch 1, join in beg sc; ch 1, turn: 8 petals.

Rnd 4: Working on wrong side, FPsc around next sc, (ch 3, FPsc around next sc) 7 times, ch 3; join in beg sc: 8 ch-3 lps; finish off rose.

Rnd 5: With right side facing, working behind petals, join off white with sl st in any ch-3 lp, ch 3, (dc, ch 3, 2 dc) all in same lp; * † ch 2, in next ch-3 lp work (dc, ch 3, dc), ch 2 †; in next lp work (2 dc, ch 3, 2 dc); rep from * 2 times more, then rep from † to † once; join in 3rd ch of beg ch-3: 24 dc counting beg ch-3 as a dc.

Rnd 6: Sl st to ch-3 sp, ch 3, in same sp work (dc, ch 3, 2 dc); * † ch 2, skip ch-2 sp, 7 dc in next ch-3 sp, ch 2, skip next ch-2 sp †; in next ch-3 sp work (2 dc, ch 3, 2 dc): shell made; rep from * 2 times more, then rep from † to † once; join as before: 4 shells, four 7-dc groups.

Rnd 7: Ch 3, dc in same st and in next dc; * † shell in shell, dc in next dc, 2 dc in next dc, ch 1, skip ch-2 sp; (dc in next dc, ch 1) 7 times, skip ch-2 sp †; 2 dc in next dc, dc in next dc: rep from * 2 times more, then rep from † to † once; join: 68 dc.

Rnd 8: Ch 3, dc in each of next 4 dc; * † shell in shell, dc in each of next 5 dc, ch 2, skip next ch-1 sp; (sc in next ch-1 sp, ch 3) 5 times, sc in next ch-1 sp, ch 2 †; skip next ch-1 sp, dc in each of next 5 dc; rep from * 2 times more, then rep from † to † once; join: 56 dc, 24 sc.

Rnd 9: Ch 3, dc in each of next 3 dc; * † ch 1, skip next dc, dc in each of next 2 dc; shell in shell, dc in each of next 2 dc, ch 1, skip next dc, dc in each of next 4 dc, ch 2; (sc in next ch-3 lp, ch 3) 4 times, sc in next ch-3 sp, ch 2 †; dc in each of next 4 dc; rep from * 2 times more, then rep from † to † once; join: 64 dc, 20 sc.

Rnd 10: Ch 3, dc in each of next 2 dc; * † ch 1, skip next dc, dc in ch-1 sp, dc in each of next 4 dc, shell in shell, dc in each of next 4 dc; dc in ch-1 sp, ch 1, skip next dc, dc in each of next 3 dc, ch 2, skip next sp, (sc in next ch-3 lp, ch 3) 3 times, sc in next ch-3 sp, ch 2 †; dc in each of next 3 dc; rep from * 2 times more, then rep from † to † once, join: 80 dc, 16 sc.

Rnd 11: Ch 3, dc in same st; * † dc in next dc, ch 1, skip next dc, dc in ch-1 lp, dc in each of next 7 dc, shell in shell, dc in each of next 7 dc; dc in ch-1 sp, ch 1, skip next dc, dc in next dc, 2 dc in next dc, ch 2, skip next sp, (sc in next ch-3 lp, ch 3) twice, sc in next ch-3 lp, ch 2 †; 2 dc in next dc; rep from * 2 times more, then rep from † to † once, join: 104 dc, 12 sc.

Rnd 12: Ch 3, dc in same st; * † dc in next dc, ch 1, skip next dc, dc in ch-1 sp, dc in each of next 9 dc, ch 1, skip next dc, shell in shell, ch 1, skip next dc, dc in each of next 9 dc; dc in ch-1 sp, ch 1, skip next dc, dc in next dc, 2 dc in next dc, ch 2; skip next sp, sc in next ch-3 sp, ch 3, sc in next ch-3 sp, ch 2 †; 2 dc in next dc; rep from * 2 times more, then rep from † to † once, join: 120 dc, 8 sc.

Rnd 13: Ch 3, dc in next dc; * † ch 1, skip next dc, dc in ch-1 sp, dc in each of next 9 dc, ch 1, skip next dc, dc in ch-1 sp, dc in next 2 dc; shell in shell, dc in next 2 dc and in ch-1 sp, ch 1, skip next dc, dc in each of next 9 dc; dc in ch-1 sp, ch 1, skip next dc, dc in next 2 dc, ch 2, skip next sp, sc in next ch-3 lp, ch 2 †; dc in next 2 dc; rep from * 2 times more, then rep from † to † once, join: 136 dc, 4 sc.

Rnd 14: Ch 4; * † skip next dc, dc in next ch-1 sp, dc in next 9 dc, ch 1, skip next dc, dc in ch-1 sp; (ch 1, skip next dc, dc in next dc) twice, ch 1, shell in shell, (ch 1, skip next dc, dc in next dc) twice; ch 1, skip next dc, dc in next ch-1 sp, ch 1, skip next dc, dc in each of next 9 dc; dc in ch-1 sp, ch 1, skip next dc, dc in next dc, ch 2, skip next 2 sps †; dc in next dc, ch 1; rep from * 2 times more, then rep from † to † once, join in 3rd ch of beg ch-4: 128 dc, 40 ch-1 sps, 4 ch 2-sps, 4 ch-3 sps.

Rnd 15: Ch 1, sc in same st; *sc in each ch-1 sp and in each dc across to corner sp, 3 sc in corner sp, sc in each dc and in each ch-1 sp across to next ch-2 sp, sc in ch-2 sp, sc in next dc; rep from * around, end with sc in last ch-2 sp, join in beg sc: 184 sc.

Rnd 16: Ch 1, sc in same st, *ch 3, (skip next sc, sc in next sc, ch 3) across to 3-sc corner group, (sc, ch 5, sc) in center sc of 3-sc corner group; rep from * around to last ch-3, join in beg sc: 23 ch-3 lps on each side between corner sps. Finish off; weave in ends

Note: *From now on, additional blocks are made and joined in 3 rows of 4 blocks each.*

Block Two

Rnds 1 through 15: Work same as First Block.

Rnd 16 (joining rnd): Work lps same as for Block One around 3 sides only.

Be sure you have exactly 23 ch-3 sps on each side between corner sps. To complete joining, hold Block One and Block Two with wrong sides tog and join last side of Block Two to one side of Block One; omit center ch of joining sps and replace with sc in corresponding sps of Block One, ending with sl st in beg sc: two blocks joined on one side.

Block Three

Work same as Block Two, joining to Block Two on side opposite previous joining. You now have one row of three blocks.

Block Four

Work same as Block Two, joining to Block One on one side to start next row.

Block Five

Work same as before but joining two sides on Rnd 16.

Blocks Six through Twelve

Work same as previous blocks joining as many sides as needed on Rnd 16 until you have joined 4 rows with 3 blocks each.

Border

Rnd 1: Working around entire outer edge of afghan, join off white with sl st in any corner ch-5 sp, ch 5 (equals first dc plus ch 2), (dc, ch 2, dc) in same sp, sc in next ch-3 sp, (dc, ch 2, dc) in next sp, (V-st made); (sc in next sp, V-st in next sp) around, working 2 V-sts in rem 3 corner sps; join with sl st in 3rd ch of beg ch-5. (Note: you may have to fudge by working sc in each of 2 lps once to ensure there are 2 V-sts in corner).

Rnd 2: Sl st in ch-2 sp, ch 1, 3 sc in same sp, ch 4, (3 sc in next ch-2 sp, ch 4) around, join beg sc. Finish off; weave in ends.

#91 ROBIN'S HOOD

Designed by Mary Jane Protus for Coats & Clark

SIZE
10" x 72"

MATERIALS
Bulky weight yarn
 15 oz navy

Note: Photographed model made with Red Heart® Light & Lofty #9387 Navy Grape

Size N (10 mm) crochet hook
 (or size required for gauge)

Yarn needle

GAUGE
8 sts = 4" in patt

INSTRUCTIONS

Ch 24.

Row 1: Skip first 5 ch, (2 dc in next ch, skip next ch) 9 times, dc in last ch; ch 3, turn.

Row 2: Skip first dc, (2 dc in sp between next 2 dc) 9 times, dc in top of turning ch; ch 3, turn.

Rep Row 2 until piece measures 72".
Finish off.

Finishing

Fold scarf in half. Beginning at the fold and using yarn needle, sew a 10" seam to form hood. Weave in ends.

#92 SHAWL OF GOLD

Designed by Suzanne Atkinson

SIZE
54" wide x 32" long

MATERIALS
Sport or DK weight yarn
 10 ¹/₂ oz gold

Note: *Photographed model made
with Patons® "Brilliant" #3023
Gold Glow*

Size G (4.5 mm) crochet hook
 (or size required for gauge)

GAUGE
18 dc = 4"

12 dc rows = 4"

INSTRUCTIONS

Ch 4.

Foundation Row: 2 dc in 4th ch from hook: 3 dc; ch 3 (counts as a dc), turn.

Row 1 (right side): Dc in first dc (inc made) , dc in next dc, 2 dc in top of ch-3 (inc made): 5 dc; ch 3, turn.

Row 2: Dc in first dc, dc in next 3 dc, 2 dc in top of ch-3: 7 dc; ch 3, turn.

Row 3: Dc in first dc, dc in each of next 5 dc, 2 dc in top of ch-3: 9 dc; ch 3, turn.

Row 4: 2 dc in first dc, ch 4, skip 3 dc, sc in next dc, ch 4, skip 3 dc, 3 dc in top of ch-3; ch 3, turn.

Row 5: Dc in first dc, dc in next dc, 2 dc in next dc, ch 3, sc in sc, ch 3, 2 dc in next dc, dc in next dc, 2 dc in top of ch-3; ch 3, turn.

Row 6: Dc in first dc, dc in next 3 dc, 2 dc in next dc, ch 2, dc in sc, ch 2, 2 dc in next dc, dc in next 3 dc, 2 dc in top of ch-3; ch 3, turn.

Row 7: Dc in first dc, dc in each 5 dc, 2 dc in next dc, ch 1, skip next dc, 2 dc in next dc, dc in next 5 dc, 2 dc in top of ch-3; ch 3, turn.

Row 8: 2 dc in first dc, ch 4, skip 3 dc, sc in next dc, ch 4, skip 4 dc, 3 dc in ch-1, ch 4, skip 4 dc, sc in next dc, ch 4, skip 3 dc, 3 dc in top of ch-3; ch 3, turn.

Row 9: Dc in first dc, dc in next dc, 2 dc in next dc, ch 3, sc in sc, ch 3, 2 dc in next dc, dc in next dc, 2 dc in next dc, ch 3, sc in sc, ch 3, 2 dc in next dc, dc in next dc, 2 dc in top of ch-3; ch 3, turn.

Row 10: Dc in first dc, dc in next 3 dc, 2 dc in next dc, ch 2, dc in sc, ch 2, 2 dc in next dc, dc in next 3 dc, 2 dc in next dc, ch 2, dc in sc, ch 2, 2 dc in next dc, dc in next 3 dc, 2 dc in top of ch-3; ch 3, turn.

Row 11: Dc in first dc, dc in next 5 dc, 2 dc in next dc, ch 1, skip next dc, 2 dc in next dc, dc in next 5 dc, 2 dc in next dc, ch 1, skip next dc, 2 dc in next dc, dc in each of next 5 dc, 2 dc in top of ch-3; ch 3, turn.

Row 12: 2 dc in first dc, ch 4, skip 3 dc, sc in next dc, ch 4, skip 4 dc, 3 dc in ch-1, ch 4, skip 4 dc, sc in next dc, ch 4, skip 4 dc, 3 dc in ch-1, ch 4, skip 4 dc, sc in next dc, ch 4, skip 3 dc, 3 dc in top of ch-3; ch 3, turn.

Row 13: Dc in first dc, dc in next dc, 2 dc in next dc; *ch 3, sc in sc, ch 3, 2 dc in next dc, dc in next dc, 2 dc in next dc; rep from * one more time; ch 3, sc in sc, ch 3, 2 dc in next dc, dc in next dc, 2 dc in top of ch-3; ch 3, turn.

Row 14: Dc in first dc, dc in next 3 dc, 2 dc in next dc; *ch 2, dc in sc, ch 2, 2 dc in next dc, dc in next 3 dc, 2 dc in next dc; rep from * one more time; ch 2, dc in sc, ch 2, 2 dc in next dc, dc in next 3 dc, 2 dc in top of ch-3; ch 3, turn.

Row 15: Dc in first dc, dc in next 5 dc, 2 dc in next dc; *ch 1, skip next dc, 2 dc in next dc, dc in next 5 dc, 2 dc in next dc; rep from * one more time; ch 1, skip next dc, 2 dc in next dc, dc in next 5 dc, 2 dc in top of ch-3; ch 3, turn.

Row 16: 2 dc in first dc, ch 4, skip 3 dc, sc in next dc, *ch 4, skip 4 dc, 3 dc in ch-1, ch 4, skip 4 dc, sc in next dc; rep from * 2 times more; ch 4, 3 dc in top of ch-3; ch 3, turn.

Rep Rows 13 through 16 nineteen more times, working one more * repeat in each row of each 4-row pattern repeat. Rep Rows 13 through 15 one more time. At end of last row, ch 1 instead of ch 3.

Edging
Working along sides of rows, *sc in side of dc at end of row, ch 3; repeat from * to lower corner; sc in bottom of center dc, ch 3; **sc in side of dc at end of row, ch 3; rep from ** to upper right corner; *** skip next dc, sc in next dc, ch 3; rep from *** across top edge of shawl to upper left corner; join in beg ch-1. Finish off and weave in ends.

#93 ALL BUTTONED UP

Designed by Tammy Hildebrand

Note: *Instructions are written for size Small; changes for sizes Medium and Large are in parentheses.*

SIZES	Small	Medium	Large
Body bust Measurements	32" - 34"	36" - 38"	40" - 42"
Finished bust Measurements	37"	41"	45"

MATERIALS

Bulky weight yarn
   18 (21, 24) oz natural

Fuzzy bulky weight yarn
   6 (7, 8) oz orange

Note: *Photographed model made with Bernat® Softee Chunky #39008 Natural and Bernat® Frenzy #55605 Outrageous Orange*

Size P (15 mm) crochet hook
   (or size required for gauge)

Six 1 ¼" long natural wooden
   shank buttons

Tapestry needle

GAUGE

9 sc = 4"

Rows 1 through 5 = 2"

INSTRUCTIONS

Note: Garment is worked vertically.

Back

With natural, ch 54.

Row 1 (right side): Sc in 2nd ch from hook and in each ch across: 53 sc; ch 1, turn.

Row 2: Sc in first st; *ch 1, skip next st, sc in next st; rep from * across: 27 sc and 26 ch-1 sps; ch 1, turn.

Row 3: Sc in each st and in each ch-1 sp across: 53 sc. Finish off; weave in ends.

Row 4: With right side facing, join orange with sc in first st; *skip next st, shell in next st, skip next st, sc in next st; rep from * across: 14 sc and 13 shells. Finish off; weave in ends.

Row 5: With right side facing, join natural with sc in back lp of first st on previous row; *working behind sts of previous row, dc in next skipped st 2 rows below, sc in back lp of center dc of next shell on previous row, dc in next skipped st 2 rows below, sc in back lp of next sc on previous row; rep from * across: 27 sc and 26 dc; ch 1, turn.

Row 6: Sc in each st across: 53 sc; ch 1, turn.

Rows 7 through 41 (46, 51): Rep Rows 2 through 6 seven (eight, nine) times more.

Rows 42 (47, 52) and 43 (48, 53): Rep Rows 2 and 3. At end of last row, finish off; weave in ends.

Left Front

Starting at side edge, with natural, ch 54.

Rows 1 through 6: Rep Rows 1 through 6 on back.

Rows 7 through 11: Rep Rows 2 through 6 on back. At end of Row 11, do not ch 1. Finish off; weave in ends.

Neck Shaping

Row 12: With right side facing, skip first 12 sts, join natural with sc in next st; *ch 1, skip next st, sc in next st; rep from * across: 21 sc and 20 ch-1 sps; ch 1, turn.

Row 13: Rep Row 3 on back: 41 sc.

Row 14: Rep Row 4 on back: 11 sc and 10 shells.

Row 15: Rep Row 5 on back: 21 sc and 20 dc.

Row 16: Sc in first st and in each st across to last 2 sts: 39 sc; ch 1, turn, leaving last 2 sts unworked.

Row 17: Sl st in first 3 sts, ch 1, sc in same sp as last sl st; * ch 1, skip next st, sc in next st; rep from * across: 19 sc and 18 ch-1 sps; ch 1, turn.

Row 18: Rep Row 3 on back: 37 sc.

Row 19: Rep Row 4 on back: 10 sc and 9 shells.

Row 20: Rep Row 5 on back: 19 sc and 18 dc.

Row 21: Rep Row 6 on back: 37 sc.

Row 22: Rep Row 2 on back: 19 sc and 18 ch-1 sps.

Row 23: Rep Row 3 on back: 37 sc.

For Size Small Only
Finish off; weave in ends.

For Sizes Medium and Large Only
Rows 24 through 26: Rep Rows 19 through 21 on left front.

For Size Medium Only
At end of last row, do not ch 1. Finish off; weave in ends.

For Size Large Only
Rows 27 and 28: Rep Rows 22 and 23 on left front. At end of Row 28, finish off; weave in ends.

Button Band (for all sizes)
Row 1: With right side facing, join natural with sc in first st on last row of left front at neck edge, sc in next st and in each st across: 37 sc; ch 1, turn.

Row 2: Sc in first st and in each st across. Finish off; weave in ends.

Right Front
Starting at side edge, with natural, ch 54.

Rows 1 through 6: Rep Rows 1 through 6 on back.

Rows 7 through 11: Rep Rows 2 through 6 on back.

Neck Shaping
Row 12: Sc in first st; *ch 1, skip next st, sc in next st; rep from * across to last 12 sts: 21 sc and 20 ch-1 sps; ch 1, turn, leaving last 12 sts unworked.

Rows 13 through 15: Rep Rows 13 through 15 on left front.

Row 16: Sl st in first 3 sts, ch 1, sc in same sp as last sl st, sc in next st and in each st across: 39 sc; ch 1, turn.

Row 17: Sc in first st; *ch 1, skip next st, sc in next st; rep from * across to last 2 sts: 19 sc and 18 ch-1 sps; ch 1, turn, leaving last 2 sts unworked.

Rows 18 through 23 (26, 28): Rep Rows 18 through 23 (26, 28) on left front.

Button Loop Band (for all sizes)
Row 1: With right side facing, join natural with sc in first st on last row of right front by bottom edge, sc in next st; *ch 5, sc in same st and in next 7 sts; rep from * across to last st; sc in last st, ch 5, sc in same st: 6 ch-3 lps and 43 sc. Finish off; weave in ends.

Sew shoulder seams. Sew side seams, leaving 17 sts below shoulder seam on each side open for armhole.

Sleeves (make 2)
With natural, ch 38 (42, 42).

Row 1 (right side): Sc in 2nd ch from hook and in each ch across: 37 (41, 41) sc; ch 1, turn.

Row 2: Rep Row 2 of back: 19 (21, 21) sc and 18 (20, 20) ch-1 sps.

Row 3: Rep Row 3 of back: 37 (41, 41) sc.

Row 4: Rep Row 4 of back: 10 (11, 11) sc and 9 (10, 10) shells.

Row 5: Rep Row 5 of back: 19 (21, 21) sc and 18 (20, 20) dc.

Row 6: Rep Row 6 of back: 37 (41, 41) sc.

Rows 7 through 31: Rep Rows 2 through 6 five times more.

Rows 32 through 35: Rep Rows 2 through 5. At end of Row 35, do not ch 1. Finish off, leaving a long length for seaming. Sew sleeve seam through Row 1 and Row 35.

Cuff

Rnd 1: With right side facing, join natural with sc in edge of any row on sleeve, sc in edge of next row, sc in edge of each row around and in sleeve seam: 36 sc; join with sl st in beg sc.

Rnd 2: Ch 1, sc in same st as joining, sc dec in next 2 sts; *sc in next st, sc dec in next 2 sts; rep from * around: 24 sc; join with sl st in beg sc.

Rnd 3: Rep Rnd 2: 16 sc.

Rnds 4 through 6: Ch 1, sc in same st as joining, sc in next st and in each st around; join with sl st in beg sc. At end of last rnd, finish off; weave in ends.

With right side facing, rep Rnd 1 of cuff on opposite edge of sleeve. Sew this end of sleeve to armhole opening left in side seam.

Neck Edging

Row 1: With right side facing, join natural with sc in neck edge of last row at top edge of button loop band on right front, sc in edge of each row and in each st around neck opening to last row of button band: 80 (91, 100) sc; ch 1, turn.

Row 2: Sc in first 6 (7, 6) sts, (sc dec in next 2 sts) twice; *sc in next st, (sc dec in next 2 sts) twice; rep from * to last 5 sts; sc in last 5 sts: 52 (59, 64) sc; ch 1, turn.

Row 3: Sc in first 4 (3, 3) sts, (sc dec in next 2 sts); *sc in next st, (sc dec in next 2 sts); rep from * to last 4 (3, 2) sts; sc in last 4 (3, 2) sts: 37 (41, 44) sc; ch 1, turn.

Rows 4 and 5: Sc in first st and in each st across; ch 1, turn. At end of Row 5, do not ch 1. Finish off; weave in ends.

Bottom Edging

Row 1: With right side facing, join natural with sc in edge of last row at bottom edge of button band, sc in edge of next row and in edge of each row around: 92 (103, 112) sc; ch 1, turn.

Row 2: Sc in first 4 (5, 4) sts, (sc dec in next 2 sts) twice; *sc in next st, (sc dec in next 2 sts) twice; rep from * to last 4 (4, 4) sts; sc in last 4 (4, 4) sts: 58 (65, 70) sc; ch 1, turn.

Row 3: Sc in first st and in each st across. Finish off; weave in ends.

Finishing

Sew buttons to button band on left front lined up with button loops on right front.

Designed by Cheryl Oxsalida

SIZE
5" long x 3 ¹/₂" tall x 2" wide

MATERIALS
Worsted weight yarn
  1 ³/₄ oz cream
  5 yds black

Note: *Photographed model made with Bernat Denim Style #3006 Canvas and Caron® Wintuk® #3009 Black*

Size F (3.75 mm) crochet hook (or size required for gauge)

2 cotton balls or small amount of fiberfill

2" round retractable tape measure

Stitch marker

Tapestry needle

GAUGE
Rnds 1 and 2 = 1 ¹/₄" diameter

INSTRUCTIONS

Body (make 2)
With cream, ch 3, join with sl st to form a ring.

Rnd 1 (wrong side): Work 8 sc in ring; join with sl st in back lp of first sc: 8 sc.

Rnd 2: Ch 1, work lp st in back lp of same st as joining, work 2 lp sts in back lp of each st around: 15 lp sts. Do not join. Place stitch marker in last st and move up to last st in each rnd.

Rnd 3: Work 2 lps sts in back lp of each st around: 30 lp sts. Do not join.

Rnd 4: *Work lp st in back lp of next st, work 2 lp sts in back lp of next st; rep from * around: 45 lp sts; join with sl st in next lp st. At end of Rnd 4 on first body piece,

240

finish off; weave in ends. At end of Rnd 4 on second body piece, do not finish off. Note: Body pieces should be about 2 ¹/₂" diameter.

Body Joining
With wrong sides of body pieces together and loopy sides facing out, work lp st in each of first 30 sts through both body pieces. Do not finish off.

Feet (make 4)
Work feet in back of 8th and 17th lp sts on joining rnd and in back of corresponding lp sts on Rnd 4 of first body piece as follows: Join black with sl st in specified st, ch 2, 2 dc in same st. Finish off; weave in ends.

Finish Body Joining
Insert tape measure between body pieces so side with desired markings is facing up, away from feet. Make sure tape pulls out and retracts without snagging body. With tape pull tab sticking out, work lp st in next 11 sts through both body pieces, leaving 4 sts unworked for tape pull tab open-

ing. Make sure tape pull tab moves freely. Finish off; weave in ends.

Additional Loops

Join cream with sl st in 19th lp st on joining rnd, insert hook in next st and draw up a lp, YO and draw through both lps on hook, pull lp on hook up about 1", slip lp off hook; *insert hook in next st and draw up a lp, YO and draw through lp on hook, pull lp on hook up about 1", slip lp off hook; rep from * 19 times more; sl st in next st. Finish off; weave in ends.

Head

With black, ch 4.

Rnd 1: Work 7 dc in 4th ch from hook (3 skipped chs count as dc): 8 dc; join with sl st in 4th ch of ch-4. Finish off. Do not weave in ends.

Rnd 2: Join cream with sl st in any dc, ch 1, sc in same st as joining, sc in next st; *2 sc in next st, sc in next 2 sts; rep from * once more: 10 sc; join with sl st in first sc.

Rnd 3: Ch 1, sc in same st as joining, 2 sc in next st; *sc in next st, 2 sc in next st; rep from * 3 times more: 15 sc; join with sl st in first sc.

Rnds 4 and 5: Ch 1, sc in same st as joining, sc in next st and in each st around; join with sl st in first sc.

Rnd 6: Ch 1, sc in same st as joining, sc in next st; *sc dec in next 2 sts, sc in next 2 sts; rep from * two times more; sc in last st: 12 sc; join with sl st in first sc.

Rnd 7: Ch 1, sc in same st as joining, sc in next st; *sc dec in next 2 sts, sc in next 2 sts; rep from * once more; sc dec in last 2 sts: 9 sc; join with sl st in first sc. Do not finish off.

Eyes, Nose and Mouth

Thread beg or end tail of black yarn in Rnd 1 into tapestry needle. Sew eyes through desired stitches on Rnd 3 as per photograph. Finish off. Thread beg tail of cream yarn into tapestry needle. Sew nose and mouth in desired positions on Rnd 1 as per photograph. Finish off.

Ears (make 2)

Join black with sl st in Rnd 5 on side of head near eye, ch 2, 2 dc in same st. Finish off; weave in ends.

Finish Head

Stuff head with 2 cotton balls or small amount of fiberfill.

Rnd 8: Ch 1, sc in same st as joining, sc dec in next 2 sts; *sc in next sc, sc dec in next 2 sts; rep from * once more: 6 sc. Finish off, leaving an 8" end.

Sew head to body through base of additional loops on opposite end from tape pull tab. Finish off; weave in ends.

#95 FUN IN THE SUN HALTER

Designed by Tammy Hildebrand

Note: *Instructions are written for size Small; changes for sizes Medium and Large are in parentheses.*

SIZES	Small	Medium	Large
Body Chest Measurements	32" - 34"	36" - 38"	40" - 42"
Finished Chest Measurements	31"	35"	39"

MATERIALS

Sport weight yarn
  1 oz turquoise
  3 (3 ½, 4) oz lime

Note: *Photographed model made with Lion Brand® Micro-Spun #148 Turquoise and #194 Lime*

Size G (4 mm) crochet hook
  (or size required for gauge)

GAUGE

14 sc = 4"

INSTRUCTIONS

With lime, ch 94 (108, 122).

Row 1: sc in 2nd ch from hook and each rem ch: 93 (107, 121) sc; ch 1, turn.

Row 2: Sc in first sc; *tr in next st, sc in next st; rep from * across: 47 (54, 61) sc, 46 (53, 60) tr; ch 1, turn.

Row 3: Sc in each st across, ch 1, turn.

For Size Small Only
Rows 4 through 21: Rep rows 2 and 3 nine more times.

For Size Medium Only
Rows 4 through 33: Rep Rows 2 and 3 fifteen more times.

For Size Large Only
Rows 4 through 45: Rep rows 2 and 3 twenty-one more times.

Rows 22 through 25 (34 through 37, 46 through 49): Skip first st (decrease made), sc in each st up to last st, ch 1, turn, leaving last st unworked: 91 (105,119) sc; ch 1. turn.

First Strap

Row 1: Skip first 2 sts, sc in next 5 sts, ch 1, turn, leaving rem sts unworked.

Row 2: Sc in first st, (tr in next st, sc in next st) twice, ch 1, turn.

Row 3: Sc in each st, ch 1, turn.

Rep Rows 2 and 3 twenty-five more times.

Finish off, leaving a long length for sewing. Sew end of strap to back opposite strap front.

Second Strap

Row 1: Join lime with sc in 7th st from end, sc in next 4 sts, ch 1, turn.

Rep Rows 2 and 3 of first strap, sew to back in same manner

Border

Rnd 1: Hold piece with right side facing and starting ch at top. Working in unused lps of starting ch, join turquoise with sc in first lp, sc in each lp to end; sc in each row end including strap, sc in each st across back, sc in each row end of opposite side, join with sl st in beg sc.

Rnd 2: Sc in same st, ch 2, (skip next st, sc in next st, ch 2) around, join with sl st in beg sc. Finish off; weave in all ends.

Tie

Row 1 (right side): With turquoise, ch 80 Finish off.

Row 2: With wrong side facing, join lime with sl st in back lp of first ch, sl st in each lp to end. Finish off.

Lace tie through ch-2 sps of front center. Sew ends of tie to inside.

SIZE

Hat: Fits 20" - 23" head

Scarf: 12" x 60" before fringe

MATERIALS

Super bulky weight boucle yarn
100 g (93 yds) multicolor for hat
300 g (279 yds) multicolor for scarf

Note: *Phototgraphed model made with Artful Yarns Circus #12 Roaring Lion*

Size N (9 mm) crochet hook (or size required for gauge)

GAUGE

8 sts = 4" over alternating rows of sc and dc

SCARF

INSTRUCTIONS

Ch 14.

Row 1 (right side): Sc in 2nd ch from hook and each ch across; ch 3, turn: 13 sc.

Row 2: Dc in each sc; ch 1, turn

Row 3: Sc in each dc; ch 3, turn.

Rep Rows 2 and 3 until scarf measures 60", ending by working a wrong-side row; turn; do not finish off.

Fringe

First End: Ch 10; *sc in next sc, ch 10; rep from * to end, join in last sc. Finish off.

Opposite End: With right side facing, join yarn in first unused lp of beg ch, ch 10; *sc in next unused lp, ch 10; rep from * to end, join in last unused lp. Finish off; weave in ends.

HAT

INSTRUCTIONS

Ch 4: join with sl st to form a ring.

Rnd 1 (right side): Ch 3 (counts as dc), 11 dc in ring, join in top of ch-3: 12 dc.

Rnd 2: Ch 3, dc in base of ch (inc made), 2 dc in each dc, join in first dc: 24 dc.

Rnd 3: Ch 1, 2 sc in first dc, sc in next 2 dc; *2 sc in next dc, sc in next 2 dc; rep from * 6 more times, join in first sc: 32 sc.

Rnd 4: Ch 3, dc in next 6 sc, 2 dc in next sc; *dc in next 7 sc, 2 dc in next sc; rep from * 2 more times, join in first dc: 36 dc.

Rnd 5: Ch 1, sc in each dc, join in first sc.

Rnd 6: Ch 3, dc in each sc, join in first dc.

Rnds 7 through 12: Rep Rnds 5 and 6.

Rnd 13: Rep Rnd 5.

Rnd 14: Ch 8; *sc in next sc, ch 8; rep from * to end of rnd; join in first ch of beg ch-8. Finish off; weave in ends. Roll up brim and tack in place if desired.

#98 TOWN & COUNTRY CAPELET

Note: *Instructions are written for size Medium; changes for Large are in parentheses.*

SIZES	Medium	Large
Length	13"	17 1/2"
Lower edge	54"	59"

MATERIALS

Light bulky weight yarn
 9 (12) oz white

Note: *Photographed model made with Lion Brand® Jiffy® #100 white*

Stitch marker or piece of
 contrast yarn

Size N (9 mm) crochet hook
 (or size required for gauge)

GAUGE

8 hdc = 4"

8 hdc rnds = 4"

INSTRUCTIONS

Starting at neck edge, loosely ch 46; join with sl st to form a ring, being careful not to twist ch.

Note: Do not join following rnds. Mark beg of each rnd.

Rnd 1: Ch 1, hdc in each ch: 46 hdc.

Rnd 2: Hdc in first hdc; *2 hdc in next hdc, hdc in next 4 hdc; rep from * 8 more times: 55 hdc.

Rnd 3: Hdc in each hdc.

Rnd 4: Hdc in first hdc; *2 hdc in next hdc, hdc in next 5 hdc; rep from * 8 more times: 64 hdc.

Rnd 5: Rep Rnd 3.

Rnd 6: Hdc in first hdc; *2 hdc in next hdc, hdc in next 6 hdc; rep from * 8 more times: 73 hdc.

Rnd 7: Rep Rnd 3.

Rnd 8: Hdc in first hdc; *2 hdc in next hdc, hdc in next 7 hdc; rep from * 8 more times: 82 hdc.

Rnd 9: Rep Rnd 3.

Rnd 10: Hdc in first hdc; *2 hdc in next hdc, hdc in next 8 hdc; rep from * 8 more times: 91 hdc.

Rnd 11: Rep Rnd 3.

Rnd 12: Hdc in first hdc; *2 hdc in next hdc, hdc in next 9 hdc; rep from * 8 more times: 100 hdc.

Rnd 13: Hdc in first hdc; *2 hdc in next hdc, hdc in next 10 hdc; rep from * 8 more times: 109 hdc.

For Size Medium Only

Rnds 14 through 26: Hdc in each hdc; at end of last rnd, join with sl st in beg hdc.

Rnd 27: Ch 1; * skip next hdc, 5 hdc in next hdc, skip next hdc, sc in next hdc; rep from * around, join in beg hdc. Finish off; weave in ends.

For Size Large Only

Rnd 14: Hdc in first hdc; *2 hdc in next hdc, hdc in next 11 hdc; rep from * 8 more times: 118 hdc.

Rnds 15 through 34: Hdc in each hdc; at end of last rnd, join with sl st in beg sc.

Rnd 35: Ch 1; *skip next hdc, 5 dc in next hdc, skip next hdc, sc in next hdc; rep from * around, skip last hdc, join in beg hdc. Finish off; weave in ends.

#99 BABY ON BOARD

Designed by Ruthie Marks

Note: *Instructions are written for size Small; changes for sizes Medium and Large are in parentheses.*

SIZES	Small	Medium	Large
Body Bust Measurements	34"	36"	38"
Finished Bust Measurement (stretched)	34"	36"	38"

MATERIALS

DK weight yarn with elastic component 8 ¾ (10 ½, 10 ¾) oz red

Note: *Photographed model made with Cascade Fixation #9210*

Size F (3.75 mm) crochet hook (or size required for gauge)

Note: *Use of an elasticized yarn is essential for the fit of this garment.*

GAUGE

10 sc = 2"

10 sc rows = 2"

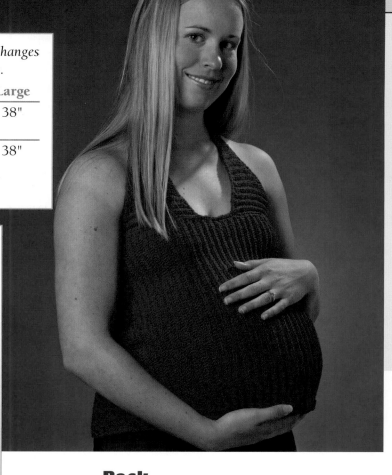

INSTRUCTIONS

Note: *Yarn is worked relaxed at all times; top is made to fit snugly with a comfortable stretch. Work all sc sts in back lp of indicated st throughout except where noted.*

Front

Row 1: Ch 80 (85, 90).

Row 2: Sc in 2nd ch from hook and in each ch across: 79 (84, 89) sc; ch 1, turn.

Rows 3 through 63 (69, 73): Sc in each sc across; ch 1, turn. At end of last row, finish off; weave in ends.

Back

Work same as front.

Side Gusset (make 2)

Row 1: Ch 2, sc in 2nd ch from hook: 1 sc; ch 1, turn.

Row 2: 2 sc in sc; ch 1, turn.

Row 3: 2 sc in first sc, sc in next sc: 3 sc; ch 1, turn.

Rows 4 through 7: Sc in each sc; ch 1, turn.

Row 8: 2 sc in first sc, sc in each sc to last sc, 2 sc in last sc: 5 sc; ch 1, turn.

Rows 9 through 12: Rep Rows 4 through 7.

Rows 13 through 37: Rep Rows 8 through 12 five times more: 15 sc at end of Row 37.

Row 38: Rep Row 8: 17 sc.

Rows 39 through 43: Sc in each sc; ch 1, turn.

Rows 44 through 61: Rep Rows 38 through 43 three times more: 23 sc at end of Row 61.

Row 62: Rep Row 8: 25 sc.

Rows 63 through 70 (75, 80): Sc in each sc; ch 1, turn. At end of last row, finish off; weave in ends.

Side Seams

With right sides facing, sew top 4 sc on front and back, insert gusset and sew rest of side seam down to bottom.

With right side facing, join yarn and sc evenly around top edge of piece: 128 (144, 152) sc. Finish off; weave in ends.

Left Front Bodice Shaping

Row 1: With right side facing, join yarn with sl st in side seam, sl st in first 4 sc, sc in both lps of next 28 sc: 28 sc; ch 1, turn.

Row 2: Working in back lps only, sc dec in first 2 sc, sc in each sc across to last 2 sc, sc dec in last 2 sc: 26 sc; ch 1, turn.

Row 3: Sc in back lp of each sc across; ch 1, turn.

Rows 4 through 21: Rep Rows 2 and 3 nine times more: 8 sc at end of Row 20.

Rows 22 and 23: Rep Row 2 twice: 4 sc at end of Row 23. Do not finish off.

Strap

Rows 24 through 83 (or desired length): Sc in back lp of each sc across: 4 sc; ch 1, turn. Finish off; weave in ends.

Right Front Bodice Shaping

Row 1: With right side facing, join with sc in back lp of 33rd sc, sc in next 27 sc: 28 sc; ch 1, turn, leaving last 4 sc unworked.

Rows 2 through 23: Work same as Rows 2 through 23 on Left Front Bodice Shaping.

Strap

Work same as Strap on Left Front Bodice Shaping.

Bottom Edging

Rnd 1: With right side facing, join with sc in any side seam, sc evenly around, sl st in beg sc; ch 1, do not turn.

Rnd 2: Skip first sc, sc in both lps of each sc around, sl st in end sl st on Rnd 1. Finish off; weave in ends.

Top Edging

With right side facing, join with sc in edge of first sc on Row 1 of Left Front Bodice, sc in edge of each row around Left and Right Front Bodice, including straps, ending in edge of last sc on Row 1 of Left Front Bodice. Finish off; weave in ends.

#100 SOPHISTICATED SHELL

Designed by Zelda K

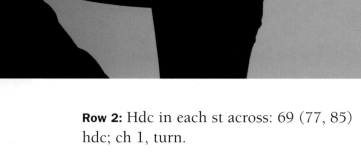

Note: *Instructions are written for size X-Small; changes for sizes Small and Medium are in parentheses.*

SIZES	X-Small	Small	Medium
Body Bust Measurements	28"	32"	36"
Finished Bust Measurement	28"	31 1/2"	35"
Length	20"	20 1/2"	21"

MATERIALS

DK weight yarn
  7 (8 3/4, 10 1/2) oz white

Short eyelash yarn
  1 3/4 oz blue

Note: *Photographed model made with Patons® Brilliant #3005 White Twinkle and Patons® Twister #05735 Bongo Blues*

Size G (4.0 mm) crochet hook
  (or size required for gauge)

Size K (6.5 mm) crochet hook

GAUGE

19 hdc = 4" with G hook and
  DK yarn

12 hdc rows = 4" with G hook
  and DK yarn

INSTRUCTIONS

Back

Beg at bottom with DK yarn and size G hook, ch 70 (78, 86).

Row 1 (right side): Hdc in 2nd ch from hook and in each ch across: 69 (77, 85) hdc; ch 1, turn.

Row 2: Hdc in each st across: 69 (77, 85) hdc; ch 1, turn.

Rows 3 through 5: Rep Row 2 three times more.

Row 6: Hdc in each st across to last st: 68 (76, 84) hdc; ch 1, turn, leaving last st unworked.

Rows 7 through 15: Rep Row 6 nine times more. At end of Row 15: 59 (67, 75) hdc.

Rows 16 through 18: Rep Row 2 three times more.

Row 19: Work 2 hdc in first st, hdc in each st across: 60 (68, 76) hdc; ch 1, turn.

Row 20: Rep Row 19: 61 (69, 77) hdc.

Rows 21 and 22: Rep Row 2 two times more.

Rows 23 and 24: Rep Row 19 two times more. At end of Row 24: 63 (71, 79) hdc.

Rows 25 through 30: Rep Row 2 six times more.

Rows 31 and 32: Rep Row 19 two times more. At end of Row 32: 65 (73, 81) hdc.

Rows 33 through 36: Rep Row 2 four times more.

Rows 37 and 38: Rep Row 19 two times more. At end of Row 38: 67 (75, 83) hdc.

Rows 39 and 40: Rep Row 2 two times more. At end of Row 40, do not ch 1.

Row 41: Sl st in first 2 sts, ch 1, hdc in next st and in each st across to last 2 sts: 63 (71, 79) hdc; turn, leaving last 2 sts unworked.

Row 42: Sl st in first 3 sts, ch 1, hdc in next st and in each st across to last 3 sts: 57 (65, 73) hdc; turn, leaving last 3 sts unworked.

Row 43: Sl st in first 1 (2, 3) sts, ch 1, hdc in next st and in each st across to last 2 sts: 54 (61, 68) hdc; turn, leaving last 2 sts unworked.

Row 44: Sl st in first 3 sts, ch 1, hdc in next st and in each st across to last 2 sts: 49 (56, 63) hdc; turn, leaving last 2 sts unworked.

Row 45: Sl st in first 1 (3, 4) sts, ch 1, hdc in next st and in each st across to last 3 sts: 45 (50, 56) hdc; turn, leaving last 3 sts unworked.

Row 46: Sl st in first 3 sts, ch 1, hdc in next st and in each st across: 42 (47, 53) hdc; ch 1, turn.

Row 47: Hdc in each st across to last 3 sts: 39 (44, 50) hdc; turn, leaving last 3 sts unworked.

Row 48: Rep Row 46: 36 (41, 47) hdc.

Row 49: Rep Row 47: 33 (38, 44) hdc.

Row 50: Rep Row 46: 30 (35, 41) hdc.

Row 51: Hdc in each st across to last 2 sts: 28 (33, 39) hdc; turn, leaving last 2 sts unworked.

Row 52: Sl st in first 4 sts, ch 1, hdc in next st and in each st across: 24 (29, 35) hdc; ch 1, turn.

Row 53: Rep Row 51: 22 (27, 33) hdc.

Row 54: Sl st in first 2 sts, ch 1, hdc in next st and in each st across: 20 (25, 31) hdc; ch 1, turn.

Row 55: Rep Row 51: 18 (23, 29) hdc; ch 1, turn.

Row 56: Hdc dec in first 2 sts, hdc in next st and in each st across: 17 (22, 28) hdc; ch 1, turn.

Row 57: Hdc in each st across to last st: 16 (21, 27) hdc; ch 1, turn, leaving last st unworked.

Row 58: Rep Row 56: 15 (20, 26) hdc; ch 1, turn.

Rows 59 through 60 (62, 64): Rep Row 2 two (four, six) times more. At end of last row, do not ch 1.

Row 61 (63, 65): Sl st in first 6 sts, ch 1, hdc in next st and in each st across: 9 (14, 20) hdc. Finish off; weave in ends.

Front
Beg at bottom with DK yarn and size G hook, ch 70 (78, 86).

Row 1 (right side): Rep Row 1 on Back: 69 (77, 85) hdc.

Row 2: Hdc in first 20 (23, 26) sts, BPdc in next st, hdc in next 27 (29, 31) sts, BPdc in next st, hdc in next 20 (23, 26) sts: 69 (77, 85) hdc; ch 1, turn.

Row 3: Hdc in first 20 (23, 26) sts, FPdc in next st, hdc in next 27 (29, 31) sts, FPdc in next st, hdc in next 20 (23, 26) sts; ch 1, turn.

Rows 4 and 5: Rep Rows 2 and 3.

Row 6: Hdc in first 20 (23, 26) sts, BPdc in next st, hdc in next 27 (29, 31) sts, BPdc in next st, hdc in next 19 (22, 25) sts: 68 (76, 84) hdc; ch 1, turn, leaving last st unworked.

Row 7: Hdc in first 19 (22, 25) sts, FPdc in next st, hdc in next 27 (29, 31) sts, FPdc in next st, hdc in next 19 (22, 25) sts: 67 (75, 83) hdc; ch 1, turn, leaving last st unworked.

Row 8: Hdc in first 19 (22, 25) sts, BPdc in next st, hdc in next 27 (29, 31) sts, BPdc in next st, hdc in next 18 (21, 24) sts: 66 (74, 82) hdc; ch 1, turn, leaving last st unworked.

Row 9: Hdc in first 18 (21, 24) sts, FPdc in next st, hdc in next 27 (29, 31) sts, FPdc in next st, hdc in next 18 (21, 24) sts: 65 (73, 81) hdc; ch 1, turn, leaving last st unworked.

Row 10: Hdc in first 18 (21, 24) sts, BPdc in next st, hdc in next 27 (29, 31) sts, BPdc in next st, hdc in next 17 (20, 23) sts: 64 (72, 80) hdc; ch 1, turn, leaving last st unworked.

Row 11: Hdc in first 17 (20, 23) sts, FPdc in next st, hdc in next 27 (29, 31) sts, FPdc in next st, hdc in next 17 (20, 23) sts: 63 (71, 79) hdc; ch 1, turn, leaving last st unworked.

Row 12: Hdc in first 17 (20, 23) sts, BPdc in next st, hdc in next 27 (29, 31) sts, BPdc in next st, hdc in next 16 (19, 22) sts: 62 (70, 78) hdc; ch 1, turn, leaving last st unworked.

Row 13: Hdc in first 16 (19, 22) sts, FPdc in next st, hdc in next 27 (29, 31) sts, FPdc in next st, hdc in next 16 (19, 22) sts: 61 (69, 77) hdc; ch 1, turn, leaving last st unworked.

Row 14: Hdc in first 16 (19, 22) sts, BPdc in next st, hdc in next 27 (29, 31) sts, BPdc in next st, hdc in next 15 (18, 21) sts: 60 (68, 76) hdc; ch 1, turn, leaving last st unworked.

Row 15: Hdc in first 15 (18, 21) sts, FPdc in next st, hdc in next 27 (29, 31) sts, FPdc in next st, hdc in next 15 (18, 21) sts: 59 (67, 75) hdc; ch 1, turn, leaving last st unworked.

Row 16: Hdc in first 15 (18, 21) sts, BPdc in next st, hdc in next 27 (29, 31) sts, BPdc in next st, hdc in next 15 (18, 21) sts; ch 1, turn.

Row 17: Hdc in first 15 (18, 21) sts, FPdc in next st, hdc in next 27 (28, 31) sts, FPdc in next st, hdc in next 15 (18, 21) sts; ch 1, turn.

Row 18: Rep Row 16.

Row 19: Hdc in first 15 (18, 21) sts, 2 hdc in next st, hdc in next 27 (29, 31) sts, 2 hdc in next st, hdc in next 15 (18, 21) sts: 61 (69, 77) hdc; ch 1, turn.

Rows 20 through 22: Hdc in each st across; ch 1, turn.

Rows 23 through 42: Rep Rows 23 through 42 on Back.

Row 43: Sl st in first 2 sts, ch 1, hdc in next st and in each st across to last 1 (2, 3) sts: 54 (61, 68) hdc; turn, leaving last 1 (2, 3) sts unworked.

Row 44: Sl st in first 2 sts, ch 1, hdc in next st and in each st across to last 3 sts: 49 (56, 63) hdc; turn, leaving last 3 sts unworked.

Row 45: Sl st in first 3 sts, ch 1, hdc in next st and in each st across to last 1 (3, 4) sts: 45 (50, 56) hdc; ch 1, turn, leaving last 1 (3, 4) sts unworked.

Row 46: Rep Row 47 on Back: 42 (47, 53) hdc.

Row 47: Rep Row 46 on Back: 39 (44, 50) hdc.

Row 48: Rep Row 47 on Back: 36 (41, 47) hdc.

Row 49: Rep Row 46 on Back: 33 (38, 44) hdc.

Row 50: Rep Row 47 on Back: 30 (35, 41) hdc.

Row 51: Rep Row 54 on Back: 28 (33, 39) hdc.

Row 52: Hdc in each st across to last 4 sts: 24 (29, 35) hdc; turn, leaving last 4 sts unworked.

Row 53: Rep Row 54 on Back: 22 (27, 33) hdc.

Row 54: Rep Row 51 on Back: 20 (25, 31) hdc.

Row 55: Rep Row 54 on Back: 18 (23, 29) hdc.

Row 56: Rep Row 57 on Back: 17 (22, 28) hdc.

Row 57: Rep Row 56 on Back: 16 (21, 27) hdc.

Row 58: Rep Row 57 on Back: 15 (20, 26) hdc.

Rows 59 through 60 (62, 64): Hdc in each st across; ch 1, turn.

Row 61 (63, 65): Hdc in first 9 (14, 20) sts: 9 (14, 20) hdc, leaving last 6 sts unworked. Finish off; weave in ends.

Assembly
Sew side seams.

Neck and Armhole Edges
With right side facing, using eyelash yarn and size K hook, work 1 rnd sc evenly spaced around neck and armhole edges, working about 1 st in every other st around; join with sl st in first sc. Finish off; weave in ends.

Bottom Edge
With right side facing, using DK yarn and size G hook, work 1 rnd sl st around bottom edge; join with sl st in first sl st. Finish off; weave in ends.

Abbreviations and Symbols

Crochet patterns are written in a special shorthand which is used so that instructions don't take up too much space. They sometimes seem confusing, but once you learn them, you'll have no trouble following them.

These are Abbreviations

BB . . . . bobble
Beg . . . . beginning
BL . . . . back loop
BPdc . . . . back post double crochet
BPsc . . . . back post single crochet
Cl(s) . . . . cluster(s)
Ch(s) . . . . chain(s)
Cont . . . . continue
Dc . . . . double crochet
Dc Cl . . . . double crochet cluster
Dc dec . . . . double crochet decrease
Dc inc . . . . double crochet increase
Dec . . . . decrease
Dtr . . . . double triple crochet
Fig . . . . figure
FL . . . . front loop
FPdc . . . . front post double crochet
FPsc . . . . front post single crochet
FPtr . . . . front post triple crochet
G . . . . grams
Hdc . . . . half double crochet
Hdc dec . . . . . half double crochet decrease
Inc . . . . Increase(ing)
LKN . . . . lover's knot
Lp(s) . . . . loop(s)
LpSt . . . . loop stitch
Long dc . . . . long double crochet
Long sc . . . . long single crochet
Oz . . . . ounces
Patt . . . . pattern
PC . . . . popcorn
Prev . . . . previous
Pst . . . . puff stitch
Rem . . . . remaining
Rep . . . . repeat(ing)
Rev sc . . . . reverse single crochet
Rnd(s) . . . . round(s)
Sc . . . . single crochet
Scdec . . . . single crochet decrease
Sc2tog . . . . single crochet 3 stitches
                              together decrease
Sl st . . . . slip stitch
Sp(s) . . . . space(s)
St(s) . . . . stitch(es)
Tog . . . . together
Tr . . . . triple crochet
V-st . . . . V-stitch
YO . . . . yarn over hook

These are Standard Symbols

* An asterisk (or double asterisks**) in a pattern row, indicates a portion of instructions to be used more than once. For instance, "rep from * three times" means that after working the instructions once, you must work them again three times for a total of 4 times in all.

† A dagger (or double daggers ††) indicates that those instructions will be repeated again later in the same row or round.

: The number of stitches after a colon tells you the number of stitches you will have when you have completed the row or round.

( ) Parentheses enclose instructions which are to be worked the number of times following the parentheses. For instance, "(ch 1, sc, ch1) 3 times" means that you will chain one, work one sc, and then chain again three times for a total of six chains and three sc's.

Parentheses often set off or clarify a group of stitches to be worked into the same space of stitch. For instance, "dc, ch2, dc) in corner sp".

[ ] Brackets and ( ) parentheses are also used to give you additional information.

Terms

Front Loop—This is he loop toward you at the top of the crochet stitch.

Back Loop—This is he loop away from you at the top of the crochet stitch.

Post—This is the vertical part of the crochet stitch

Join—This means to join with a sl st unless another stitch is specified.

Finish Off—This means to end your piece by pulling the cut yarn end through the last loop remaining on the hook. This will prevent the work from unraveling.

Continue in Pattern as Established— This means to follow the pattern stitch as it has been set up, working any increases or decreases in such a way that the pattern remains the same as it was established.

Work even—This means that the work is continued in the pattern as established without increasing or decreasing.

Right Side—This means the side of the garment that will be seen.

Wrong Side—This means the side of the garment that is inside when the garment is worn.

Right hand side—This means the side of the garment that is near the right hand when worn.

Left hand side—This means the side of the garment that is near the left hand when worn.

Gauge

This is probably the most important aspect of crocheting!

GAUGE simply means the number of stitches per inch, and the numbers of rows per inch that result from a specified yarn worked with a hook in a specified size. But since everyone knits or crochets differently-some loosely, some tightly, some in between-the measurements of individual work can vary greatly, even when the crocheters or knitters use the same pattern and the same size yarn and hook.

If you don't work to the gauge specified in the pattern, your garment will never be the correct size, and you may not have enough yarn to finish your project. The hook size given in the instructions is merely a guide and should never be used without a gauge swatch.

To make a gauge swatch, crochet a swatch that is about 4" square, using the suggested hook and the number of stitches given in the pattern. Measure your swatch. If the number of stitches is fewer than those listed in the pattern, try making another swatch with a smaller hook. If the number of stitches is more than is called for in the pattern, try making another swatch with a larger hook. It is your responsibility to make sure you achieve the gauge specified in the pattern.

The patterns in this book have been written using the crochet terminology that is used in the United States. Terms which may have different equivalents in other parts of the world are listed below.

United States	International
Double crochet (dc)	treble crochet (tr)
Gauge	tension
Half double crochet (hdc)	half treble crochet (htr)
Single crochet	double crochet
Skip	miss
Slip stitch	single crochet
Triple crochet (tr)	double treble crochet (dtr)
Yarn over (YO)	yarn forward (yfwd)
Yarn over (YO)	yarn around needle (yrn)

Crochet Hooks Conversion Chart

U.S.	B-1	C-2	D-3	E-4	F-5	G-6	H-8	I-9	J-10	K-10 12	N	P	Q
Metric	2.25	2.75	3.25	3.5	3.75	4	5	5.5	6	6.5	0	10	15

Steel Crochet Hooks Conversion Chart

U.S.	00	0	1	2	3	4	5	6	7	8	9	10	11	12	13	14
Metric	3.5	3.25	2.75	2.25	2.1	2	1.9	1.8	1.65	1.5	1.4	1.3	1.1	1.0	0.85	0.75

Fringe

Basic Instructions

Cut a piece of cardboard about 6" wide and half as long as specified in the instructions for strands, plus $1/2$" for trimming allowance. Wind the yarn loosely and evenly lengthwise around the cardboard. When the card is filled, cut the yarn across one end. Do this several times; then begin fringing. You can wind additional strands as you need them.

Single Knot Fringe

Hold the specified number of strands for one knot of fringe together, and then fold in half.

Hold the project with the right side facing you. Using a crochet hook, draw the folded ends through the space of stitch from right to wrong side.

Pull the loose ends through the folded section.

Draw the knot up firmly.

Space the knots evenly and trim the ends of the fringe.

Abbreviations, 254

Accessories
Flower Garden Scarf, 53
Fun Hat and Scarf, 244
Glitzy Capelet, 12
Loopy Tape Measure, 240
Pinning Up Roses, 197
Scarf in Style, 41
Snowflake Earring, 153
Soft 'n Sweet, 62
Sweet Sachet, 171

Afghans
Dutch Treat, 56
Flowers and Bears in the
Dell, 214
Lazy Daisies for Baby, 202
Merry-Go-Round Blanket, 190
Pineapple Roses, 230
Plum Granny Ripple, 82
Rock-A-Bye Baby, 61
Rose Garden, 120
Stripes on Parade, 146
Texas Roses, 160

A La Foo-Foo Potholder, 188
All Buttoned Up, 236
Asymmetrical Poncho, 159
Awesome Blossom,110
Baby on Board, 248
Beary Cute Jacket, 165
Beauty in Geometry, 76

Bedspreads
Bedtime Roses, 68
Romance of Yesteryear, 132

Bedtime Roses, 68
Big Scary Spider Cat Toy, 21
Bronze Beauty, 209
Bucket Bag, 96
By The Sea, 198

Children's
Baby Sweater, 205
Bonnet, 206
Booties, 207
Flowers and Bears in the Dell,
214
Lazy Daisies for Baby, 202
Lazy Daisies Layette, 204
Little Friend's Backpack, 27
Merry-Go-Round Blanket, 190
Pretty Posies, 154
Rock-A-Bye Baby, 61
Rows of Bows, 42
Sheep Mittens, 176
Teddy Bears, 214

Citrus Chic, 6
Cozy Shrug, 218
Cute Combo, 148
Dad's Doily, 90

Doilies
Dad's Doily, 90
Pretty Petals, 10

Dutch Treat, 56
Entrelac Skull Cap, 47
Falling Leaves Wrap, 225
Fast and Fun T-Top, 66
Felted Purse, 64
Floral Potholder
and Dish Cloth Set, 24
Flower Garden Scarf, 53
Flower Squares, 220
Flowers and Bears in the Dell, 214
Four-Way Poncho, 108
Fringe, 255
Fun Hat and Scarf, 244
Fun in the Sun Halter, 242
Gauge, 254
General Directions, 254
Glitter Girl Bolero, 16
Glitzy Capelet, 12
Grin and Bear It, 72
Harlequin Vest, 86

Hats
Awesome Blossom, 110
Entrelac Skull Cap, 47
Fun Hat, 245
Pretty Posies, 158
Robin's Hood

International Terms, 255

Jackets
All Buttoned Up, 236
Citrus Chic, 6
Cute Combo, 148
Magnificent in Mesh, 98
Tiny Bubbles Jacket, 162

Kitchen Angel Dish Cloth, 36

Kitchen Projects
A La Foo-Foo Potholder, 236
Coaster, 106
Dish Cloth, 26
Floral Potholder
and Dish Cloth Set, 24
Kitchen Angel Dish Cloth, 36
Let's Do Lunch, 104
Place Mat, 105
Potholder, 107

Lazy Daisies for Baby, 202
Lazy Daisies Layette, 204
Let's Do Lunch, 104
Little Friend's Backpack,27
Little Something, A, 101
Loopy Poncho, 216
Loopy Tape Measure, 240
Lover's Knot Shrug, 58
Magnificent in Mesh, 98
Maternity Top, 248
Merry-Go-Round Blanket, 190
Mesh Tunic, 92
Patchwork Tote, 113
Pick a Pretty Pair, 172

Pillows
Quilt Block Pillow, 123
Round Pillow, 136
Square Pillow, 135

Pineapple Roses, 230
Pinning Up Roses, 197
Plum Granny Ripple, 82

Ponchos and shawls
Asymmetrical Poncho, 159
Bronze Beauty, 209
Falling Leaves Wrap, 225
Four-Way Poncho, 108
Loopy Poncho, 216
Pick a Pair, 175
Ribbon Fringe Shawl, 178
Shawl of Gold, 234
Soft 'n Sweet, 62
Town & Country Capelet, 246
Wrap Up, 22

Pretty Petals Doily, 10
Pretty Posies, 154
Prom Purses, 14

Purses
Bucket Bag, 96
Felted Purse, 64
Patchwork Tote, 113
Prom Purses, 14
Rows of Bows, 46
Summer Escape Tote, 184

Quilt Block Pillow, 123
Rainbow Cover-up, 168
Ribbon Fringe Shawl, 178
Robin's Hood, 233
Rock-A-Bye Baby, 61
Romance of Yesteryear, 132
Rose Garden, 120
Rows of Bows, 42
Scarf in Style, 41
Shawl of Gold, 234
Sheep Mittens, 176

Shrugs
Cozy Shrug, 218
Glitter Girl Bolero, 16
Lover's Knot Shrug, 58
Simply Shrug, 126
Surely Chic, 33

Simply Shrug, 126

Skirts
Pick a Pair, 173
Summer Escape Sarong, 180
Surely Chic, 30
Sweet Summer Suit, 118

Slinky Tunic, 50
Snowflake Earring, 153
Soft 'n Sweet, 62
Sophisticated Shell, 250
Square Deal Vest, 38
Stripes on Parade, 146
Summer Escape, 180

Summer Outfits
Fun in the Sun Halter, 242
Rainbow Cover-Up, 168
Summer Escape, 180
Sweet Summer Suit, 116

Sunshine and Waves, 192
Surely Chic, 30
Sweet Sachet, 171
Sweet Summer Suit, 116
Terms, 254
Texas Roses, 160
Tiny Bubbles Jacket, 162

Tops
Baby on Board, 248
Beauty in Geometry, 76
By The Sea, 198
Cute Combo, 151
Diagonal Stripe Top, 143
Drawsting Top, 139
Fast and Fun T-Cloth, 66
Flower Squares, 220
Grin and Bare It, 72
Little Something, A, 101
Mesh Tunic, 92
Slinky Tunic, 50
Sophisticated Shell, 250
Square Deal Vest, 38
Summer Escape Halter Top, 182
Sunshine and Waves, 192
Sweet Summer Suit, 116
Trendy Tank, 128

Town and Country Capelet, 246

Toys
Big Scary Spider Cat Toy, 21
Teddy Bears in the Dell, 214

Trendy Tank, 128
Two Trendy Tops. 138

Vests
Harlequin Vest, 86
Square Deal Vest, 38

Wrap Up, 22